Arthur Schnitzler

PLAYS AND STORIES

The German Library : Volume 55

Volkmar Sander, General Editor

Arthur Schnitzler

PLAYS
AND
STORIES

Edited by Egon Schwarz
Foreword by Stanley Elkin

CONTINUUM · NEW YORK

1982

The Continuum Publishing Company
575 Lexington Avenue, New York, NY 10022

Printed in the United States of America

Library of Congress Cataloging in Publication Data

Schnitzler, Arthur, 1862–1931.
Plays and Stories.

(The German library; v. 55)
Contents: Flirtations—La Ronde—Countess
Mitzi, or The family reunion—[etc.]
I. Schwarz, Egon, 1922–   II. Title.
III. Series.
PT2638.N5A2 1982   833'.8   82-18263
ISBN 0-8264-0270-4
ISBN 0-8264-0271-2 (pbk.)

For acknowledgments of published material, please see page 280,
which constitutes an extension of the copyright page.

Contents

* This translation appears here for the first time in print

Foreword

If I could come back it would be as a playwright. For the amiability of the thing, for the backstage and greenroom nexus and the gag telegrams on opening night. For the parties and endless, hopeful toasts and generally companionable, even intimate, round robin life. To be collegial and pally. To be thick as a thief and bussed by the showgirls. To be part, I mean, of a small idea.

But not for the art. Almost certainly not for the art. There is, I think, a natural constraint on playwrights, on drama, the form itself. For one, there is the constraint of time. The play—and movies and music, too—is essentially a social form, invented, may be, as they tell you in the sophomore anthologies, to be performed on the back of the church truck, or in the amphitheater on the Greek high holidays, but that was social, too, of course, and we know in our hearts it's done today, as it may have been done then, for the night-out of the thing, for its dinner-and-a-show aspects and ramifications, its birthday and anniversary ones—our own high holidays, I mean—theater, or at least going to it, a moveable feast, the sense we have of occasion. And the playwright's commitment is as much to his audience as to any fancy notion he has of any fancy notion. The busses stop running, the subways. The babysitter has to be back by midnight and the eight-thirty curtain is no accident, I think, but some cozy tie-in with the deli guys and restaurateurs—been to Broadway? the West End?—possibly even with the babysitters. There's this mutual understanding that the playwright will get you in and get you out in something under two and a half hours—Eugene O'Neill's long nights' journeys into days were windbag exceptions; *Nicholas Nickleby* was—and this whole business of time limitation opens the play up to its vulnerabilities. Indeed, it *becomes* its vulnerabilities—a format for one idea, often enough drawn out even at that, padded as togs about some kernel of Eskimo; knee-deep in time as in mud. Or the constraint of structure—why who-done-its (but all plays are who-done-its, *Oedipus* no less than *The Mouse Trap*, *King Lear* no less than *Sleuth*) run years—when structure (scenes, acts, the explosive lines that bring down curtains, the frozen moments and dimmed lights which end an act) itself tends toward form, almost genre, as westerns are a genre, as science fiction is, and theater entertaining in relation, like westerns, like science fiction, to how it rings the changes, how it presumes to do it this time, turning on itself, on expectation, with a twist and resolution like some closing couplet slamming a door in a sonnet. Or an excuse—this now, not then, other playwrights, not Schnitzler—for "production values," how the thing is "mounted," its hi-tech arrangements and willful media mixing—how plays try to burst their bonds and become, well, movies. Or the other excuse—not the well-made play so much as the well-acted one, "a vehicle," voice and carriage a substitute for—well, *two* ideas.

But finally those two-and-a-half hours which constrict playwrights, which hole-and-corner them into convention—theater is a *smorgasbord* of convention; even musical comedy, which, when it works, is possibly the most satisfying theatrical form there is, if only because of the presence of singers and dancers with their immediate access to the communal lyrical, musical theater's marvelous ability to dispense with logic and go with little or no preparation for the jugular emotions, even musical comedy has its clichés and conventions, here masked by movement and melody, the distraction of pure and pointless energy—to close them off from an exploitation of character and situation and story and even language—astonishingly, "language," high rhetoric, I mean, finds no *natural* home in plays—the only proper considerations of fiction, forcing them into a kind of "issue dependency," those hundred eighty minutes which make a false virtue of economy and an iron-clad, no loopholes law of Chekhov's dictum that any gun hung on the wall in Act 1 must by and by be fired. Such "economy" is, of course, a sort of penny wise, pound foolishness, a mean and mingy, wasteful thrift. Because it clips the wings of possibility and seals, mint and airtight, what ought to remain open-ended. The theater, one cannot breathe there. (I'm thinking of plays like *A Man For All Seasons;* I'm thinking of plays like *Amadeus,* where all that's allowed is the argument, some shuttlecock notion of confrontation, the obsessive back-and-forths of accusation and denial.) And because, finally, in drama it is always the present tense. Even in flashbacks it is the present tense for, unlike the novel, plays do not have the gift of tense. In a novel or short story all half dozen tenses are available to the writer all together all at once, and not just within a single scene, or even paragraph, but, if he chooses, within a sentence, within a single clause from simple past through all the perfect future, a pluperfect perpetual calendar of handled time. Do that in a play and you have reminiscence, a set-piece, a *speech.*

One goes to the theater then—or *I* do—as to a museum, as a conscious act of secular archaelogy. And reads plays like Arthur Schnitzler's as one might read an old newspaper—for an amusing account of the types and times. For the nostalgia, that is. To find out about the shopgirls and young men (*Flirtations*); the married ladies and cuckold husbands, the poets and chippies, housemaids and actresses, enlisted men, noblemen and whores (*La Ronde*); to find out about the professional people, the professors and doctors, the priests, the lawyers, the journalists and political comers (*Professor Bernhardi*)—to learn about Vienna at the turn of the century.

But for all that a roll call of Schnitzler's Vienna with its immense cast of characters suggests operetta, what he gives us finally is not operetta at all. His playboys and young officers depict nothing if not the dark side of the Chocolate Soldier, and his view, if not tragic—it isn't; it's street wise and cynical—is at least afflicting. He writes about the wide flaws and crabbed comeuppances of silly people. In a way, his tragedy is venereal—you pays your money and you takes your chancres—brought on not by love but urge, not conviction but dumb, even reluctant, obstinacy, not individuals caught up in their beliefs but in their culture's practices, all of which make Schnitzler a sort of consummate playwright, for his scolds and pulpiteering are pitched at a collective audience in the snug snuffbox, safe and social circumstances of theater, and feed off a fixed, governing idea—the dramatic conceit—convention—of hypocrisy. Audiences are suckers for hypocrisy. They love *all* the easy discrepancies, all ducks-in-a-barrel morality and pot-shotted shortcomings. They love, that is, to lick the finger that points at them.

Although *Professor Bernhardi* is not included in this collection, it is instructive to cast a glance at it. In *Professor Bernhardi* Schnitzler is working the tradition of what can only be called "integrity drama." The trick is to present a character in a tight situation and turn all the screws, bring on all the big guns of circumstances. It's man-against-the-lynch-mob theater, the theater of choices, of the protagonist in Kiplingesque "If-ian" contingency where a hero absorbs all the mean-spirited low blows his enemies can dish out, takes all those rabbit punches to his integrity, and remains a man, my son. These are crises not so much of conscience as of punishment and, in *Professor Bernhardi,* did not Schnitzler meddle with his own premises, would reveal a character so smitten with his martyrdom that the play might almost have become a set-piece of heroically smug dimensions. What saves it, I think—and what saves a great deal of Schnitzler—is the subtle reversal that occurs at the end of the play, a reversal that suddenly introduces a real, and far more interesting, possibility—that we have been duped into philosophy, fooled into philosophy. Startlingly, we are presented with the idea that Bernhardi may have been wrong. The doctor, back from a two-month prison term to which he's been sentenced on trumped-up, antisemitically motivated charges that he'd physically interfered with a priest come to grant absolution to a young girl about to die in the septic aftermath of an illegal abortion—Bernhardi had intended to allow the girl to die in a state of narcotically induced bliss, the sudden appearance of the priest, or so the questionable premise goes, needlessly forcing her down from her high to die in despair—has an interview with Councillor Winkler, an administrator with the Ministry of Education. Bernhardi is loaded for self-righteous bear.

> BERNH: . . . all at once it seemed as though the broadest ethical issues were at stake; responsibility and revelation, and finally the question of free will—

WINKLER: Oh yes, you always end up with that if you dig down to the root of things. But it's better to break off before you get so far, otherwise one fine day it may happen that you begin to understand everything and forgive everything. . . . Undoubtedly you were not born to be a reformer—

BERNH: Reformer—? My dear sir—

WINKLER: As little as I—We are not prepared, deep down, to follow up our principles to the final consequences—to stake our lives, if necessary, for our convictions. And therefore the best thing, in fact the only decent thing, is for men of our sort—to leave such matters alone—

BERNH: But—

WINKLER: No good results from meddling. What end would have been attained after all, my dear Professor, had you spared that poor creature a last shock on her deathbed? . . .

BERNH: . . . I simply did what I held to be right in one specific instance.

WINKLER: That is where you went wrong. If we always did only the right thing, or rather started off one day at breakfast time, without further reflection, to do only the right thing all day long, we should certainly land in jail before supper time.

BERNH: And shall I tell you something, Councillor? In my place you would have acted exactly as I did.

WINKLER: Possibly. Then I should have been—you'll forgive me, Professor—just such an ass as you—

Curtain

This is the curtain speech and opens the play's ends as it were, permitting if not genuine ambiguity then at least a sort of theatrical counterpart—textual double take.

Which—opening ends, fiddling dramatic form—Schnitzler, though I think his strong suit was fiction, may have had some real interest in. Despite the fact that his plays remain chiefly, well, charming and conventional, there is the feeling in Arthur Schnitzler's work that he was at odds with his countrymen, with the Vienna that may have been, at least for him and at least symbolically, almost as much the city-state as the Venice to which his worn out Casanova returns under the humiliating terms of his lifted exile, a sense of odd man out, of exclusion, a rift as deep as the sexual one between men and women which pervades his plays, which, indeed, is largely the subject of them. Yet—his plays *are* conventional—*La Ronde* is certainly an exception if only for its pas de deux arrangements—and it is an interesting exercise to count the convenient encounters between characters in the entrances and exits in a given play. They seem, in their dependable comings and goings, scheduled as trains. The second act of *Flirtations* is simply an example.

Christine is dressing to go out. Katharine enters. They talk. Christine's father, Weiring, enters. All three talk. Christine leaves. Katharine and Weiring talk. Mitzi, Christine's friend, enters. The three are talking (mostly about having to leave) when Christine enters. Weiring and Katharine leave together. Mitzi and Christine talk. Fritz, Christine's lover, enters. Mitzi leaves. Fritz and Christine have, for this act, at least, a longish talk. (A little about the picture on Christine's wall, "Parting and Return.") Theodore, Fritz's friend, enters. The two friends whisper together while Christine "busies herself at the window" (the stage direction) until she "is near them again" (another stage direction). The three talk together. Theodore and Fritz leave. Christine, "uneasy, remains standing, then goes to the door left ajar. She is subdued," calls Fritz. Fritz enters and holds her. He says "Farewell."

Six characters appear in this brief act; there are seven separate entrances; two characters leave individually, two others exit together. While important information is obviously exchanged, much of the dialogue—since Schnitzler, not even excluding the deliberate experimentation of *La Ronde,* is essentially a realistic, even a naturalistic, playwright—is necessarily small talk, the Hi's and How-are-ya's of ordinary life. (And much talk of weather and, since characters leave as well as come on board, there is leave*taking,* not only a Hello for each Goodbye but regards to the wife and all the polite conversation of primarily civilized people.)

What we're talking about here is plot by conversation, some Aristotle-grounded Law of the Off-Stage; life in the wings. (Here *La Ronde is* an exception, though, at least in reading the play, one gets an impression—all those asterisks where the good parts go— of staging by ellipses, of the partners going to the shadows to do their business.) Because what we're talking about *finally* is melodramatics, soap opera, the peculiar pulled punches of all distinctly social art forms.

And yet— And yet— And yet there is his fiction.

Schnitzler's use of stream-of-consciousness in *Lieutenant Gustl,* though certainly innovative, is, on the face of it, clumsy, his use of the "I" in his silly, blustering young officer's interior monologue unfortunate, probably impossible (rather like trying to sustain in even so short a piece of fiction as the short story the second person point-of-view).

> How much longer is this thing going to last? Let's see what time it is . . . perhaps I shouldn't look at my watch at a serious concert like this. But no one will see me. If anyone does, I'll know he's paying just as little attention as I am. In that case I certainly won't be embarrassed. . . . Only quarter to ten? . . . I feel as though I'd been here for hours. I'm just not used to going to concerts. . . . What's that they're playing? I'll have a look at the program. . . . Yes that's what it is: an oratorio. Thought it was a mass. That sort of thing belongs in church.

People do not think to themselves syntactically; they don't remind themselves—"That was funny a week ago when she was at the Gartenbau Café with him, and I was sitting opposite Kopetzky; she kept winking at me"—of what they already know. The effect is not only unnatural, it is insane, as talking to oneself is supposed to be insane. Yet in Schnitzler's remarkable novella all sense of the innate falseness of the point-of-view drops almost immediately away, and it is as if the author had invented for this particular character in this particular situation a diction and tense and viewpoint entirely, and distinctively, and *perfectly,* his own, as if Schnitzler were taking the affidavit of Lieutenant Gustl's soul. Indeed, that seems to be precisely what he's doing, giving the reader privileged information to another man's character. The effect is extraordinary and very powerful, for Gustl, with his straight, humorless failure of perception and highfalutin' notions of himself, makes a terrible witness and becomes, before our eyes, a sort of witless, unforgivable Falstaff, unregenerate and unforgettable. That this is a consequence of the very clumsiness of the point-of-view in hand-glove relation with Gustl's measly character is almost certainly the case, granting the reader not only his inside information about Gustl (and advancing, incidentally, the difficult technique of the "unreliable narrator") but a kind of licensed omniscience, and not only creating, within the small compass of a brief book, a memorable character but turning his voice into what is possibly a unique trope in literature.

Schnitzler's Casanova, in *Casanova's Homecoming,* is an even greater achievement if for no other reasons than that he has a more interesting mind than Gustl and finds himself in a more interesting situation, Casanova's problems being "real," while Gustl's are only made up, self-inflicted, the product of a locked-in imagination engined by an unrelenting egoism. But there *are* other reasons.

The character of a great man, now aging, whose deeds are "by degrees passing into oblivion" is not an unfamiliar one. Movies have rendered him for years—broken-down sheriffs and old gunfighters, all the worn-out spies come in from the cold, all the drunk docs called to draw upon depleted skills in times of crisis, have become stick stock figures in the literature. What Schnitzler has going for him in *Casanova's Homecoming* is the conception of using a legendary character—though this isn't new either; Shaw had recycled Don Juan; Joyce Odysseus—with whom we're already familiar so that neither the protagonist nor the other characters have constantly to remind us how the mighty are fallen. We know because he is in our heads. What he has going for him further is that Casanova *isn't* called upon in emergency and, further still, that his particular depleted skills are only personal, and that all Casanova wants is to have a last fling and go home. The "only personal" is, of course, the best and most difficult situation of all, not more valuable to literature than its great other half—going home, coming to terms, resignation and acceptance—not more valuable because, finally, they are the same.

If the cliché about novelists not making good playwrights is true, as I think it is in the case of Arthur Schnitzler, it isn't because talent lapses or undergoes some radical sea-change as the writer turns his attention from one form to the other, but because of something in the nature of the forms themselves—that, broadly and vastly oversimplified, theater is public and political—an actor's lines are even *called* "speeches"—an occasion, while fiction, with its disregard for time—or at least length—and its concomitant gifts of extension and an almost holographic ability to project in the round is essentially private and personal, an occasion, too, of sorts, but lonelier, no occasion at all, really. Which is why, if I *could* come back, it would be as a playwright.

STANLEY ELKIN

Introduction

There are, in nature and culture, suggestive sites and atmospheres that have traditionally invited a great deal of mythologizing. This can be easily observed in some cities, such as Rome, New York, and Paris, whose legendary fame defies time and space. Art and literature abound in images, *topoi*, evocations, descriptions, transfigurations, and even demonizations, all engendered by these places. The mythology thus created serves artists of many media in analyzing and interpreting life. The imaginative force field irradiated by the city of Venice has been so potent in the course of its variegated history that it has given rise to a series of divergent projections in writing and painting. These irresistible emanations inspired, for example, Rainer Maria Rilke to designate Venice as "the world's beautiful counterweight" and Arthur Schnitzler, who followed another tradition, to use it as a sordid background for the degradation of his aging adventurer in one of the most impressive short novels of world literature, *Casanova's Homecoming* (1918), thereby disowning the favorite figure of fin-de-siècle aestheticism.

Imperial Vienna has always been a sought-after milieu for myth-makers. In song and operetta, in poems and on canvas, in novels, plays and films, its qualities, fed by fiction as much as fact, have been celebrated a thousandfold. The splendor of the Habsburg court, the artistic sponsorship of ambitious families, the motley crowds of a multi-ethnic empire, its role as mediator between East and West, the late intrusion of capitalist enterprise and liberal ideas into an essentially feudal order, the relative affluence of the middle classes, the ceaseless arrival of foreign artists, diplomats, fortune hunters, travelers, lured to Vienna by the rumor of a light-hearted, sybaritic life—all of these factors contributed to an historic fame the last reflections of which are still visible today.

They are richly present in Arthur Schnitzler's works, so much so that his books could be said to "physically contain the Vienna of 1900, just as Balzac's novels harbor the Paris of the Restoration period." But it would be a regrettable mistake to assume, as has often been the case, that his purpose was to glorify his native city. A physician and the son of a physician, he viewed his milieu with a clinical eye. It was not his fault if a smug public not only chose to ignore the critical edge in his studiously satirical writings, but even regarded them as complicitous reinforcements of their own hedonistic or melancholic attitudes. To make the misunderstanding complete, Schnitzler was attacked and vilified by other segments of his society. On account of a brilliant stream-of-consciousness story, *Lieutenant Gustl* (1900), in which the fetish of duelling was revealed in all its anachronistic absurdity, Schnitzler was deprived of his officer's commission in the Austro-Hungarian army. By exposing to view the vacuous, prejudice-ridden mind of one of its typical representatives, Schnitzler can be credited with being among the first to portray pre-Fascist inauthenticity. No wonder that he incurred the implacable wrath of certain groups who succeeded, either by censorship or organized riots, in preventing the performance of some of his most incisive plays.

This is demonstrated all too clearly by the history of *La Ronde* (1900). Aware of its explosive untimeliness Schnitzler permitted only a private printing of two hundred copies, which he sent to friends. It could not be performed in pre-war Europe, and even after 1918 it caused veritable scandals wherever an attempt was made to stage the play. The most virulent of these uproars occurred in Vienna. Prominent personalities of public life were implicated. The comedy became the plaything of politics as well as the object of stormy scenes in Parliament and violent demonstrations in the streets. The theater was stormed, stink-bombs were thrown, benches destroyed, spectators and actors assaulted. The play was kept from being performed, then, under heavy police protection, brought back on stage and all the while vilified by the press as "the most vulgar bordello piece," written for the purpose of "inciting the prurience of Asiatic intruders [meaning the Jews of Vienna]," a verdict echoed by the highest authorities in government. Ironically, today one has learned to understand the ten dialogues not at all as a celebration of free sex but as a denunciation of lovelessness in a corrupt society.

Among the finest contributions of the novelist and dramatist Schnitzler is the empathetic portrayal of women and their lot in "Victorian" Vienna, an analysis which was greatly aided by the invention of his famous *"süsses Mädel,"* the character of the "sweet wench." She first appears in *Anatol* (1894) and can be seen in *La Ronde* and other works right through to *Countess Mitzi* (1906) where she quite logically reappears as a somewhat more seasoned and delightfully emancipated woman. Schnitzler described the figure from every aspect—demure and saucy, tragic and frivolous. Her many-sidedness is especially evident in *Flirtations* because there the social alternatives to the *"süsses Mädel"* for the woman of the lower classes are analyzed with awesome precision.

First of all there is the vivacious Mitzi Schlager, who lightheartedly accepts the role in which the male world casts her—that of the willing and eternally cheerful toy of their whims, a swift conquest who can be abandoned with no trouble at the right moment. Another variant is that of Christine's aunt who, protected by her brother from any encounters, any seduction, and in the long run any happiness, eventually dies as a depleted and resigned old maid. A third type is represented by Katharine Binder, who tried to find refuge from erotic insecurity in an unexciting marriage to a hosier, and now no longer permits herself even a memory of a more colorful youth. Finally there is Christine herself, earnest and affectionate, whose fate demonstrates that, in this world of halfheartedness, a woman who commits herself with her whole being is likely to come to a tragic end. This tragedy is all the more convincing since she is contrasted with the sister figures who have already failed in a non-tragic manner.

It has often been said that Arthur Schnitzler was less interested in social than in psychological matters. In this extreme form the statement is misleading. Who would deny that he was a profound authority on, and interpreter of, involved and often terrifying emotional conditions? But since he understood the human mind as a complex which translates the general into the particular, and thus the social into the individual, his analysis of the psyche always has a societal depth that can be ignored only at the risk of intellectual impoverishment.

Despite the long-faded period color of the turn of the century for which he became justly famous, despite his counts and coaches, his handsome officers and horse-drawn trams, his Jewish artists and Jewish upper middle class, none of which exist any more, despite his being the shrewd diagnostician of his age, I should like to express the seemingly paradoxical opinion that Schnitzler projected the consciousness of a future epoch as accurately as that of his own. In his autobiography *A Youth in Vienna* the author describes his plan for a drama: "My piece was to bear the title 'Aristocrat and Democrat,' and as characters there should appear the Prince, the Princess, the Count, the Countess, the Baron, the Baroness, and a middle-class youth who is simply called Robert and has to bring the prologue to its high point with a fulminating revolutionary sentence, while the entire aristocracy . . . are assigned the most miserable roles."

That was "around the year '70" according to the autobiography, when Arthur Schnitzler was about eight years old. This piece was never written—fortunately, one might add. As a mature writer he never permitted himself to deal with social problems in such a crude manner, and thus the irony with which he derides his youthful plan is not entirely unjustified. But in consideration of everything we know about his work today, we can safely conclude that as a whole it has served the emancipatory ideals of his youth in more subtle and consequently more effective ways.

E.S.

FLIRTATIONS

CHARACTERS

HANS WEIRING, *violinist at the Josefstadt Theatre*
CHRISTINE, *his daughter*
MITZI SCHLAGER, *a milliner*
KATHARINE BINDER, *wife of a stocking weaver*
LINA, *her nine-year-old daughter*
FRITZ LOBHEIMER ⎱ *young men*
THEODORE KAISER ⎰
A GENTLEMAN

SCENE: *Vienna, spring 1895*

Act I

Fritz's apartment. Elegant and comfortable. Fritz and Theodore enter, Theodore first, carrying his topcoat over his arm; he takes off his hat after entering. He carries a cane.

FRITZ (*offstage*): So, no one was here?

SERVANT'S VOICE: No, sir.

FRITZ (*entering*): We could probably send the carriage away?

THEODORE: Of course. I thought you already had.

FRITZ (*crossing to door*): Send the carriage away. Oh and—you can leave now, too. I won't be needing you anymore today. (*to Theodore*) Why don't you put your things down?

THEODORE (*at the desk*): Here are some letters.
      (*He throws his topcoat and hat on an armchair, but still carries his cane.*)

FRITZ (*goes hastily to desk*): Ah! . . .

THEODORE: Hey! There! . . . You look positively upset.

FRITZ: From Papa . . . (*Opens the other.*) From Lensky . . .

THEODORE: Don't let me disturb you.
                    (*Fritz skims the letters.*)
      What does Papa have to say?

FRITZ: Nothing special . . . I'm supposed to spend a week at the estate later this spring.

THEODORE: That would be very sensible. I'd like to send you there for half a year.
            (*Fritz, standing at the desk, turns to him.*)

3

I really would!—Horseback riding, fresh air, farmers' daughters—

FRITZ: Look, I'm going to my father's estate . . .

THEODORE: All right, but you know what I mean . . .

FRITZ: Would you like to come along?

THEODORE: I can't.

FRITZ: Why not?

THEODORE: My dear Fritz, I have exams to take! If I went along it would only be to make sure you stayed there.

FRITZ: Come on, don't worry about me.

THEODORE: What you need—if you ask me—is just a bit of fresh air! —I saw that today. Outside in the fresh, green spring you were a very charming and pleasant human being again.

FRITZ: Thanks.

THEODORE: And now—now, of course, you're going to pieces. This dangerous atmosphere is closing in again.
>   (*Fritz reacts with irritation.*)
You simply don't know how cheerful you were out there—you were actually making sense—it was like the good old days. . . . And just the other day, when we were with those two adorable girls, you were very agreeable—but now—that's all over, of course, and you find it absolutely necessary . . . (*with ironic pathos*) to think about "that woman."
>   (*Fritz stands up, irritated.*)
You don't know me, my dear friend. I have no intention of putting up with this any longer.

FRITZ: My God, you're worked up today . . . !

THEODORE (*ironically*): Understand, I'm not asking you to forget—*that* woman—I only want (*cheerfully*), my dear Fritz, this unfortunate affair to mean no more to you than any other intrigue. . . . I constantly tremble for you. Look, Fritz, one day, when you stop worshiping "that woman," you'll be astonished to see that you really *like* her. And then you'll realize that she's not an enchantress at all. Instead you'll see that she's a very sweet little woman full of fun and no different from any other woman who is young and pretty and has a little spirit.

FRITZ: Why did you say "tremble for me?"

THEODORE: You know . . . I can't hide my fear that one fine day the two of you will run off together.

FRITZ: That's what you've been thinking . . . ?

THEODORE (*after a short pause*): And that's not the only danger.

FRITZ: You're right, Theodore—there are others.

THEODORE: People like us just don't act stupidly.

FRITZ (*to himself*): There are others.

THEODORE: What's wrong . . . ? You're thinking of something quite specific.

FRITZ: Oh no, I'm not thinking of anything in particular. . . . (*as he glances toward the window*) After all, she was mistaken once before.

THEODORE: What . . . ? I don't understand.

FRITZ: It's nothing.

THEODORE: What is this? Why don't you make sense.

FRITZ: These past few days she's been frightened . . . on and off.

THEODORE: Why? There must be some reason.

FRITZ: Absolutely not. Nerves—(*ironically*) Guilty conscience, if you like.

THEODORE: You said that she'd been mistaken once before—

FRITZ: Well, yes—and again today. Probably.

THEODORE: Today—What does all this mean?

FRITZ (*after a short pause*): She thinks . . . we're being watched.

THEODORE: What?

FRITZ: She sees things that frighten her, really . . . actual hallucinations. (*At the window, parting the curtains.*) Standing here, she sees somebody down there on the corner, and she thinks. . . . (*Interrupts himself.*) Is it really possible to recognize a face from this far away?

THEODORE: Hardly.

FRITZ: That's what I said, too. But that is what makes it so awful. She doesn't dare leave. She gets herself all worked up. She cries hysterically. Then she wants to die with me—

THEODORE: Naturally.

FRITZ (*short pause*): Today I had to go downstairs, to check. Casually, as if I were going out myself; of course there wasn't a familiar face to be seen, anywhere. . . . (*Theodore remains silent.*) That's completely reassuring, isn't it . . . ? Nobody just suddenly vanishes into thin air, right . . . ? Well, why don't you answer me!

THEODORE: What sort of answer do you want to a question like that? Naturally nobody vanishes into thin air. But people do hide in doorways sometimes.

FRITZ: I looked into every one of them.

THEODORE: Well, you must have certainly looked the innocent.

FRITZ: No one was there. I told you, she's having hallucinations.

THEODORE: Certainly. But this ought to teach you to be more careful.

FRITZ: I couldn't have helped noticing if *he* was suspicious. Yesterday, in fact, I dined with them after the theater—both of them—and I tell you, it was so pleasant. . . . Ridiculous!

THEODORE: I beg you, Fritz—do me a favor, be sensible. Give up this whole damned business—if only for *my* sake. I have nerves, too. . . . I know perfectly well you're not the type to escape easily from an affair; so I've made it very easy for you and given you the opportunity to escape into *another* affair.

FRITZ: You?

THEODORE: Now, didn't I take you to my rendezvous with Mitzi a few weeks ago? And didn't I ask her to bring along her prettiest girl friend? And can you deny that you liked the little dear?

FRITZ: Certainly she's a dear . . . ! Very dear! You have no idea how I've longed for such tenderness without melodrama, for someone so sweet, so quiet, someone kind to me, someone who can help me recover from these endless tempests and martyrdoms.

THEODORE: That's it, you're right! Recovery. That's what it's all about. They're here to help us recover. That's why I'm not in favor of these so-called interesting women. Women aren't meant to be interesting, they're meant to be pleasant. You must look for your happiness where I've already looked and found it, where there are no big scenes, no dangers, no tragic complications. Where the beginning has no particular difficulties and the end has no torment. Where you take your first kiss with a smile and you say good-bye with touching emotion—

FRITZ: Yes, that's it.

THEODORE: Women are so happy in their simple humanity—what compels us to turn them into demons or angels at all costs?

FRITZ: She really is a sweetheart. So devoted, so dear. Sometimes it almost seems that she's too dear for me.

THEODORE: You're incorrigible. If you intend to turn even *this* situation into something serious—

FRITZ: That's the last thing in my mind. We agree: recovery.

THEODORE: Otherwise I would have to wash my hands of you. I'm fed up with your tragic love affairs. You bore me with them. And if you should ever want to come to me with that famous conscience of yours, I'll let you know now what my basic principle is in these situations: I'd rather have it be me than some other fellow. Because that other fellow is out there waiting, as sure as fate itself.

(*Doorbell rings.*)

FRITZ: Who can that be . . . ?

THEODORE: Take a look. —You've gone pale again! Pull yourself together right now. It's just those two sweet girls.

FRITZ (*pleasantly surprised*): What . . . ?

THEODORE: I took the liberty of inviting them here today.

FRITZ (*exiting*): Go on—why didn't you tell me! And now I've sent my man away.

THEODORE: All the cozier.

FRITZ (*outside*): Well, hello, Miss Mitzi!

(*Mitzi enters, carrying a package in her hand. Fritz follows.*)

FRITZ: And where is Christine?—

MITZI: She'll be along right away. And hello to you, Teddy. (*Theodore kisses her hand.*) You must excuse us, Mr. Fritz, but Theodore invited us to come over—

FRITZ: But that was a wonderful idea. Theodore *did* forget one thing, however—

THEODORE: Theodore forgot nothing! (*Takes the package from Mitzi.*) Did you bring everything I wrote down?

MITZI: Sure did. (*to Fritz*) Where can I put this?

FRITZ: Just give it to me, Mitzi. For the time being we'll put it on the sideboard.

MITZI: I bought a few extras you didn't write down, Teddy.

FRITZ: Give me your hat, Miss Mitzi. There—
            (*Puts hat as well as her boa on the piano.*)

THEODORE (*skeptically*): What else?

MITZI: A mocha cream torte.

THEODORE: You little glutton!

FRITZ: So tell me, why didn't Christine come directly with you?

MITZI: Christine went with her father to the theatre. Then she'll take the streetcar over here.

THEODORE: That's a considerate daughter for you. . . .

MITZI: That's right, and especially now since the death in the family.

THEODORE: Who died?

MITZI: The old gentleman's sister.

THEODORE: Oh, you mean the married aunt!

MITZI: No, it was the old spinster sister who's always lived with them—and now he misses her so much.

THEODORE: Isn't Christine's father the small gentleman with short gray hair?

MITZI (*shaking her head*): No, he has long hair—

FRITZ: Where do you know him from?

THEODORE: I was at the theater the other day with Lensky and took a look at the people playing bass viol.

MITZI: He doesn't play the bass. He plays violin.

THEODORE: Aha, I thought he played bass. (*To Mitzi, who laughs*) It's not funny. I can't know everything, child!

MITZI: Mr. Fritz, you have a beautiful place—just beautiful! What is the view like?

FRITZ: That window overlooks the Strohgasse and the next room—

THEODORE (*interrupting*): Hey, now, why are you both being so formal! Why don't you just call him Fritz!

MITZI: We'll toast our friendship at supper.

THEODORE: Solid principles! At least it's reassuring. . . . And how is your dear mother getting along?

MITZI (*turns toward him, suddenly, with a concerned look*): Do you know, she has a—

THEODORE: Toothache—I know, I know. Your mother always has a toothache. Someday she ought to see a dentist.

MITZI: But the doctor says it's only rheumatism.

THEODORE (*laughing*): Well, if it's only rheumatism—

MITZI (*holding a photo album*): You have so many beautiful things here. (*Leafing through the book*) Who is this . . . ? Oh, this is you, Mr. Fritz. . . . In uniform!? You're in the military?

FRITZ: Yes.

MITZI: In the dragoons! Are you with the yellows or the blacks?

FRITZ (*smiling*): The yellow regiment.

MITZI (*dreamily*): The yellow regiment!

THEODORE: Look at her, all starry-eyed! Mitzi, wake up!

MITZI: But now you're a lieutenant in the reserves, aren't you?

FRITZ: I certainly am.

MITZI: You must look so handsome in your shako.

THEODORE: A veritable encyclopedia! Hey, Mitzi, I'm in the military too, you know.

MITZI: Are you also in the dragoons?

THEODORE: Yes—

MITZI: Why don't you tell a person . . .

THEODORE: I want to be loved for myself alone.

MITZI: Oh, Teddy, some time soon, when we're going out together, you must wear your uniform.

THEODORE: I'll be having military exercises in any case in August.

MITZI: Oh, God, by August—

THEODORE: You're right—eternal love doesn't last quite *that* long.

MITZI: Who thinks about August in May. Isn't that right, Mr. Fritz? —Mr. Fritz, why did you slip away from us yesterday?

FRITZ: What do you mean?

MITZI: Well, you know—after the theater.

FRITZ: Didn't Theodore give you my apologies?

THEODORE: Of course, I did.

MITZI: What good are all your apologies to me or rather to Christine! When you make a promise, you keep it.

FRITZ: I would honestly have preferred to be with you.

MITZI: Is that true. . . ?

FRITZ: But I couldn't. You saw that. I had company in my box, and afterward I simply couldn't get away from them.

MITZI: You mean you couldn't get away from the lovely ladies. Do you think we couldn't see you from where we sat in the gallery?

FRITZ: I saw you, too. . . .

MITZI: You were sitting at the back of the box—

FRITZ: Not all the time.

MITZI: Most of the time. Behind a lady in a black velvet dress and you were always peering out (*mocking his movements*)—like this.

FRITZ: My! You certainly kept a close eye on me.

MITZI: It's not my affair! But if I was Christine . . . Why does Theodore have time for us after the theater? Why doesn't he have to dine with friends?

THEODORE (*proudly*): Why don't I have to dine with friends. . . ?

(Doorbell rings.)

MITZI: That's Christine.

(Fritz hurries out.)

THEODORE: Mitzi, you could do me a favor.

(Mitzi gives him a questioning look.)

For the time being—forget your military memories.

MITZI: But I don't have any.

THEODORE: Well, it's obvious you didn't learn your facts from a textbook.

(Fritz and Christine enter; she is carrying a bouquet in her hands.)

CHRISTINE *(with slight shyness)*: Good evening. Greetings.

(to Fritz)

Are you happy that we're here?—You're not angry?

FRITZ: But child! —Sometimes Theodore is more clever than I am.

THEODORE: Well, is dear Papa fiddling away?

CHRISTINE: Of course; I took him to the theater.

(to Mitzi)

And then Katharine Binder held me up a little while longer.

MITZI: Oh Lord, that hypocrite.

CHRISTINE: She's not a hypocrite. She's very good to me.

MITZI: You trust everyone.

CHRISTINE: Why should she lie to me?

FRITZ: Who is this Katharine?

MITZI: The wife of a stocking maker. And she's jealous of anybody who's younger than she is.

CHRISTINE: But she's still young herself.

FRITZ: Let's forget about Katharine—what have you got there?

CHRISTINE: Some flowers I brought for you.

(Fritz takes them from her and kisses her hand.)

FRITZ: You're a little angel. Just a second, here's a vase, we should—

THEODORE: Oh no! You have no talent at all for party decorations—they're supposed to be strewn informally all over the table. Later, of course, when the table has been set, you should actually arrange for them to fall from the ceiling. But I suppose, that can't be really done.

FRITZ *(laughing)*: Hardly.

THEODORE: Meanwhile they can be kept in here after all.
>   (*Puts them in the vase.*)

MITZI: Children, it's getting dark!
>   (*Fritz has helped Christine out of her jacket; she has also taken off her hat. He removes the things to a chair upstage.*)

FRITZ: We'll light the lamp in a minute.

THEODORE: Lamp! You're joking! We're going to light candles. It makes things much prettier. Come on, Mitzi, you can help me.
>   (*He and Mitzi light the candles; in the two candelabra, on the chest, one on the desk, then two on the sideboard. Meanwhile Fritz and Christine are speaking together.*)

FRITZ: How are you, my treasure?

CHRISTINE: I'm fine, now—

FRITZ: And otherwise?

CHRISTINE: I've been missing you so much.

FRITZ: We just saw each other yesterday.

CHRISTINE: Yes . . . from a distance . . . (*shyly*) Fritz, it wasn't nice of you to . . .

FRITZ: Yes, I know. Mitzi's already told me. But as usual you're acting like such a child. I couldn't get away. You have to understand things like that.

CHRISTINE: Yes . . . Fritz, dear . . . Who were those people in your box?

FRITZ: Acquaintances—it doesn't matter at all who they are.

CHRISTINE: Who was the lady in the black velvet dress?

FRITZ: My child, I have no memory at all for the way ladies dress.

CHRISTINE (*coaxingly*): Come on now!

FRITZ: What I mean is . . . I do remember sometimes—under certain circumstances. For example, I remember very clearly the dark gray blouse that you wore the first time we saw each other. And the white and black bodice, yesterday . . . at the theater—

CHRISTINE: I'm wearing it again today!

FRITZ: Oh, so you are! . . . Well, you know, from a distance it looks completely different. Seriously! And I recognize that locket, too.

CHRISTINE (*smiling*): When was I wearing it?

FRITZ: Well—during—yes, when we were strolling in the park near where all the children were playing . . . isn't that right? . . .

CHRISTINE: Yes . . . You do think of me sometimes.

FRITZ: Quite often, my pet . . .

CHRISTINE: Not as often as I think of you. I'm always thinking of you . . . all day long . . . I'm never happy unless I see you!

FRITZ: Don't we see each other often enough?

CHRISTINE: Often . . .

FRITZ: But of course, we'll be seeing less of each other in the summer. . . . What would you say if I told you that I would be going away for a few weeks?

CHRISTINE (*worried*): What? What do you mean? Are you planning to take a trip?

FRITZ: No . . . Of course, it is possible that I might be in the mood to be all by myself for a week. . . .

CHRISTINE: Yes, but why?

FRITZ: I'm only talking about a possibility. I know myself, I do have such moods. And, you—sometime you might not feel like seeing me either for a few days. I'd always understand that.

CHRISTINE: I will never feel that way, Fritz.

FRITZ: You never know.

CHRISTINE: *I* know. I love you.

FRITZ: And of course I love you too. Very much.

CHRISTINE: You're everything to me, Fritz, you are my all. For you I could—

(*She interrupts herself.*)

No, I can't imagine that there would ever be a time when I wouldn't want to see you. As long as I live, Fritz—

FRITZ (*interrupting*): Dear child, please . . . it's better not to say things like that . . . Those big words—I don't like them. Let's not talk about . . . "forever."

CHRISTINE (*with a sad smile*): Don't worry, Fritz. Of course, I know it's not forever . . .

FRITZ: You don't understand what I'm saying, dear child. It is possible (*laughing*) that one day we won't be able to live without each other but we can't really know that yet, right? We're only human.

THEODORE (*pointing to the candles*): Would you be so kind as to have a look at this? . . . Now isn't this much better than some silly lamplight?

FRITZ: You really were born with the touch.

THEODORE: Children, how would it be if we started . . . thinking about supper? . . .

MITZI: Yes . . . ! Come on, Christine! . . .

FRITZ: Wait, I'll show you where you can find everything.

MITZI: First we must have a tablecloth.

THEODORE (*with an exaggerated accent*): "That is a cloth of the table."

FRITZ: What?

THEODORE: Don't you remember the clown at the Orpheum? "That is a cloth of the table. . . ." "That is a piece from tin." . . . "That is a little piccolo. . . ."

MITZI: Hey, Teddy, when are you going to take me to the Orpheum? You promised just the other day. And when we go, Christine will come along and Mr. Fritz, too.
   (*She takes the tablecloth from Fritz, who has removed it from the sideboard.*)
Then *we'll* be the company in your box. . . .

FRITZ: Yes, yes. . . .

MITZI: And the lady in the black velvet dress can go home all by herself.

FRITZ: Why do you and Christine keep dwelling on this lady in black? It's really stupid.

MITZI: Oh, *we* don't dwell on her at all . . . Now then . . . the silverware?
   (*Fritz shows her where everything is kept.*)
Yes . . . And the plates? . . . yes, thank you . . . so now the two of us will take care of the rest ourselves. . . . Now go . . . go on, you'll only be in the way.
   (*Theodore meanwhile has lain down full length on the sofa; as Fritz crosses downstage to him, he speaks.*)

THEODORE: With your permission . . .
   (*Mitzi and Christine set the table.*)

MITZI: Have you ever seen the picture of Fritz in his uniform?

CHRISTINE: No.

MITZI: Oh, you have to see it. So smart!
   (*They continue speaking.*)

THEODORE (*on the sofa*): You see, Fritz, I live for evenings like this.

FRITZ: Yes, they *are* nice.

THEODORE: They put me so at ease. . . . You too? . . .

FRITZ: I wish I could always be so content.

MITZI: Tell me, Mr. Fritz, is there coffee?

FRITZ: Yes . . . You can light that now because it takes a while to brew. . . .

THEODORE (*to Fritz*): I'd give ten of your "enchantresses" for one sweet little girl like her.

FRITZ: You can't compare them.

THEODORE: You know, we hate the woman we love and we only love the women to whom we are indifferent.

(*Fritz laughs.*)

MITZI: What's so funny? We want to hear it too!

THEODORE: It's not for your ears, children. We're philosophizing. (*To Fritz*) Even if this were the last time we were with them, we wouldn't be having any less fun, right?

FRITZ: "The last time"—That's a bit melancholy, isn't it? Parting is always painful, even when you've been looking forward to it for a long time!

CHRISTINE: Fritz, where are the small forks?

(*Fritz goes upstage to the sideboard.*)

FRITZ: Here they are, sweetheart.

(*Mitzi comes downstage, runs her fingers through Theodore's hair. He is still lying on the sofa.*)

You pussycat, you!

FRITZ (*opening Mitzi's package*): Superb . . .

CHRISTINE (*to Fritz*): How tidy you keep everything here.

FRITZ: Yes . . .

(*Sorts out the things Mitzi has brought: tin of sardines, cold cuts, butter, cheeses.*)

CHRISTINE: Fritz . . . Won't you tell me?

FRITZ: Tell you what?

CHRISTINE (*very shyly*): Who the lady was?

FRITZ: No. Don't make me angry. (*milder*) Look here, we came to a clear understanding: No questions. That's what makes it all so beautiful! When I'm alone with you, the rest of the world vanishes—period. I don't ask you any questions, either.

CHRISTINE: You can ask me about everything.

FRITZ: But I don't. I don't want to know anything.

(*Mitzi crosses to them again.*)

MITZI: God, you're making a mess here. (*Takes over and arranges the food on the plates.*) There . . .

THEODORE: Fritz, do you have anything to drink in the house?

FRITZ: Of course, I'm sure something can be found.

(*He walks offstage to the anteroom.*)

THEODORE (*rising and inspecting the table*): Good.—

MITZI: So, I think everything's set! . . .

(*Fritz comes in with several bottles.*)

FRITZ: Well here we have something we might like to drink.

THEODORE: Where are the roses that are supposed to fall from the ceiling?

MITZI: Yes! Right! We forget the roses! (*She takes the roses out of the vase, climbs on a chair, and lets them fall on the table.*) There!

CHRISTINE: Lord, she stops at nothing.

THEODORE: Please! Not on the plates . . .

FRITZ: Where do you want to sit, Christine?

THEODORE: Where's a corkscrew?

(*Fritz brings one from the sideboard.*)

FRITZ: Here's one.

(*Mitzi attempts to open the wine bottle.*)

FRITZ: Give that to me.

THEODORE: Let me open it. . . . (*Takes the bottle and corkscrew out of her hands.*) Meanwhile you could . . . (*Mimes piano playing.*) . . . a little.

MITZI: Yes! Yes! That'll be nifty! . . . (*She walks to the piano, opens it after she's removed the things on it and placed them on a chair.*)

FRITZ (*to Christine*): Should I?

CHRISTINE: Oh please do. I've been wanting to hear you play for so long.

FRITZ (*at the piano*): You can play a little too, can't you?

CHRISTINE (*awkwardly*): Oh Lord . . .

MITZI: She can play beautifully—Christine can—she can sing, too.

FRITZ: Really? You never told me that! . . .

CHRISTINE: Did you ever ask me?

FRITZ: Where did you learn?

CHRISTINE: Well, I never really studied. Father gave me a few lessons—but I don't have much of a voice. And, you know, ever since my aunt died, the one that always lived with us, it's much quieter at home than it was.

FRITZ: What do you really do all day long?

CHRISTINE: Oh Lord, I have plenty to do!

FRITZ: Around the house—right?

CHRISTINE: Yes. And I copy music quite a lot.

THEODORE: Music?

CHRISTINE: Of course.

THEODORE: That must pay terrifically well. (*as the others laugh*) Well, I would pay you terrifically well. I think copying must be an awful job!

MITZI: It's ridiculous the way she drives herself with that work. (*To Christine*) If I had a voice like yours, I would have gone on the stage a long time ago.

THEODORE: You don't even need much voice. . . . I suppose you do absolutely nothing all day long, right?

MITZI: I beg your pardon! I have two little brothers who go to school. In the morning I dress them, and later I help them with their homework—

THEODORE: Not a word of that is true.

MITZI: Well, you don't have to believe me! —And up until last fall I even had a job in a store from eight in the morning until eight at night—

THEODORE (*in a gentle mocking tone*): And where was that?

MITZI: In a milliner's shop. My mother wants me to go back there.

THEODORE (*as above*): So why did you leave then?

FRITZ (*to Christine*): You must sing something for us!

THEODORE: Children, why don't we eat now, and later on you can perform, all right? . . .

FRITZ (*standing up, to Christine*): Come, sweetheart! (*Leads her to the table.*)

MITZI: The coffee! It's boiling over, and we haven't even eaten anything yet!

THEODORE: It doesn't make any difference now!

MITZI: But it's boiling over! (*Blows out the spirit lamp; everyone sits at the table.*)

THEODORE: What would you like, Mitzi? But let me tell you right now, the torte comes last . . . ! First you must eat all the sour things.

(*Fritz pours the wine.*)

Not that way! Nowadays it's done differently. Don't you know the latest fashion? (*Stands up, with affected elegance, bottle in hand, and speaks to Christine.*) Voeslauer Ausstich eighteen hundred . . . (*The next sentences are spoken unintelligibly as he pours for Mitzi.*) Voeslauer Ausstich eighteen hundred . . . (*again, to Fritz*) Voeslauer Ausstich eighteen hundred . . . (*and again, at his own place*) Voeslauer Ausstich eighteen hundred . . . (*He sits down.*)

MITZI (*laughing*): He's always such a clown.

(*Theodore raises his glass and they all clink glasses.*)

THEODORE: Cheers!

MITZI: Long life, Theodore . . .

THEODORE (*rising*): Ladies and gentlemen . . .

FRITZ: Not right now!

THEODORE (*sitting down*): All right, I can wait.

(*Everyone eats.*)

MITZI: I love it when speeches are made at the table. I have a cousin who always talks in rhymes.

THEODORE: What regiment is he with?

MITZI: Go on, stop it. . . . He knows his speeches by heart and even rhymes them. I tell you, Christine, they're just wonderful. And he's actually quite an elderly gentleman.

THEODORE: Well, it happens now and again that elderly gentlemen still speak in rhymes.

FRITZ: Why, you're not even drinking, Christine!

(*He clinks glasses with her.*)

THEODORE (*Clinks glasses with Mitzi*): Here's to all the old gentlemen who speak in rhymes.

MITZI (*merrily*): Here's to the young gentlemen even if they don't speak at all . . . for example, here's to Fritz. . . . Now, Mr. Fritz, we'll drink to friendship, if you'd like to—and Christine must also drink to friendship with Theodore.

THEODORE: But not with this wine. I have something better for toasting friendship. (*Rises, takes another bottle—same performance as previously.*) Xeres de la Frontera mille huit cent cinquante—Xeres de la Frontera—Xeres de la Frontera, etc.

MITZI (*sips*): Ah—

THEODORE: Can't you wait for us all to drink? . . . Well then, children . . . Before we solemnly toast our friendship, let us drink to the lucky coincidence that, that . . . and so on. . . .

MITZI: All right, that's enough!

(*They drink. Fritz links arms with Mitzi, Theodore with Christine, glasses in hand, as is done when drinking to friendship. Fritz kisses Mitzi. Theodore is about to kiss Christine.*)

CHRISTINE: Do we have to?

THEODORE: Absolutely, otherwise it doesn't count. . . . (*kisses her*) Well then, and now *à place!* . . .

MITZI: It's terribly hot in here.

FRITZ: That's because of all the candles Theodore lit.

MITZI: And because of the wine. (*She leans back on the easy chair.*)

THEODORE: Now, come here, we've saved the best for last. (*He cuts a small piece of torte and puts it in her mouth.*) Here pussycat—good?

MITZI: Very!

(*He gives her another piece.*)

THEODORE: Come on Fritz, this is the right moment! Now you can play something!

FRITZ: Would you like me to, Christine?

CHRISTINE: Please do!

MITZI: But something smart!

(*Theodore fills the glasses.*)

MITZI: I can't drink any more!

(*She drinks.*)

CHRISTINE (*sipping*): The wine is so strong!

THEODORE (*pointing to wine*): Fritz!

(*Fritz empties his glass, goes to the piano. Christine sits down next to him.*)

MITZI: Mr. Fritz, play "The Double Eagle."

FRITZ: The "Double Eagle"—how does it go?

MITZI: Teddy, can't you play "The Double Eagle?"

THEODORE: I can't play the piano at all.

FRITZ: I know it, but I just can't remember it right now.

MITZI: I'll sing it for you. La . . . la . . . lalalala . . . la . . .

FRITZ: Ah ha! Now I remember!

(*But he does not get it quite right. Mitzi goes to the piano.*)

MITZI: No, like this . . .

(*She plays the melody with one finger.*)

FRITZ: Yes, yes . . .

(*He plays, Mitzi sings along.*)

THEODORE: This brings back sweet memories, doesn't it . . . ?

    (*Fritz plays inaccurately again and stops.*)

FRITZ: That's not right. I have no ear at all.

    (*He improvises. Mitzi speaks immediately after the first chord.*)

MITZI: That's nothing at all!

FRITZ (*laughing*): Don't scold, that's my own!

MITZI: But it's no good for dancing!

FRITZ: Just give it a try. . . .

THEODORE: (*to Mitzi*): Come on, let's give it a try.

    (*Takes her by the waist, they dance. Christine stands by the piano watching him play. Doorbell. Fritz suddenly stops playing; Theodore and Mitzi continue dancing. They speak at the same time.*)

THEODORE: What's that—Oh, Dear!

MITZI: What's that?—O-o-o-o-h!

FRITZ: The doorbell just rang. . . . (*to Theodore*) Did you invite somebody else?

THEODORE: Certainly not—you don't even have to answer.

CHRISTINE (*to Fritz*): What's the matter?

FRITZ: Nothing.

    (*Doorbell again. Fritz stands up, but does not move.*)

THEODORE: You're simply not at home.

FRITZ: You can hear the piano all the way out in the hall. . . . And you can see from the street that the room is lit.

THEODORE: Don't be ridiculous! You're just not at home.

FRITZ: But it makes me nervous.

THEODORE: Well what can it be, then? A letter! —Or a telegram—You're not expecting company at—(*looks at clock*) nine o'clock.

    (*Doorbell rings again.*)

FRITZ: All right, I'll have to go see—

    (*Exits.*)

MITZI: Well, the two of you certainly aren't acting with any class—

    (*Hits a few notes on the piano.*)

THEODORE: Go on, now stop it—

    (*to Christine*)

What's the matter? Does the doorbell make you nervous, too?

(*Fritz returns with forced composure.*)

THEODORE & CHRISTINE: Who was it?

(*Fritz forces himself to smile.*)

FRITZ: You must be good enough to excuse me for a moment. For the time being you can stay in there.

THEODORE: What is going on, then?

CHRISTINE: Who is it?

FRITZ: It's nothing, child, I just need to have a few words with a gentleman. . . . (*He opens the door to the adjoining room, escorts the girls inside. Theodore exits last, giving Fritz an inquiring look. Fritz speaks quietly, with a horrified expression.*) Him . . . !

THEODORE: Ah . . . !

FRITZ: Go in, go in . . .

THEODORE: I beg you, don't do anything stupid. It could be a trap. . . .

FRITZ: Go . . . go . . .

(*Theodore exits to the adjoining room. Fritz hurries out of the room to the hall, so that the stage remains empty for a short time. Then he enters again, preceded by an elegantly dressed gentleman, about thirty-five years old. The gentleman wears a yellow topcoat, gloves, and holds a hat in his hand. Fritz speaks as they enter.*)

Excuse me for having made you wait . . . please . . .

GENTLEMAN (*very lightly*): Oh, that doesn't matter. I'm very sorry to have disturbed you.

FRITZ: It's of no concern. Please won't you . . . (*points to a chair*).

GENTLEMAN: I see that I *have* disturbed you. A little party—is that right?

FRITZ: A few gentlemen friends.

GENTLEMAN (*sitting down, still friendly*): Probably a masquerade?

FRITZ (*disconcerted*): How's that?

GENTLEMAN: Well, your gentlemen friends have ladies' hats and shawls.

FRITZ: Well yes . . . (*smiling*) It's possible that there are also lady friends present. . . .

(*Silence.*)

GENTLEMAN: Life is occasionally quite entertaining. . . . Yes . . . (*He fixes Fritz with his gaze. Fritz stares back for a moment, then looks away.*)

FRITZ: I presume I may take the liberty of asking you to what I owe the honor of your visit?

GENTLEMAN (*calmly*): Certainly . . . You know, my wife forgot her veil. Here. With you.

FRITZ: Your wife, here . . . ? her . . . (*Smiles.*) Your joke is a little odd. . . .

GENTLEMAN (*suddenly standing up, very forceful, almost fierce, as he supports himself with his hand on the back of the chair*): She *did* forget it. (*Fritz also stands up, and the two face each other. The gentleman raises his fist, as if he wanted to strike Fritz; . . . in rage and disgust, he speaks.*) Oh!

(*Fritz defends himself, retreating a step. There is a long pause.*) Here are your letters. (*He throws a parcel that he has pulled out of his topcoat pocket, on to the desk.*) May I please have the ones you have received . . . ?

(*Fritz steps back again. The gentleman, violently, and with insinuation, continues.*) I don't want them to be found here —*later.*

FRITZ (*forcefully*): No one will find them.

(*The gentleman looks at him. Long pause.*)

Is there anything else you wish?

GENTLEMAN (*scornfully*): Anything *else* I wish . . . ?

FRITZ: I am at your service.

(*The gentleman bows coldly.*)

GENTLEMAN: Good.

(*He looks around the room and as he again sees the festive table, ladies' hats, etc., a strong emotion passes over his face, as if there would be another explosion of rage. Fritz, seeing this, speaks again.*)

FRITZ: I am entirely at your service—I shall be home tomorrow until noon.

(*The gentleman bows and turns to leave. Fritz accompanies him to the door, the gentleman resists this. When he has gone, Fritz walks to the desk, remaining there a moment. Then he hurries to the window, looks outside through a crack in the blind, and follows the gentleman with his eyes. The gentleman is now on the sidewalk below. Fritz withdraws from the window, remains staring at the floor for a second, then walks to the door of the adjoining room and opens it halfway and calls.*)

. . . Can I have a word with you, Theodore? Just one moment.
(*The following scene is to be played rapidly.*)

THEODORE: Well . . .

FRITZ: He knows.

THEODORE: He knows nothing. Sure enough, you fell into his trap.
In the end you confessed. You're a fool, I tell you . . . You're—

FRITZ (*pointing to letters*): He brought my letters back to me.

THEODORE (*stunned*): Oh . . .

(*after a pause*)
I always say you shouldn't write letters.

FRITZ: It was him, this afternoon, down there.

THEODORE: Well then, what happened? —Tell me.

FRITZ: Now you have to do me a great service, Theodore.

THEODORE: Don't worry, I'll put everything in order.

FRITZ: There isn't any question of that anymore.

THEODORE: What then . . .

FRITZ: No matter what happens, it will be for the best. . . . (*interrupts himself*) But we can't keep those poor girls waiting any longer.

THEODORE: Let them wait. What were you going to say?

FRITZ: It would be good if you could still manage to see Lensky today.

THEODORE: Right away, if you'd like.

FRITZ: You won't find him now . . . but between eleven and twelve he will certainly be at the café. . . . Maybe then the two of you can come back here. . . .

THEODORE: Come on, don't make such a face. . . . In ninety-nine cases out of a hundred these things come out fine.

FRITZ: It's been seen to that *this* isn't going to end well.

THEODORE: I beg you, just remember last year the affair between Dr. Billinger and Herz. That was exactly the same thing.

FRITZ: Stop it, you know yourself—he might as well have shot me dead here in this room: it'll all be the same in the end.

THEODORE (*forced*): Oh that's just great! That's a wonderful way of taking it. . . . And Lensky and I, we count for nothing? Do you think that we will just stand by and permit . . .

FRITZ: Please, stop it! You will simply accept what they propose to do.

THEODORE: Ah—

FRITZ: What's the point, Theodore? As if you didn't know all along.

THEODORE: Nonsense. Anyway, it's all a matter of luck. . . . You're just as likely to win as . . .

FRITZ (*without listening*): She sensed it. We both sensed it. We knew it. . . .

THEODORE: Come on Fritz . . .

FRITZ (*going to the desk, locking the letters inside*): I wonder what *she*'s doing at this very moment. I wonder if he intends to harm . . . Theodore . . . Tomorrow you must find out what happened there.

THEODORE: I'll try . . .

FRITZ: Also, see to it that there won't be any unnecessary delay. . . .

THEODORE: It can hardly take place before the morning of the day after tomorrow.

FRITZ (*almost frightened*): Theodore!

THEODORE: Now then . . . chin up. There's something to be said for inner conviction, isn't that right?—and I'm firmly convinced, that everything . . . will end well. (*Talks himself into being cheerful.*) I don't know why myself, but I am just convinced of it.

FRITZ (*smiling*): You're such a good friend! —But what are we going to tell the girls?

THEODORE: That really isn't important. We'll simply send them away.

FRITZ: Oh no. We'll be as cheerful as possible. Christine must not suspect anything. I'm going to sit down at the piano again. And you can call them back in here.

(*Theodore turns to do so, his expression dissatisfied.*)

And what are you going to tell them?

THEODORE: That this is none of their business.

FRITZ (*who has sat down at the piano, turns toward him*): No, no—

THEODORE: Tell them it has to do with a friend—we'll think of something.

(*Fritz plays a few notes.*)

Ladies, please. (*He has opened the door; Mitzi and Christine enter.*)

MITZI: Well, finally! Has he gone?

CHRISTINE (*hurrying to Fritz*): Who was here, Fritz?

FRITZ (*still playing piano*): You never stop being curious.

CHRISTINE: I beg you, Fritz, tell me.

FRITZ: Treasure, I can't tell you. It really has to do with people you don't know at all.

CHRISTINE (*coaxingly*): Come on, Fritz, tell me the truth!

THEODORE: Naturally, she won't leave you alone. . . . Just be sure you don't tell her anything! You promised him!

MITZI: Come on, don't be so boring, Christine. Let them have their fun. They're just showing off, anyhow.

THEODORE: I must finish my waltz with Miss Mitzi. (*Clowning*) Maestro, please—a bit of music.

(*Fritz plays. Theodore and Mitzi dance; after a few bars they stop.*)

MITZI: I can't! (*She collapses in an easy chair. Theodore kisses her and sits down with her on the arm of the easy chair. Fritz remains at the piano but takes Christine's hands in his, looking at her.*)

CHRISTINE (*as if coming out of a trance*): Why don't you go on playing?

FRITZ (*smiling*): Enough for today. . . .

CHRISTINE: Oh, if I could only play like that . . .

FRITZ: Do you play much? . . .

CHRISTINE: I don't get much chance to. There's always something to do at home. And then, you see, we have such a bad little piano.

FRITZ: Well I'd like to try it out one day. Actually, I'd really like to see your place.

CHRISTINE (*smiling*): It's not as beautiful as it is here! . . .

FRITZ: And there's another thing I'd like: One day I want you to tell me a lot about yourself . . . a whole lot . . . I really know so little about you.

CHRISTINE: There's not much to tell. I don't have any secrets either—like someone else I know . . .

FRITZ: You've never loved anyone else?

(*Christine just looks at him; he kisses her hands.*)

CHRISTINE: And I will never love anyone else. . . .

FRITZ (*with an almost painful expression*): Don't say that . . . don't say that. . . . What do you know? . . . Does your father care for you a great deal, Christine?

CHRISTINE: Oh Lord! . . . There was a time when I told him everything.

FRITZ: Now, my child, don't reproach yourself. . . . Now and then one does have secrets. That's the way of the world.

CHRISTINE: . . . If I only knew that you liked me—then everything would be just fine.

FRITZ: Don't you know that then?

CHRISTINE: If only you would always speak to me this way, yes . . .

FRITZ: Christine! You can't be comfortable sitting like that.

CHRISTINE: Oh forget it—it's perfectly comfortable. (*She rests her head on the piano. Fritz stands up and caresses her hair.*) Oh, that's good.

(*Silence in the room.*)

THEODORE: Where are your cigars, Fritz?

(*Fritz goes over to him; Theodore standing by the sideboard has already been searching. Mitzi has dozed off. Fritz hands him the cigar box.*)

FRITZ: And the black coffee!

(*He pours two cups.*)

THEODORE: Children, wouldn't you like some black coffee, too?

FRITZ: Mitzi, should I pour you a cup?

THEODORE: Let's let her sleep. . . . Fritz, by the way, don't drink any coffee now. You should get to bed as soon as possible and see to it that you get a good night's sleep.

(*Fritz looks at him and laughs bitterly.*)

Well, now, things are as they are. . . . And it's no longer a matter of acting as grandly or profoundly as possible, but as sensibly as possible . . . that's what's important . . . in these matters.

FRITZ: You'll still come by tonight with Lensky, right?

THEODORE: That's nonsense. There'll be enough time tomorrow morning.

FRITZ: I beg you.

THEODORE: Well then, all right . . .

FRITZ: Will you walk the girls home?

THEODORE: Yes and as a matter of fact, right now . . . Mitzi! . . . Get up!

MITZI: You're drinking coffee! Give me a cup too!

THEODORE: Here you are, child! . . .

FRITZ (*going to Christine*): Tired, my sweetheart? . . .

CHRISTINE: How sweet it is when you talk this way.

FRITZ: Very tired?

CHRISTINE (*smiling*): The wine. —And I have a little headache, too. . . .

FRITZ: Well the fresh air will make you feel better.

CHRISTINE: Are we going so soon? —Will you walk us home?

FRITZ: No, my pet. I'm staying now. . . . I still have a few things left to do.

CHRISTINE (*trying to remember*): Now . . . What do you have to do now?

FRITZ (*almost sternly*): Christine, you must learn not to do this! (*mildly*) I'm just exhausted. . . . Today Theodore and I went walking out in the country for hours—

THEODORE: Oh, that was delightful. One of these days we'll all go into the country together.

MITZI: Oh how smart! And you'll put on your uniforms.

THEODORE: There's a real nature lover for you.

CHRISTINE: When will we see each other again?

FRITZ (*somewhat nervous*): Don't worry. I'll write you.

CHRISTINE (*sadly*): Good-bye. (*She turns to leave and Fritz notices her sadness.*)

FRITZ: *Tomorrow* we'll see each other, Christine.

CHRISTINE (*happily*): Yes?

FRITZ: In the park . . . there like the last time . . . at—let's say, six o'clock. . . . Yes? Is that all right with you?
(*Christine nods.*)

MITZI: Are you coming with us, Fritz, darling?

THEODORE: She really does have a talent for informality!

FRITZ: No, I'm staying home.

MITZI: He's lucky! The long trip we have ahead of us . . .

FRITZ: Mitzi, you're leaving almost all of that delicious torte. Wait, I'll wrap it up for you—all right?

MITZI (*to Theodore*): Would that be all right?

(Fritz picks up the torte.)

CHRISTINE: She's like a little child. . . .

MITZI *(to Fritz)*: Wait, I'll help you put out the candles.
(Puts out one candle after the other, the candle on the desk remains lit.)

CHRISTINE: Shouldn't I open the window for you? It's so stuffy.
(She opens the window, looks at the house directly across the street.)

FRITZ: And, children, now I will light your way.

MITZI: Are the lights out so soon in the staircase?

THEODORE: Yes, of course.

CHRISTINE: Oh, the fresh air from the window is good! . . .

MITZI: A little spring breeze . . .
(At the door, Fritz has the candlestick in his hand.)
Well, thank you for your kind hospitality!

THEODORE *(pushing Mitzi)*: Go, go, go . . .
(Fritz accompanies the others out. The inner door remains open, they can be heard talking outside. The outer door opens.)

MITZI: Oh, stop it!

THEODORE: Be careful of the steps there.

MITZI: Thank you very much for the torte. . . .

THEODORE: Shhhhh, you'll wake up the neighborhood!

CHRISTINE: Good night!

THEODORE: Good night!
(Fritz can be heard closing and locking the apartment door. As he enters and places the candle on the desk, the downstairs door can be heard opening and closing. Fritz walks to the window and waves farewell. Christine calls from the street.)

CHRISTINE: Good night!

MITZI *(in equally high spirits)*: Good night, my sweet little pet . . .

THEODORE *(scolding)*: Now, Mitzi . . .
(He can be heard speaking, she laughs, their footsteps fade away. Theodore whistles "The Double Eagle," which is the last sound to fade away. Fritz looks outside for a few more seconds, then he sinks into the easy chair by the window.)

(Curtain.)

Act II

Christine's room, neat and modest. She is getting dressed to go out. Katharine enters, after she has knocked outside.

KATHARINE: Evening, Miss Christine.

CHRISTINE (*standing in front of a mirror, turns*): Good evening.

KATHARINE: You were just going out?

CHRISTINE: I'm in no hurry.

KATHARINE: Because my husband and I wonder if you'd like to go out to supper with us in the Lehnergarten. There'll be music there tonight.

CHRISTINE: Oh, thank you, Mrs. Binder . . . But I can't tonight . . . some other time, maybe? —Now I hope you're not angry, are you?

KATHARINE: Don't be silly—why should I be? I'm sure you can find more entertaining company than us.

(*Christine gives her a look.*)

KATHARINE: Is your father already at the theater. . . ?

CHRISTINE: Oh no, he comes home before he goes to work. These days it starts at seven thirty!

KATHARINE: That's right, I always forget that. Well then, I'll just wait for him here because I've been meaning to ask him a long time now for free tickets to the new play. I shouldn't have any trouble getting them now, I guess?

CHRISTINE: Of course . . . Hardly anyone is going now that the evening weather is so fine.

KATHARINE: People like us hardly ever get a chance to go otherwise unless we happen to have friends who work in the theater. . . . But don't stay here on my account, Miss Christine, if you have to leave. Of course, my husband is going to be very disappointed . . . and somebody else too. . . .

CHRISTINE: Who?

KATHARINE: My husband's cousin is going to be with us, naturally. . . . You know, Miss Christine, he has a steady job now.

CHRISTINE (*indifferently*): Oh.

KATHARINE: And with a very nice salary. He's such an upright young man. And he admires you so much—

CHRISTINE: Well then—good-bye, Mrs. Binder.

KATHARINE: No matter what anyone says about you—he won't believe a word of it. . . .

> (*Christine gives her a look.*)

There really are men like that. . . .

CHRISTINE: *Good-bye*, Mrs. Binder.

KATHARINE: Good-bye . . . (*not too nasty a tone of voice*) Better make sure you're not too late for your rendezvous, Miss Christine!

CHRISTINE: What is it you really want from me?

KATHARINE: Nothing, you're right! You're only young once.

CHRISTINE: Good-bye.

KATHARINE: But I would like to give you a small piece of advice, Miss Christine. You ought to be a little more careful!

CHRISTINE: What is that supposed to mean?

KATHARINE: Look, Miss Christine—Vienna is a very big city. . . . Do you really have to have your rendezvous just down the street from your own home?

CHRISTINE: That's nobody's business.

KATHARINE: At first I didn't even want to believe it when my husband told me. He saw you, you know. . . . "Go on," I said to him, "you probably saw somebody else. Miss Christine, she's not the kind of girl to go strolling in the evening with elegant young gentlemen, and even if she is, she'd be smart enough not to do it in her own backyard." "Well," he says, "you can ask her yourself." And then he says, "It wouldn't surprise me at all—she doesn't come to see us anymore. Instead she's always running around with that Schlager girl, Mitzi. And what kind of company is that for such a proper young girl?" —Men have their minds in the gutter, Miss Christine! —Naturally he had to go and tell Franz all about it right away, but Franz got really angry—he'd put his hand in the fire for Miss Christine, and anyone who says anything about you is going to have to answer to him. He's always talking about how you're such a homebody and how sweet you were always with your old Aunt—may her soul rest in peace—and how modest and quiet you are, and so on. . . . (*Pause.*) Now maybe you will come with us to the concert . . . ?

CHRISTINE: No . . .

> (*Hans Weiring enters carrying a branch of lilac.*)

WEIRING: Good evening . . . Oh, Mrs. Binder. How are you?

KATHARINE: Fine, thank you.

WEIRING: And little Lina? —And your dear husband? . . .

KATHARINE: They're all healthy—thank the Lord.

WEIRING: Well, that's nice—(*to Christine*) You're still home—in this beautiful weather?

CHRISTINE: I was just going out.

WEIRING: That's a good idea—The air is so wonderful outside today, isn't it, Mrs. Binder, it's absolutely wonderful. I was just walking through the park. The lilac is in bloom there—a feast for the eyes! I also broke the law a little bit. (*Gives Christine the lilac branch.*)

CHRISTINE: Thank you, Father.

KATHARINE: Be thankful that the watchman didn't catch you.

WEIRING: Why don't you go there, Mrs. Binder? It still smells just as good there as if I hadn't picked this little branch.

KATHARINE: But if everyone did that—

WEIRING: That *would* be a problem!

CHRISTINE: Good-bye, Father!

WEIRING: If you'd like to wait just a few minutes you could walk with me to the theater.

CHRISTINE: I . . . I promised Mitzi that I would come by for her. . . .

WEIRING: I see. —That's a better idea. Young people belong together. Good-bye, Christine . . .

CHRISTINE (*kisses him*): Good-bye, Mrs. Binder!
    (*Exits. Weiring watches her tenderly as she leaves.*)

KATHARINE: She and Miss Mitzi have become very intimate friends.

WEIRING: Yes—I'm really happy that Tina has some company and isn't always sitting at home. What else does her life have to offer her! . . .

KATHARINE: Yes, of course.

WEIRING: I really can't tell you, Mrs. Binder, how much it hurts me sometimes to come home from a rehearsal—and see her sitting and sewing—and then, in the afternoon, when we've hardly finished eating she sits down right away and begins to copy her music. . . .

KATHARINE: Well, well, millionaires, of course, have it better than we do. How about her singing?

WEIRING: She's not doing very much. Her voice is good enough for the living room, and she sings sweetly enough for her father—but she couldn't make a living out of it.

KATHARINE: Oh, that's too bad.

WEIRING: I'm happy she realizes it herself. At least she'll be spared the disappointment. —Of course, I could find her a place in the theater chorus.

KATHARINE: Yes indeed, with *her* figure!

WEIRING: But that's no future.

KATHARINE: You really have to worry with girls! When I think that in five or six years my Lina will also be a young lady—

WEIRING: Why don't you sit down, Mrs. Binder?

KATHARINE: Oh, no thank you, my husband is coming for me soon. I just came up to invite Christine out.

WEIRING: Invite her out?

KATHARINE: Yes, to the concert in the Lehnergarten. I thought that would cheer her up a little bit. She really needs it.

WEIRING: It certainly couldn't harm her—particularly after this dreary winter. Why isn't she going with you?

KATHARINE: I don't know. . . . Maybe because Binder's cousin will be along.

WEIRING: Well that's possible. She can't stand him, you know. She told me so herself.

KATHARINE: Oh? Why not? Franz is a very fine man—he even has a steady job now. These days that's a godsend for a—

WEIRING: For a . . . poor girl . . .

KATHARINE: For every girl it's a godsend.

WEIRING: Now, tell me, Mrs. Binder, is such a lovely creature good for nothing beside some "fine" man, who happens to hold a steady job?

KATHARINE: It is the best thing! You can't wait for a count, and even if one day he does come, he'll probably take off without marrying the girl. . . .

(*Weiring is standing at the window. There is a pause.*)

Well . . . that's why I always say you can never be too careful with young girls—particularly with friends like that—

WEIRING: Is that all she's meant to do, just toss her youth out the window?—What does a poor creature get for all her virtue when she waits for years—and only a stocking weaver comes along!

KATHARINE: Mr. Weiring, even if my husband is only a stocking weaver, he's still a good honest man, and in all these years I've never had any reason to complain about . . .

WEIRING (*soothingly*): But Mrs. Binder—did you think I was talking about you! . . . you didn't just toss your youth out the window, either.

KATHARINE: I don't remember those days anymore.

WEIRING: Don't say that—you can say anything you like—but memories are the best things we have in life.

KATHARINE: I don't have any memories at all.

WEIRING: Now, now . . .

KATHARINE: And even if you have these memories, what are you left with? . . . Regret.

WEIRING: Well, and what will she be left with—if she doesn't have anything at all to remember—? If all your life has just passed you by—(*said very simply, not dramatically*) one day just like the next, without happiness, without love—is that any better perhaps?

KATHARINE: But, Mr. Weiring, think about the old lady—your sister! . . . But it still pains you to hear people talk about her, Mr. Weiring. . . .

WEIRING: Yes, it still hurts me. . . .

KATHARINE: Of course . . . When two people were so close to one another . . . I've always said, you'd have to go a long way to find a brother like you.

(*Weiring waves off the compliment.*)

It's true. You had to be a father and a mother to your sister at such a young age.

WEIRING: Yes, yes—

KATHARINE: That must be of some comfort to you. Just to know that you've always looked after that poor creature—

WEIRING: Yes, I used to think that way—when she was still a young and pretty girl—and God knows I thought of myself as clever and noble. But later as the gray hairs slowly came, and the wrinkles, and the days just slipped away—and her youth, too—that young girl became bit by bit—you hardly notice—that spinster. It wasn't until then that I began to realize what I had actually done!

KATHARINE: But Mr. Weiring—

WEIRING: I can still see her the way she used to sit across from me in the evening. There by the lamp, in this very room. She would look at me with that quiet smile of hers, accepting God's will—as if she still felt gratitude toward me—and I—all I wanted to do was throw myself at her feet and beg her forgiveness for having protected her so well from life's dangers—and life's happiness!

(Pause.)

KATHARINE: Well, anyhow, there are lots of women who would have been happy with a brother like you at their side . . . and happy to have nothing to regret. . . .

(Mitzi enters.)

MITZI: Good evening! . . . My, it's already so dark in here . . . you can't see anything. —Ah, Mrs. Binder. Your husband is downstairs waiting for you. . . . Isn't Christine home . . . ?

WEIRING: She left fifteen minutes ago.

KATHARINE: Didn't you meet her? Didn't she have a rendezvous with you?

MITZI: No . . . well anyway we missed each other. . . . Your husband told me that you're going to the concert—?

KATHARINE: Yes, he adores these things. Oh my, Miss Mitzi, that's a charming little hat you're wearing. New, isn't it?

MITZI: Certainly not. —Don't you recognize the style anymore? From last spring; all that's new is the trimming.

KATHARINE: You make the trimming yourself?

MITZI: Well, of course I did.

WEIRING: How clever!

KATHARINE: You know, I always forget that you worked for a year as a milliner.

MITZI: I'll probably go back someday. Mother wants me to—what can you do?

KATHARINE: How is your mother?

MITZI: All right—has a little toothache—but the doctor says it's only rheumatism. . . .

WEIRING: Well, it's high time that I leave. . . .

KATHARINE: I'll go downstairs with you, Mr. Weiring. . . .

MITZI: I'll come too. . . . Now bring your topcoat, Mr. Weiring, it'll be chilly later.

WEIRING: You think so?

KATHARINE: Of course . . . How can anyone be so careless.
(*Christine enters.*)
MITZI: Well, here she is. . . .
KATHARINE: Already back from your walk?
CHRISTINE: Yes. Hello, how are you, Mitzi. . . . I have such a headache. . . . (*She sits down.*)
WEIRING: What?
KATHARINE: It's probably from the spring air. . . .
WEIRING: Come on, what's the matter, Christine! . . . Miss Mitzi, please light a lamp.
(*Mitzi is about to do so.*)
CHRISTINE: I can do that myself.
WEIRING: Let me look at you, Christine . . . !
CHRISTINE: It's nothing, father. I'm sure it's from the spring air outside.
KATHARINE: Sometimes spring air just doesn't agree with some people.
WEIRING: Miss Mitzi, will you stay here with Christine?
MITZI: Of course, I'll stay here. . . .
CHRISTINE: But it's nothing, father.
MITZI: My mother doesn't make such a fuss over me when I have a headache. . . .
WEIRING (*to Christine, who is still sitting*): Are you very tired. . . ?
CHRISTINE (*getting up from the chair*): Look, I'm already back on my feet! (*She smiles.*)
WEIRING: There—you already look much better—(*to Katharine*) She looks completely different when she smiles, right . . . ? Well then, good-bye, Christine. (*Kisses her.*) And be sure your headache is all gone when I come home tonight. . . !
KATHARINE (*quietly to Christine. Weiring is at the door*): Did the two of you have a quarrel?
(*Christine makes an impatient gesture.*)
WEIRING (*at the door*): Mrs. Binder. . . !
MITZI: Good-bye. . . !
(*They exit.*)
You know where you got that headache, don't you? All the sweet wine yesterday. I'm amazed that I haven't felt it at all— oh but we had fun, didn't we. . . ?

(*Christine nods.*)

They're both such smart people—both of them—we certainly can't complain, right?—And Fritz has a beautiful home, really magnificent! At Teddy's . . . (*interrupts herself*) Never mind . . . Hey, do you really have such a bad headache? Why aren't you talking? . . . What's wrong with you . . .

CHRISTINE: Would you believe it—he didn't come.

MITZI: He stood you up? Serves you right!

CHRISTINE: What do you mean by that? What have I done?—

MITZI: You spoil him. You're too good to him. That's bound to make a man arrogant.

CHRISTINE: You don't know what you're talking about.

MITZI: I know very well what I'm saying.—I've been annoyed with you the whole time. He's too late for your rendezvous, he doesn't walk you home, he sits with strangers in the theater, and he's stood you up—you put up with everything, and to top it off you look at him—(*mocking her look*) with those lovesick eyes.—

CHRISTINE: Come on, don't talk like that, don't be worse than you are. You care very much for Theodore, too.

MITZI: Care for—of course, I care for him. But not Teddy or any other man will ever live to see the day that I'm upset because of him. If you put them all together, they still wouldn't be worth that (*snaps fingers*).

CHRISTINE: I've never heard you talk like this, never!

MITZI: Well, Tina—we never used to speak about this at all—I didn't dare. Do you realize how I looked up to you? You see, I always thought: If you ever fell for someone, you'd really fall hard. The first time always knocks you for a loop!—You can be thankful though that you have me for such a good friend to help you through your first love.

CHRISTINE: Mitzi!

MITZI: Don't you know that I'm a good friend to you? If I weren't here to tell you, "My child, he's not different from any other man, and all men put together aren't worth one rotten hour," you'd start thinking God knows what. But I'm always telling you: you should never believe one word a man says.

CHRISTINE: What are you talking about—men, men.—What do I care about men!—I'm not asking about any other men. All my life, I'll only think of him. . . .

MITZI: . . . Well, then what are you thinking. . . . Has he . . . of course . . . anything can happen and has. . . . In that case you should have started this whole business differently. . . .

CHRISTINE: Oh, be quiet!

MITZI: Well, what do you want from me? I can't do anything about it—you should have thought of it earlier. Now you'll just have to wait until someone comes along with serious intentions written all over his face.

CHRISTINE: Mitzi, I can't stand to hear this today, it only hurts me.—

MITZI (*goodnaturedly*): Now, come on—

CHRISTINE: You'd better go . . . don't be angry . . . just leave me alone!

MITZI: Why should I be angry? I'm going. I didn't want to hurt you, Christine, really. . . . (*as she turns to leave*) Oh, Mr. Fritz!

FRITZ (*Fritz enters.*): Good evening.

CHRISTINE (*shouts with joy.*): Fritz, Fritz!
　　(*Runs into his arms. Mitzi sneaks out with an expression that says "three's a crowd."*)

FRITZ: (*freeing himself*): What's this. . . ?

CHRISTINE: Everyone's saying that you're going to leave me! You're not, are you?—not yet—not yet . . .

FRITZ: Who says that? . . . What's the matter. . . . (*caressing her*) Sweetheart! . . . I really thought you'd be startled if I suddenly walked in here.—

CHRISTINE: Oh—just as long as you're here now.

FRITZ: Come on, calm down—did you wait long for me?

CHRISTINE: Why didn't you come?

FRITZ: I was delayed and got there late. I went to the park and couldn't find you—and I was about to go home again. But suddenly I felt such a longing, a longing for this dear sweet little face. . . .

CHRISTINE (*happily*): Is that true?

FRITZ: And then all of a sudden I felt such an indescribable desire actually to see where you live—really, it's the truth—All at once I just had to see it—I couldn't stand it any longer and came up here . . . you're not angry with me, are you?!

CHRISTINE: Oh, Lord!

FRITZ: No one saw me—and I knew that your father was at the theater.

CHRISTINE: What do I care about other people!

FRITZ: So this is it? (*Looks about the room.*) So this is your place? Very pretty . . .

CHRISTINE: How can you see anything? (*Is about to take the shade off the lamp.*)

FRITZ: No, don't. It will be too bright, this is better. . . . So this is it? This is the window you told me about, where you always do your work, right? And the beautiful view! (*smiling*) How many rooftops you can see from here. . . . And over there— What's that?—the dark thing I see over there?

CHRISTINE: That's the Kahlenberg!

FRITZ: Right! You have a prettier view here than I do.

CHRISTINE: Oh!

FRITZ: I'd like to live this high up, above all those roofs. I find this very beautiful. And is it quiet in these little streets?

CHRISTINE: Oh, it's noisy enough in the daytime.

FRITZ: Do any carriages ever drive by here?

CHRISTINE: Rarely, but there's a blacksmith shop right over there.

FRITZ: Oh, that's not very pleasant. (*He has sat down.*)

CHRISTINE: You get used to it. We don't even hear it anymore.

FRITZ (*standing up again, quickly*): Am I really here for the first time? It all seems so familiar! . . . It looks exactly the way I thought it would. (*He's about to take a closer look at the room.*)

CHRISTINE: No, you mustn't look at any of those things—

FRITZ: What sort of pictures are these? . . .

CHRISTINE: Come on . . . !

FRITZ: Oh, I'd like to look at them. (*He takes the lamp and illuminates the pictures.*)

CHRISTINE: . . . "Parting"—and "Homecoming."

FRITZ: That's right—"Parting"—and "Homecoming"!

CHRISTINE: I know they aren't pretty—there's one in father's room. It's much better.

FRITZ: What is it?

CHRISTINE: There's a girl, looking out the window, and outside, you know, it's winter—and it's called "Forsaken."—

FRITZ: Yes . . . (*Puts the lamp back.*) Ah, and here's your library. (*Sits down next to the small book stand.*)

CHRISTINE: Don't bother with those—

FRITZ: Why not? Ah!—Schiller . . . Hauff . . . The Encyclopedia . . . Quite a collection!

CHRISTINE: It only goes through *G* . . .

FRITZ (*smiling*): Oh, I see . . . "The Home Companion" . . . You look at the pictures, right?

CHRISTINE: Of course.

FRITZ (*still sitting*): And who's that gentleman on the stove?

CHRISTINE (*like a teacher*): That's Schubert, of course.

FRITZ (*rising*): Of course.

CHRISTINE: Because father likes him so much. Father used to compose songs, very pretty ones.

FRITZ: He doesn't anymore?

CHRISTINE: Not anymore.

(Pause.)

FRITZ (*sitting*): It's so comfortable here . . .

CHRISTINE: You really like it?

FRITZ: Very much . . . Now what's this. (*Takes a vase of artificial flowers that is standing on the table.*)

CHRISTINE: Now he's found something else!

FRITZ: No, no, my child, these don't belong here . . . they look so dusty.

CHRISTINE: They're certainly not dusty. . . .

FRITZ: Artificial flowers always look dusty. . . . There should be real flowers in your room, fragrant and fresh. From now on I'll send—(*Interrupts himself, turns away to hide his emotions.*)

CHRISTINE: What is it? . . . What were you about to say?

FRITZ: Nothing . . . nothing . . .

CHRISTINE (*stands, speaks tenderly*): What?

FRITZ: That I'll send you fresh flowers tomorrow. That's what I was about to say. . . .

CHRISTINE: Well, and do you regret that already?—Naturally by tomorrow you won't be thinking of me.

(Fritz makes a gesture of denial.)

Certainly—when we're not together, you don't think about me.

FRITZ: Now what are you talking about?

CHRISTINE: Oh, yes, I know. I feel it.

FRITZ: How can you even imagine such a thing?

CHRISTINE: It's your own fault. Because you always keep secrets from me! . . . Because you never tell me anything at all about yourself. —What do you do all day long?

FRITZ: Sweetheart, it's very simple. I go to lectures—on and off—then I go to the café . . . then I read . . . sometimes I play the piano—then I chat with someone or other . . . then I go visiting. . . . It's all so unimportant. It's so boring to talk about— Well, now I have to go, my child. . . .

CHRISTINE: So soon—

FRITZ: Your father will be home shortly.

CHRISTINE: Not for a long time, Fritz. Stay—for just a minute— Do stay—

FRITZ: And then I have . . . Theodore's expecting me. . . . I still have something to discuss with him.

CHRISTINE: Today?

FRITZ: Absolutely today.

CHRISTINE: But you could see him tomorrow, instead!

FRITZ: Tomorrow I may not even be in Vienna.

CHRISTINE: Not in Vienna?—

FRITZ (*noticing her fear, calmly—cheerfully*): Well, now, that happens doesn't it? I'm going away for a day—or maybe for two—

CHRISTINE: Where?

FRITZ: Where . . . ! Where . . . Anywhere—Oh God, don't make such a face. . . . I'm going to the estate to see my parents . . . now . . . is that so mysterious?

CHRISTINE: You see, you never even tell me about them!

FRITZ: Oh what a child you are! . . . You don't understand at all how sweet it is that we're completely alone. Tell me, don't you feel the same?

CHRISTINE: No, it's not sweet at all that you never tell me anything about yourself. . . . I'm interested in everything that concerns you, oh yes. . . . everything—I want more of you than the one hour in the evening we sometimes spend together. But then you're gone again, and I don't know anything about you at all . . . Then a whole night passes and a whole day with all those long hours—and I don't know anything. It makes me so sad.

FRITZ: Why does it make you sad?

CHRISTINE: Well, because I miss you so much, as if you weren't even in the same city, as if you were in some totally unknown place. It's as if I'd lost you, you're so far away. . . .

FRITZ (*somewhat impatiently*): But . . .

CHRISTINE: Well, look, it's true!

FRITZ: Come here, to me!

(*She goes to him.*)

You know only one thing, how I—how you—you love me at this moment. . . . (*As she's about to speak, he continues.*) Don't speak about forever. (*More to himself*) Maybe there are moments that give you glimpses of eternity . . . that is the only thing we can understand. The one thing that belongs to us. . . . (*He kisses her. There is a pause. He stands up. Bursts out.*) Oh how beautiful it is here, with you, how beautiful! . . . (*He stands by the window.*) How far away the world is, even with all these houses around . . . I feel as if I'm all by myself, alone here with you. . . . (*quiet*) So protected . . .

CHRISTINE: If you only spoke like that all the time . . . I could almost believe. . . .

FRITZ: What, my child?

CHRISTINE: That you love me the way I dreamed you did—on the day you gave me the first kiss . . . Do you remember?

FRITZ (*passionately*): I *do* love you! (*He embraces her, tears himself from her.*) But now let me go—

CHRISTINE: Are you already sorry that you said that to me? You're free, yes, you're free—you can leave me whenever you want. . . . You haven't promised me anything—and I haven't asked you for anything. . . . Whatever happens to me—*just doesn't matter*—I was happy once, I can't ask any more of life. I only want you to know this and believe me: I've never loved any man before you and will never love any man again—when you don't want me anymore—

FRITZ (*to himself*): Don't say that, don't say that—it sounds . . . too beautiful. . . .

(*A knock at the door. Fritz starts.*)

That must be Theodore. . . .

CHRISTINE (*taken aback*): He knows you're here with me—?
(*Theodore enters.*)

THEODORE: Good evening. —Shameless, aren't I?

CHRISTINE: You have such important things to talk to him about?

THEODORE: I certainly do—and I've been looking for him everywhere.

FRITZ (*quietly*): Why didn't you wait downstairs?

CHRISTINE: What are you whispering about?

THEODORE (*deliberately loud*): Why didn't I wait downstairs? . . . Well, if I'd known for certain that you were here . . . But I couldn't afford to walk back and forth down there for two hours. . . .

FRITZ (*giving him the cue*): So . . . You're going with *me* tomorrow?

THEODORE (*understanding him*): That's right . . .

FRITZ: Good.

THEODORE: I'm so out of breath from running here that I must ask your permission to sit down for a few seconds.

CHRISTINE: Please do. (*Busies herself at the window.*)

FRITZ (*quietly*): Anything new . . . ? Did you find anything out about her?

THEODORE (*quietly to Fritz*): No. I only came to get you because you're so foolish. Why get yourself worked up unnecessarily like this? You should be in bed resting . . . . You need peace and quiet . . . !
(*Christine joins them again.*)

FRITZ: Tell me, don't you find this room as sweet as can be.

THEODORE: Yes, it's very nice. . . . (*to Christine*) Are you hidden away in this room all day long? —It's incidentally very livable here. A little high up for my taste.

FRITZ: That's just what I find so nice about it.

THEODORE: Well, now I'm going to kidnap Fritz from you. We have to get up very early tomorrow.

CHRISTINE: Then you're really going away?

THEODORE: He'll come back, Miss Christine.

CHRISTINE: Will you write to me?

THEODORE: But if he's home again tomorrow—

CHRISTINE: Oh, I know he'll be away quite a long time. . . .

(*Fritz winces and Theodore notices.*)

THEODORE: And does that immediately call for letters? I wouldn't have thought you were so sentimental, Miss Christine. . . . *Christine,* I mean—we are good friends . . . now . . . Well, then . . . kiss each other good-bye, since you are going to be apart for so—(*interrupts himself*) Pretend I'm not here.

(*Fritz and Christine kiss. Theodore takes out a cigarette case, puts a cigarette in his mouth, searches his topcoat for a match. When he does not find one, he speaks.*)

THEODORE: Tell me, my dear Miss Christine, don't you have a match?

CHRISTINE: Oh, yes, you'll find some over there. (*Points to the bureau.*)

THEODORE: There aren't any here.

CHRISTINE: I'll bring you one.

(*She goes into the adjoining room; Fritz watches her leave.*)

FRITZ: Oh, God, how full of lies such moments are!

THEODORE: What are you talking about!

FRITZ: At this very minute I could almost believe I could find my happiness here, that this sweet little girl—(*interrupting himself*) But this moment is one great lie. . . .

THEODORE: Banalities . . . How you'll laugh about this some day.

FRITZ: I doubt that I'll ever have the opportunity.

CHRISTINE (*returning with matches*): Here you are!

THEODORE: Thank you very much . . . Well, then, good-bye.—
(*to Fritz*) Now what are you waiting for?—

(*Fritz looks around the room, as if he wanted to take it all in one more time.*)

FRITZ: It's almost impossible to leave.

CHRISTINE: Go on, just make fun of me.

THEODORE (*forcefully*): Come on. —Good-bye, Christine.

FRITZ: Farewell.

CHRISTINE: Till we meet again.

(*Theodore and Fritz leave. Christine uneasy, remains standing, then she goes to the door, left ajar. She is subdued. She calls.*)

Fritz!

(*Fritz returns and presses her against his heart.*)

FRITZ: Farewell!

(*Curtain.*)

Act III

The same room as Act II. Noontime. Christine is alone, sitting by the window, sewing. She puts her work down. Lina, Katharine's nine-year-old daughter, enters.

LINA: Good day, Miss Christine!

CHRISTINE (*very distracted*): Hello there, how are you, my child? What do you want?

LINA: Mother sent me to see if we can have the theater tickets now. —

CHRISTINE: Father isn't home yet. Do you want to wait?

LINA: No, Miss Christine. I'll come back after dinner.

CHRISTINE: Fine.

LINA (*Starting to leave, turns*): Mother sends her greetings and wants to know if you still have your headache?

CHRISTINE: No, my dear.

LINA: 'Bye, Miss Christine!

CHRISTINE: 'Bye!

(*As Lina exits, Mitzi enters.*)

LINA: Good afternoon, Miss Mitzi!

MITZI: Hi there, you little scamp!

(*Lina exits.*)

CHRISTINE: Mitzi—

(*Christine rises as Mitzi crosses to her.*)

Well, are they back?

MITZI: How should I know?

CHRISTINE: You don't have a letter, nothing?

MITZI: No.

CHRISTINE: *You* don't have a letter? Either?

MITZI: What would we be writing each other about?

CHRISTINE: They've been gone since the day before yesterday!

MITZI: Well, yes, that's not such a long time! That's no reason to make such an issue out of this. I don't understand you at all. . . . Just look at you. You look like you've been crying all day long. Your father will notice something's wrong with you when he comes home.

CHRISTINE (*simply*): My father knows everything.

MITZI (*almost shocked*): What?

CHRISTINE: I've told him.

MITZI: Well, wasn't that clever of you. But of course your face can't hide a thing, anyway. And I suppose he even knows *who* it is?

CHRISTINE: Yes.

MITZI: And did he scold you?

           (*Christine shakes her head.*)

Well then, what did he say?

CHRISTINE: Nothing . . . He walked away very quietly, the way he always does.

MITZI: Well, it was stupid anyway that you told him. You'll see. . . . Do you know why your father didn't say anything about it? Because he thinks that Fritz is going to marry you.

CHRISTINE: Why do you have to talk about it.

MITZI: Do you know what I think?

CHRISTINE: What do you think?

MITZI: I think the whole story about their trip is just a fake.

CHRISTINE: What?

MITZI: Maybe they didn't go away at all.

CHRISTINE: They went away—I know they did. Last night I went past his house, and the blinds were drawn; he is not there.

MITZI: I believe that. They're away somewhere all right. But they just won't be coming back—at least not to us.

CHRISTINE (*fearfully*): Mitzi . . .

MITZI: Well, it's possible!

CHRISTINE: You can say that so calmly—

MITZI: Well, whether it happens today or tomorrow, or six months from now, it's all the same in the end.

CHRISTINE: You don't know what you're talking about. . . . You don't know Fritz—he's not like that—he's not the way you think he is—I saw that the other day when he was here, in this room. He just sometimes pretends to be indifferent—but he loves me . . . (*as if she could guess Mitzi's answer*) Yes, yes—not forever, I know—but love just doesn't stop from one day to the next!

MITZI: Well, I don't know Fritz that well.

CHRISTINE: He'll come back, and Theodore will come back too. For certain!

    (*Mitzi makes a gesture that says "it doesn't really matter to me."*)

Mitzi . . . do me a favor.

MITZI: Don't be so upset—well what do you want?

CHRISTINE: Go to Theodore's house, it's not far. Just stop in. . . . Ask if he's already home, and if he's not, does anyone in the house know when he'll be back.

MITZI: I'm not going to run after a man.

CHRISTINE: He doesn't need to know. Maybe you'll just happen to meet him. It's almost one o'clock; he might be going out to eat.

MITZI: Why don't *you* go to Fritz's house to see if *he's* there?

CHRISTINE: I don't dare—he can't stand things like that. . . . And anyway he's certainly not home yet. But maybe Theodore's already home and would know when Fritz will be back. I beg you, Mitzi.

MITZI: Sometimes you're so childish—

CHRISTINE: Do it for my sake! Go there! That's not asking so much.

MITZI: Well, if it means so much to you, then I'll go. But it's not going to be much use. They're certainly not home yet.

CHRISTINE: You'll come right back . . . won't you?

MITZI: Well, Mother will just have to wait a little with dinner.

CHRISTINE: Oh, thank you, Mitzi, you're so kind. . . .

MITZI: Of course, I'm kind; but now you better be sensible . . . all right? . . . Well then, 'bye.

CHRISTINE: Thank you!

> (*Mitzi leaves. Christine, alone, tidies up the room. She puts away the sewing things, then she walks to the window and looks out. After a minute Weiring enters. She doesn't see him at first. He is in a state of extreme agitation and anxiously observes his daughter, who is still standing at the window.*)

WEIRING: She doesn't know yet . . . (*He remains by the door, not daring to enter further. Christine turns, sees him, is startled. He attempts to smile, then enters the room.*) Christine . . . (*As if he were calling her to him. She goes to him as if she wanted to sink down at his feet. He stops her.*) Well then . . . what are you doing, Christine? We—(*He comes to a decision.*) —we'll just forget all about this, won't we?—

> (*She lifts her head.*)

Well . . . yes . . . I will, and you will.

CHRISTINE: Father, didn't you understand what I was telling you this morning . . . ?

WEIRING: But, what do you want, Christine? . . . I have to tell you what I think about all this! Isn't that what you want? Well, then . . .

CHRISTINE: What does this mean, father?

WEIRING: Come here, my child . . . listen to me calmly. Look, I listened calmly to you when you told me all you had to say— We must—

CHRISTINE: Please don't speak to me like this, father. . . . if you've thought this over and realize now that you can't forgive me, then throw me out—but don't speak to me like this. . . .

WEIRING: Listen to me calmly, Christine! Then you can still do whatever you like. . . . You're so young Christine. —Haven't you ever thought . . . (*with great hesitation*) . . . that the whole thing could be a mistake—

CHRISTINE: Why are you saying this to me, father? —I know what I've done—and I'm not asking anything—of you or any other person in the world—if it has been a mistake. . . . I told you you can throw me out, but . . .

WEIRING (*interrupting*): How can you talk like that. . . . Even if it was a mistake, is there any reason for someone as young as you to be so desperate? Just think how beautiful, how truly beautiful life is. —Just think how much there is to be happy about, how much youth, how much joy lies ahead of you. . . . Look, I can't expect much more from this world, but even for me life is still beautiful—and there is so much I can still look forward to. The way you and I will be together—how we'll plan the life we want—you and I . . . how you'll—now, when there's beautiful weather coming, now you'll begin to study singing again, and how when the holidays are here, we'll drive out into the country and spend the whole day there—yes—oh, there are so many beautiful things . . . so much. —It's ridiculous to—it's senseless to throw all this away just because you have to sacrifice your first bit of happiness, or something that you thought was that—

CHRISTINE (*fearfully*): Why . . . what do you mean, sacrifice?

WEIRING: Was it ever happiness? Do you really believe, Christine, that you had to wait until today to tell your father about this?

I've known it for a long time! —and I've known that you would tell me. I knew that. No. It was never happiness! . . . Don't I know these eyes? They would never have been so full of tears, your cheeks would never have been this pale if you had loved someone who deserved your love.

CHRISTINE: How can you . . . What do you know. . . . What have you found out?

WEIRING: Nothing . . . nothing at all . . . You told me, yourself, what he is . . . A young man, like that— What does he know?— Does he have any idea what's fallen into his lap—does he know the difference between true and false—and all of your crazy love—did he understand anything about that?

CHRISTINE (*more and more frightened*): You saw . . . —You went to see him?

WEIRING: What are you thinking of! He's away, isn't he? But Christine, I still have a head on my shoulders. I still have eyes in my head! Look, child, forget about him! Forget about him! Your future lies completely elsewhere! You can and you will have all the happiness you deserve. And someday you'll find someone who knows what he has in you—

(*Christine has hurried to the bureau to get her hat.*)

What do you want? —

CHRISTINE: Leave me alone, I want to go. . . .

WEIRING: Where do you want to go?

CHRISTINE: To him . . . to him . . .   } *Simultaneously*

WEIRING: But what are you thinking of . . .

CHRISTINE: You're keeping something from me—let me go to him—

(*Weiring holds her back.*)

WEIRING: Come to your senses, child. He's not there. . . . He may be gone for a long while. . . . Please stay here with me. What will you do there. . . . Tomorrow or even this evening I'll go over there with you. You can't go out on the street like this . . . do you know what you look like? . . .

CHRISTINE: You want to go there with me—?

WEIRING: I promise you— Only now just stay here calmly. Sit down and pull yourself together. It's enough to make you laugh to see you like this for absolutely nothing. Can't you stand it here with your father anymore?

CHRISTINE: What do you *know*?

WEIRING (*increasingly at a loss*): What should I know . . . I know that I love you, that you are my only child, that you should stay here with me—that you should always have stayed here with me—

CHRISTINE: Enough—let me go—(*She tears herself away from him and opens the door, in which Mitzi appears and later, Theodore. Mitzi lets out a little scream as Christine runs into her.*)

MITZI: What a scare you gave me . . . !

(*Christine pulls back when she sees Theodore, who remains standing in the doorway. He is dressed in black.*)

CHRISTINE: What . . . what's happened. . . . (*Receiving no answer, she looks at Theodore who averts his gaze.*)Where is he, where is he? . . . (*In great fear she looks about at the uneasy and sad expressions.*)Where is he? (*to Theodore*) Tell me, then!

(*Theodore attempts to speak. Christine stares at him, stares at the others, understands the meaning of their expressions. Her face displays a gradual realization of the truth, after which she gives a terrible scream.*)

Theodore! . . . He's . . .

(*Theodore nods. Christine clutches at her forehead, she doesn't understand, she walks over to Theodore, takes him by the arm—as if insane; and speaks as if she were asking herself.*)

. . . He's . . . dead . . . ?

WEIRING: My child—

CHRISTINE (*Pushes him away*): Speak to me, Theodore!

THEODORE: You know everything.

CHRISTINE: I know nothing. . . . I don't know what's happened. . . . Do you think . . . I can't hear all this now . . . how did this happen . . . Father . . . Theodore . . . (*to Mitzi*) You know, too. . . .

THEODORE: An unfortunate accident—

CHRISTINE: What, what?

THEODORE: He has fallen . . .

CHRISTINE: What does that mean: He was—

THEODORE: He fell in a duel.

CHRISTINE:

> (*She shrieks and is about to faint. Weiring supports her and gives Theodore a sign that he should leave now. Christine sees this and grabs Theodore.*)

Stay . . . I must know everything. Do you think that you can keep something from me even now. . . .

THEODORE: What else do you want to know?

CHRISTINE: Why—why did he fight a duel?

THEODORE: I don't know the reason.

CHRISTINE: With whom, with whom—? Who killed him—surely you must know that? . . . Well, well—

THEODORE: No one you know . . .

CHRISTINE: Who, who?

MITZI: Christine!

CHRISTINE (*to Mitzi*): Who? Tell me—. . . You, father!

> (*No answer. She tries to leave. Weiring holds her back.*)

I ought to be able to know who killed him, and for what—

THEODORE: It was . . . for a . . . pointless reason.

CHRISTINE: You're not telling the truth. . . . Why, why . . .

THEODORE: My dear Christine . . .

> (*Christine, as if she wanted to interrupt him, walks over to him—at first she doesn't speak, looking at him, and then she suddenly screams.*)

CHRISTINE: Because of a woman?

THEODORE: No—

CHRISTINE: Yes—for a woman. . . . (*She has turned toward Mitzi.*)—for *that* woman—for that woman, the one that he *loved*—And her husband—yes, yes, her husband killed him . . . and I . . . what am I? What did I mean to him . . . ? Theodore . . . don't you have anything at all for me . . . didn't he write anything down . . . ? Didn't he give you any message for me . . . ? Didn't you find anything . . . a letter . . . a scrap of paper—

> (*Theodore shakes his head.*)

And that evening . . . when he was here, when you came to get him . . . he already knew then, he already knew, that he might never see me. . . . And he walked away from here, to let himself be killed for someone else—no, no—it's not possible . . . didn't he know, what he meant to me . . . didn't he . . .

THEODORE: He knew. —That last morning when we drove out there . . . he talked about you, too.

CHRISTINE: He talked about me *too*! About me too! And what else did he talk about? About how many other people, about how many other things, that meant just as much to him as I did —He talked about me *too*! Oh God! . . . And about his father and about his mother and about his friends, and about his room and about the spring and about the city and about everything, about everything that just happened to be a part of his life and which he just happened to have to say good-bye to, the way he did to me . . . he talked about everything with you . . . and he talked about me, too. . . .

THEODORE (*moved*): He surely loved you.

CHRISTINE: Love! —Him?—I was nothing but a way to pass the time—and he died for someone else!—And I—I worshiped him!—Didn't he know that? . . . That I gave him everything that I had to give—that I would have died for him—that he was my God and my salvation—didn't he notice that at all? And he could leave me, with a smile, leave this room and let himself be shot down for someone else. . . . Father, Father—can you understand that?

WEIRING (*crossing to her*): Christine!

THEODORE (*to Mitzi*): See here, my dear, you could have spared me this. . . .

(*Mitzi gives him a nasty look.*)

I've had enough excitement . . . these last few days. . . .

CHRISTINE (*with sudden decision*): Theodore, take me there. . . . I want to see him—I want to *see* him one last time—his face. Theodore, take me there.

THEODORE (*hesitantly*): No . . .

CHRISTINE: Why no? —You can't deny me that?—Surely I am permitted to see him one last time—?

THEODORE: It's too late.

CHRISTINE: Too late? —To see his body . . . is it too late? Yes . . . yes . . . (*She doesn't understand.*)

THEODORE: He was buried this morning.

CHRISTINE (*with an expression of the most extreme horror*):

Buried . . . And I didn't know? They shot him . . . and they put him in a coffin and they carried him out and they buried him in the ground—and I wasn't even allowed to see him one last time? —He's been dead for two days—and you didn't come and you didn't tell me—?

THEODORE (*very moved*): In these two days. . . . You have no idea all the things, in these two days. . . . You must consider that it was also my responsibility to inform his parents—I had so much to think about—and on top of that, my own personal feelings . . .

CHRISTINE: Your . . . own . . .

THEODORE: Also, it was . . . we kept it very quiet. . . . Only the closest relatives and friends . . .

CHRISTINE: Only the closest—! And me—? . . . What am I . . . ?

MITZI: They would have asked the same question there.

CHRISTINE: What am I—? Less than all the others—? Less than his relatives, less than . . . you?

WEIRING: My child, my child. Come to me, come to me. . . . (*He embraces her. Speaks to Theodore.*) Go . . . leave me alone with her!

THEODORE (*with a tearful voice*): I'm very . . . I had no idea. . . .

CHRISTINE: No idea!? — That I *loved* him?—
(*Weiring pulls her to him; Theodore stares into space. Mitzi stands next to Christine, who frees herself from Weiring.*) Take me to his grave!

WEIRING: No, no—

MITZI: Don't go there, Christine—

THEODORE: Christine . . . later . . . tomorrow . . . when you've calmed down . . .

CHRISTINE: Tomorrow? —When I have calmed down! —And in a month when I am completely recovered, is that right? —And in half a year I can start laughing again, is that right — (*Burst out laughing.*) And when is the next lover going to come along? . . .

WEIRING: Christine . . .

CHRISTINE: Just stay here . . . I'll find my way alone.

WEIRING: Don't go.

MITZI: Don't go.

CHRISTINE: It's even better . . . if I . . . leave me alone, let me
  go . . .

WEIRING: Christine, stay . . .

MITZI: Don't go there! —Maybe the other woman will be there
  . . . praying.

CHRISTINE (*to herself, glassy-eyed*): I'm not going there to pray
  . . . no . . . (*She dashes away . . . the others are speechless.*)

WEIRING: Hurry after her.

> (*Theodore and Mitzi exit after her.*)

I can't, I can't . . . (*He walks painfully from the door to the
window.*) What will she do . . . what will she do. . . . (*He looks
out the window into nothingness.*) She won't come back—she
won't come back!

> (*He sinks to the floor, sobbing loudly.*)

(*Curtain.*)

Translated by
Arthur S. Wensinger and Clinton J. Atkinson
(based on a working translation by Susanne Mrozik)

LA RONDE

CHARACTERS

THE WHORE
THE SOLDIER
THE PARLOR MAID
THE YOUNG GENTLEMAN
THE YOUNG WIFE
THE HUSBAND
THE LITTLE MISS
THE POET
THE ACTRESS
THE COUNT

THE TIME: *The 1890s.*

THE PLACE: *Vienna.*

1 The Whore and the Soldier

Late in the evening. On the Augarten Bridge. Soldier on his way home, whistling.

WHORE: Want to come with me, Angel Face?

           (Soldier turns round, then walks on.)

    Wouldn't you like to come with me?

SOLDIER: You mean me? Angel Face?!

WHORE: Who do you think? Come on. Come with me. I live near here.

SOLDIER: No time. Have to get back to the barracks.

WHORE: You'll get back to the barracks all right. But it's nicer with me.

SOLDIER *(near her now)*: Yeah. Could be.

WHORE: Uh, uh! A cop might come.

SOLDIER: Nonsense! What's a cop? I got my sword on.

WHORE: Come on with me!

SOLDIER: Leave me alone. I got no money anyhow.

WHORE: I don't need any money.

SOLDIER *(Stops. They are under a street lamp.)*: You don't need any money? Who are you for God's sake?

WHORE: Civilians have to pay, sure. A guy like you can get it from me for nothing.

SOLDIER: So you're the one Huber told me about. . . .

WHORE: I don't know any Huber.

SOLDIER: Yes, you're the one. That's right. The café in the Schiff Gasse. Then he went home with you.

WHORE: The café in the Schiff Gasse! I've taken plenty of guys home from there. Eh! (*Her eyes tell how many.*)

SOLDIER: Let's go then, let's go.

WHORE: What? You're in a hurry now?

SOLDIER: Well, what are we waiting for? I gotta be back in the barracks at ten.

WHORE: How long you been in the army?

SOLDIER: What business is that of yours? Live far from here?

WHORE: Ten minutes' walk.

SOLDIER: Too far. How about a little kiss?

WHORE (*kisses him*): I like that part the best. When I like a guy.

SOLDIER: I don't. No. I can't go with you. Too far.

WHORE: Tell you what. Come tomorrow. In the afternoon.

Soldier: Okay. Give me the address.

WHORE: Only—I bet you won't come.

SOLDIER: I told you I would, didn't I?

WHORE: Tell you what—if it's too far tonight—how about over there? (*She points toward the Danube.*)

SOLDIER: What's over there?

WHORE: Lovely and quiet there, too. No one around this late.

SOLDIER: Aw, that's no good.

WHORE: It's always good—with me. Come on, stay with me. Who knows if we'll still be around tomorrow?

SOLDIER: Okay, then. But let's make it snappy.

WHORE: Easy. It's so dark there. One slip, and you're in the Danube.

SOLDIER: Might be the best thing.

WHORE: Pst! Hey, wait a second. We're just coming to a bench.

SOLDIER: You know your way around.

WHORE: Wish I had a guy like you for a boyfriend.

SOLDIER: I'd make you jealous too much.

WHORE: I'd know how to take care of that.

SOLDIER: Think so?

WHORE: Not so loud. Could be a cop around at that—he might be lost. Who'd think we were right in the middle of Vienna?

SOLDIER: Over here. Come on over here!

WHORE: What's got into you? If we slip, we're in the river!

SOLDIER (*has grabbed hold of her*): Ah! now . . .

WHORE: Hold on tight now.
SOLDIER: Don't worry . . .

* * * * *

WHORE: It'd have been a lot better on the bench.
SOLDIER: On the bench, off the bench . . . Well, you getting up?
WHORE: Where are you rushing off—
SOLDIER: Got to get back to the barracks. I'm late anyhow.
WHORE: Tell me, soldier—what's your name?
SOLDIER: What's my name got to do with you?
WHORE: Mine's—Leocadia.
SOLDIER: Ha! That's a new one!
WHORE: Soldier . . .
SOLDIER: Well, what do you want?
WHORE: How about a dime for the janitor?
SOLDIER: Ha! . . . What do you think I am? 'Bye now! Leocadia . . .
WHORE: You crook! You son of a bitch!
(He is gone.)

2 The Soldier and the Parlor Maid

*The Prater. Sunday evening. A path leading from the Wurstelpra-
ter—or amusement park—out into dark avenues of trees. The din
of the amusement park is audible. So is the sound of the Fünf-
kreuzertanz—a banal polka—played by a brass band. The Soldier.
The Parlor Maid.*

PARLOR MAID: Yes, but now you must tell me. Why were you in
such a hurry to leave?
   (Soldier laughs stupidly; he is embarrassed.)
I thought it was marvelous. I love dancing.
   (Soldier takes her by the waist. Parlor Maid lets him.)
But we're not dancing *now*. Why are you holding me so tight?
SOLDIER: What's your name? Kathi?
PARLOR MAID: You've got a Kathi on your mind.
SOLDIER: I know. I've got it: Marie.
PARLOR MAID: Look, it's dark here. I get so scared.

SOLDIER: Nothing to be afraid of with me around. Just leave it to uncle.

PARLOR MAID: But where are we going to, though? There's no one around at all. Let's go back, come on! How *dark* it is!

SOLDIER (*pulling at his Virginia cigar till the tip glows*): See it get lighter? Ha! My little treasure!

PARLOR MAID: Ooh! What are you doing? If I'd known *this*. . . .

SOLDIER: Nice and soft! Damned if you're not the nicest and softest one in the whole bunch, Fräulein!

PARLOR MAID: What whole bunch?

SOLDIER: In there—in the Swoboda.

PARLOR MAID: You tried all of them?

SOLDIER: Oh, you notice. Dancing. You notice a lot of things. Ha!

PARLOR MAID: You danced with that blonde more than with me. The one with the crooked face.

SOLDIER: An old friend of a buddy of mine.

PARLOR MAID: You mean of that corporal with the turned-up mustache?

SOLDIER: Nah. The civilian. You know—the one at the table with me before. With the hoarse voice?

PARLOR MAID: Oh, yes. I know. He's pretty fresh.

SOLDIER: Did *he* try something with you? I'll show the bastard. What did he try?

PARLOR MAID: Oh, nothing. I just saw how he was with the other girls.

SOLDIER: Now, Fräulein, tell me. . . .

PARLOR MAID: Ooh! You'll burn me with that cigar.

SOLDIER: Oh, so sorry! Fräulein—or can I call you . . . Marie?

PARLOR MAID: We haven't known each other very long.

SOLDIER: Hell, there's lots of people can't stand each other and still use first names.

PARLOR MAID: Let's make it next time, when. . . . You see, Herr Franz . . .

SOLDIER: You remembered my name!

PARLOR MAID: You see, Herr Franz. . . .

SOLDIER: Make it just—Franz, Fräulein.

PARLOR MAID: Well then don't be so fresh. Sh! What if somebody comes!

SOLDIER: What if they do? You can't see two feet in front of you.

PARLOR MAID: But, heavens, where are we going?

SOLDIER: Look! There's two just like us.

PARLOR MAID: Where? I can't see a thing.

SOLDIER: There. Right up there.

PARLOR MAID: What do you say like *us* for?

SOLDIER: Oh, I only mean—they kinda like each other.

PARLOR MAID: Hey, watch out! What was that? I nearly fell.

SOLDIER: It's these railings they put round the grass.

PARLOR MAID: Don't push so hard. I'll fall right over.

SOLDIER: Sh! Not so loud!

PARLOR MAID: Look now I'm *really* going to scream! What are
you doing . . . hey . . .

SOLDIER: There's no one for miles around.

PARLOR MAID: Let's go back with the rest of them.

SOLDIER: But we don't need them, Marie, what we need is . . .
uh, huh . . .

PARLOR MAID: Herr Franz, please! For Heaven's sake!! Now listen, if I'd had . . . any idea . . . oh! . . . oh!! . . . yes . . .

* * * * *

SOLDIER (*blissfully*): Jesus Christ Almighty! . . . Ah-h! . . .

PARLOR MAID: . . . I can't see your face at all.

SOLDIER: My face? . . . Hell!

* * * * *

SOLDIER: Now look, Fräulein, you can't stay in the grass all night.

PARLOR MAID: Oh, come on, Franz, help me up!

SOLDIER: Okay. (*He grabs her.*) Oops!

PARLOR MAID: Oh dear, Franz!

SOLDIER: Yes, yes? What's the matter with Franz?

PARLOR MAID: You're a bad man, Franz.

SOLDIER: Oh, so that's it? Hey, wait for me!

PARLOR MAID: What do you let me go for?

SOLDIER: Can't I get this cigar lit for God's sake?

PARLOR MAID: It's so dark.

SOLDIER: Well, tomorrow it'll be light again.

PARLOR MAID: At least tell me—do you like me?

SOLDIER: I thought you might have noticed! (*He laughs.*)

PARLOR MAID: Where are we going?

SOLDIER: Why, back!

PARLOR MAID: Oh, please, Franz, not so quick!

SOLDIER: What's the matter? I don't like running around in the dark.

PARLOR MAID: Tell me, Franz, do you . . . like me?

SOLDIER: I just told you I liked you.

PARLOR MAID: Come on then, give me little kiss.

SOLDIER (*condescending*): Here . . . listen! You can hear that music again.

PARLOR MAID: You probably want to go dancing again.

SOLDIER: Sure. What else?

PARLOR MAID: Well, Franz, look, I must be getting back. They'll gripe anyhow, the lady of the house is such a . . . she'd like it best if we never went out at all.

SOLDIER: Sure. You go home then.

PARLOR MAID: Herr Franz! I thought . . . you might take me.

SOLDIER: Home? Eh! (*The open vowel indicating disgust.*)

PARLOR MAID: Oh, please, it's so dreary—going home alone!

SOLDIER: Where do you live?

PARLOR MAID: It's not far—Porzellan Gasse.

SOLDIER: Oh! Then we go the same way. . . . But it's too early for me! I want some fun. I got a late pass tonight. Don't have to be back in the barracks till twelve. I'm going dancing.

PARLOR MAID: *I* see how it is. It's that blonde. The one with the crooked face.

SOLDIER: Ha! . . . Her face ain't so bad.

PARLOR MAID: Heavens, you men are wicked! I bet you do this to every girl.

SOLDIER: That'd be too much!

PARLOR MAID: Franz, do me a favor. Not tonight—stay just with me tonight, look . . .

SOLDIER: Okay, okay. But I can dance for a while first, I suppose?

PARLOR MAID: Tonight I'm not dancing with anyone else.

SOLDIER: Here it is.

PARLOR MAID: What?

SOLDIER: The Swoboda! How quickly we got back, huh? And they're still playing *that* thing. (*Singing with the band.*) Tatata-tum, tatatatum! . . . All right, if you want to wait, I'll take you home. If you don't, I'll be saying good night. . . .

PARLOR MAID: I think I'll wait.

SOLDIER: Why don't you get yourself a glass of beer? (*Turning to a blonde, dancing by with her boy, putting on a "refined" accent.*) May I have the pleasure?

3 The Parlor Maid and the Young Gentleman

A hot summer afternoon. His parents are off in the country. The cook is having her half-day. In the kitchen the Parlor Maid is writing the Soldier a letter; he is her lover. There is a ring from the Young Gentleman's room. She gets up and goes into the Young Gentleman's room. The Young Gentleman is lying on the sofa with cigarette and French novel.

PARLOR MAID: You rang, Herr Alfred?

YOUNG GENTLEMAN: Oh, Yes . . . Marie . . . yes, I did ring as a matter of fact. . . . Now what was it? . . . Oh, I know, let the blinds down, Marie, will you? . . . It's cooler with the blinds down . . . don't you think? . . .

(*Parlor Maid goes to the window and lets the Venetian blinds down.*)

YOUNG GENTLEMAN (*goes on reading*): What are you doing, Marie? That's right. Oh, but now I can't see to read.

PARLOR MAID: The way you always study so, Herr Alfred!

YOUNG GENTLEMAN (*passing over this loftily*): That'll be all, thanks.

(*The Parlor Maid goes out.*
The Young Gentleman tries to go on reading; soon lets the book fall; rings again.
The Parlor Maid is in the doorway.)

YOUNG GENTLEMAN: Look, Marie . . . now, um, what I was going to say . . . well . . . yes, is there any cognac in the house?

PARLOR MAID: Yes, Herr Alfred. But it's locked up.

YOUNG GENTLEMAN: Oh. Well, who has the key?

PARLOR MAID: Lini has the key.

YOUNG GENTLEMAN: Who's Lini?

PARLOR MAID: The cook, Herr Alfred.

YOUNG GENTLEMAN: Oh. Then go and tell Lini.

PARLOR MAID: Well . . . Lini's having her half day.

YOUNG GENTLEMAN: Oh.

PARLOR MAID: Shall I run over to the café for you, Herr Alfred?

YOUNG GENTLEMAN: Oh, no . . . hot enough as it is. I don't need cognac anyway. Listen, Marie, just bring me a glass of water. Wait, Marie—let it run, hm? Till it's quite cold?

(*The Parlor Maid goes.*

The Young Gentleman is watching her go when the Parlor Maid turns round at the door. The Young Gentleman stares into space. The Parlor Maid turns the faucet on and lets the water run. Meanwhile she goes to her little room, washes her hands, and arranges her curls in the mirror. Then she brings the Young Gentleman the glass of water. She walks to the sofa.

The Young Gentleman raises himself part way. The Parlor Maid puts the glass in his hand. Their fingers touch.)

YOUNG GENTLEMAN: Oh. Thanks . . . Well, what is it? Now be careful. Put the glass back on the tray. . . . (*He lies back and stretches out.*) What's the time?

PARLOR MAID: Five o'clock, Herr Alfred.

YOUNG GENTLEMAN: I see. Five. Thank you.

(*The Parlor Maid goes; at the door, she turns; the Young Gentleman is looking; she notices and smiles.*

The Young Gentleman lies where he is for a while, then suddenly gets up. He walks to the door; then returns and lies down on the sofa. He tries to read again. In a couple of minutes, he again rings.

The Parlor Maid enters with a smile which she makes no attempt to hide.)

YOUNG GENTLEMAN: Look, Marie, what I was going to ask you . . . didn't Dr. Schueller call this morning?

PARLOR MAID: No. No one called this morning.

YOUNG GENTLEMAN: Well. That's strange. So Dr. Schueller didn't call? You know him—Dr. Schueller?

PARLOR MAID: Oh, yes. The tall gentleman with the big black beard.

YOUNG GENTLEMAN: Yes. Then maybe he *did* call?

PARLOR MAID: No. No one called, Herr Alfred.

YOUNG GENTLEMAN (*taking the plunge*): Come here, Marie.

PARLOR MAID (*coming a little closer*): Yes, Herr Alfred?

YOUNG GENTLEMAN: Closer . . . yes . . . um . . . I only thought . . .

PARLOR MAID: Yes, Herr Alfred?

YOUNG GENTLEMAN: Thought . . . I thought . . . about that blouse. What kind is it? . . . Oh, come on, closer. I won't bite you.

(Parlor Maid comes.)

PARLOR MAID: What's this about my blouse? You don't like it, Herr Alfred?

YOUNG GENTLEMAN *(takes hold of the blouse and, in so doing, pulls the Parlor Maid down on him)*: Blue, is it? Yes, what a lovely blue! *(Simply.)* You're very nicely dressed, Marie.

PARLOR MAID: But, Herr Alfred!

YOUNG GENTLEMAN: Well, what? *(He's opened the blouse. Matter-of-fact.)* You've got lovely white skin, Marie.

PARLOR MAID: I think you're flattering me, Herr Alfred.

YOUNG GENTLEMAN *(kissing her bosom)*: This can't hurt you, can it?

PARLOR MAID: Oh no!

YOUNG GENTLEMAN: How you're sighing! Why do you sigh like that?

PARLOR MAID: Oh, Herr Alfred . . .

YOUNG GENTLEMAN: And what nice slippers you have on . . .

PARLOR MAID: . . . but . . . Herr Alfred . . . if the doorbell rings . . .

YOUNG GENTLEMAN: Who'd ring at this hour?

PARLOR MAID: But, Herr Alfred . . . you see, it's so light!

YOUNG GENTLEMAN: Oho, you needn't be embarrassed with me! *You* needn't be embarrassed with anybody . . . pretty as you are! I swear you *are*, Marie! You know, your hair has such a pleasant smell.

PARLOR MAID: Herr Alfred . . .

YOUNG GENTLEMAN: Don't make such a fuss, Marie. I've seen you . . . quite different. When I came in late the other night, and went for a glass of water, the door to your room was open . . . yes . . .

PARLOR MAID *(hides her face)*: Heavens, I'd no idea you could be so naughty, Herr Alfred.

YOUNG GENTLEMAN: I saw a great, great deal . . . this . . . and this . . . and this . . . and . . .

PARLOR MAID: Herr Alfred!

YOUNG GENTLEMAN: Come on . . . here . . . that's right, yes . . .

PARLOR MAID: But if anyone rings . . .

YOUNG GENTLEMAN: Now stop it, for Heaven's sake. We won't go to the door. . . .

* * * * *

The doorbell rings.

YOUNG GENTLEMAN: Christ Almighty! . . . What a racket the man makes! Maybe he rang before, and we just didn't notice anything.

PARLOR MAID: Oh, I kept my ears open the whole time.

YOUNG GENTLEMAN: Well, now, go and see—through the peephole.

PARLOR MAID: Herr Alfred . . . You *are* . . . No! . . . a naughty man!

YOUNG GENTLEMAN: Now please, go take a look.

> (*The Parlor Maid goes. The Young Gentleman quickly pulls up the Venetian blinds.*)

PARLOR MAID (*comes back*): Whoever it was, he's gone away again. There's no one there. Maybe it was Dr. Schueller.

YOUNG GENTLEMAN (*disagreeably affected*): That'll be all, thanks.

> (*The Parlor Maid comes closer.*)

YOUNG GENTLEMAN (*retreating*): Look, Marie, I'm going. To the café.

PARLOR MAID (*tenderly*): So soon . . . Herr Alfred?

YOUNG GENTLEMAN (*severely*): I'm going to the café. If Dr. Schueller should come here . . .

PARLOR MAID: He won't be here today.

YOUNG GENTLEMAN (*more severely*): If Dr. Schueller should come here, I . . . I . . . I'm—in the café. (*He goes into the next room.*) (*The Parlor Maid takes a cigar from the smoking table, slips it in her pocket, and goes out.*)

4 The Young Gentleman and the Young Wife

Evening. A drawing room in a house in the Schwind Gasse, furnished with cheap elegance.

The Young Gentleman has just come in and, still in hat and overcoat, lights the candles. Then he opens the door into the next room and glances in. The glow of the candles in the drawing room falls on the parquet floor and makes its way to the four-poster against the rear wall; a reddish glow from the fireplace in a corner of the bedroom is thrown on the bed curtains.

The Young Gentleman also inspects the bedroom. He takes an atomizer from the dressing table and sprays the pillows with a fine stream of violet perfume. Then he goes with the spray through both rooms, squeezing the little bulb the whole time, so that soon the whole place smells of violets. He takes off hat and overcoat, sits down in a blue velvet armchair, lights a cigarette, and smokes. After a short while he gets up to make sure that the green shutters are drawn. Suddenly he goes back to the bedroom, opens the drawer of the bedside table, feels around till he finds a tortoise shell hairpin. He looks round for a place to hide it and finally puts it in his overcoat pocket. Then he opens a cupboard in the drawing room, takes out a silver tray, a cognac bottle, and two liqueur glasses, and puts it all on the table. He goes back to his overcoat and fishes out a small white parcel, which he opens and puts next to the cognac bottle. He returns to the cupboard and takes out two dessert plates, knives, and forks. From the small parcel he extracts a marron glacé and eats it. Then he pours himself a glass of cognac and quickly drinks it down. He looks at his watch. He paces the room. In front of the large mirror on the wall he stops for a while, smoothing his hair and little moustache with a pocket comb. He goes to the door to the hall and listens—not a sound. He draws the blue curtains screening the door to the bedroom. The doorbell rings. The Young Gentleman gives a start. He drops into an armchair and only rises when the door opens and the Young Wife enters.

The Young Wife thickly veiled, shuts the door behind her and stands for a moment with her left hand on her heart, as though she had to master intense emotion.

YOUNG GENTLEMAN (*goes to her, takes her left hand, and imprints a kiss on the white, black-trimmed glove; softly*): I thank you.

YOUNG WIFE: Alfred—Alfred!

YOUNG GENTLEMAN. Come in, dear lady . . . come in, Frau Emma.

YOUNG WIFE: Let me alone for a moment, please—oh, please, Alfred!

(*She stays close by the door.*
The Young Gentleman stands before her, holding her hand.)

YOUNG WIFE: But where am I, actually?

YOUNG GENTLEMAN: In my flat.

YOUNG WIFE: This building is a horror, Alfred.

YOUNG GENTLEMAN: Why? It's very dignified.

YOUNG WIFE: I met two men on the stairs.

YOUNG GENTLEMAN: People you know?

YOUNG WIFE: I don't know. Maybe.

YOUNG GENTLEMAN: Forgive me—you must know who you know!

YOUNG WIFE: But I didn't see a thing.

YOUNG GENTLEMAN: Even if they'd been your best friends, they couldn't have recognized you. Even I . . . if I didn't know it was you . . . this veil . . .

YOUNG WIFE: There are two.

YOUNG GENTLEMAN: Won't you come a bit closer in? And anyway do take off your hat.

YOUNG WIFE: What are you thinking of, Alfred? I told you—five minutes. No, not a second more! I swear . . .

YOUNG GENTLEMAN: Then the veil!

YOUNG WIFE: There are two.

YOUNG GENTLEMAN: Oh, well, both veils then—at least I'm allowed to see you!

YOUNG WIFE: Do you really love me, Alfred?

YOUNG GENTLEMAN (*deeply hurt*): Emma, can you ask . . . ?

YOUNG WIFE: It's so hot in here.

YOUNG GENTLEMAN: But you still have your fur cape on—you're going to catch cold!

YOUNG WIFE (*at last steps into the room, throwing herself into an armchair*): I'm dead tired.

YOUNG GENTLEMAN: Permit me.

(*He takes her veils off, takes out the hatpin, puts hat, pin, and veils down side by side on the sofa.*
The Young Wife lets it happen.
The Young Gentleman stands before her, shaking his head.)

YOUNG WIFE: What's the matter with you?

YOUNG GENTLEMAN: Never were you so beautiful!

YOUNG WIFE: How's that?

YOUNG GENTLEMAN: Alone . . . alone with you . . . Emma . . .
(He sinks on one knee beside the armchair, takes both her hands and covers them with kisses.)

YOUNG WIFE: And now . . . let me go. I have done what you asked.
(The Young Gentleman drops his head on to her lap.)

YOUNG WIFE: You promised me that you'd be good.

YOUNG GENTLEMAN: Yes.

YOUNG WIFE: This room's stifling.

YOUNG GENTLEMAN *gets up.* You still have your cape on.

YOUNG WIFE: Put it with my hat.
(The Young Gentleman takes off her cape and puts it on the sofa along with the hat and the other things.)

YOUNG WIFE: And now—adieu—

YOUNG GENTLEMAN: Emma!

YOUNG WIFE: The five minutes are up.

YOUNG GENTLEMAN: No, no! You haven't been here one minute yet!

YOUNG WIFE: Alfred, please, tell me exactly what time it is.

YOUNG GENTLEMAN: Quarter past six, on the nose.

YOUNG WIFE: I should have been at my sister's long ago.

YOUNG GENTLEMAN: You can see your sister any time. . . .

YOUNG WIFE: Oh God, Alfred, why did you get me to do this?

YOUNG GENTLEMAN: Because I . . . worship you, Emma.

YOUNG WIFE: How many women have you said that to?

YOUNG GENTLEMAN: Since I saw you, to none.

YOUNG WIFE: What a frivolous woman I am! If anyone had told me—a week ago . . . or even yesterday . . .

YOUNG GENTLEMAN: It was the day before yesterday you promised . . .

YOUNG WIFE: Because you kept tormenting me. But I didn't want to, God is my witness—I didn't want to. Yesterday I'd made up my mind. . . . Do you know I even wrote you a long letter last night?

YOUNG GENTLEMAN: I didn't get it.

YOUNG WIFE: I tore it up. I should have sent it after all!

YOUNG GENTLEMAN: It's better like this.

YOUNG WIFE: No, it's scandalous . . . of me. I can't understand myself. Good-bye, Alfred, let me go.

(The Young Gentleman takes her in his arms and covers her face with hot kisses.)

YOUNG WIFE: So this is . . . how you keep your promise?

YOUNG GENTLEMAN: One more kiss! Just one.

YOUNG WIFE: The last!

(He kisses her, she reciprocates, and their lips stay together a long time.)

YOUNG GENTLEMAN: May I tell you something, Emma? It is only now that I know what happiness is.

(The Young Wife sinks back in an armchair.)

YOUNG GENTLEMAN *(sits on the arm of the chair, putting his arm gently round her neck.)* . . . Or rather, only now do I know what happiness *might* be.

(The Young Wife gives a profound sigh.
The Young Gentleman kisses her again.)

YOUNG WIFE: Alfred, Alfred, what are you making me into?

YOUNG GENTLEMAN: It's not really so uncomfortable here, is it? And we are so safe. It's a thousand times better than meeting in the open air.

YOUNG WIFE: Oh, don't remind me.

YOUNG GENTLEMAN: Even those meetings I shall think of with delight! Every minute I've had the privilege of spending at your side will linger forever as a sweet memory.

YOUNG WIFE: You remember the Industrial Ball?

YOUNG GENTLEMAN: Do I remember? . . . But didn't I sit next to you during supper—right up close? The champagne your husband—

(The Young Wife gives him a look of protest.)

YOUNG GENTLEMAN: I was only going to mention the champagne! Tell me, Emma, wouldn't you like a glass of cognac?

YOUNG WIFE: Maybe just a drop. But first let me have a glass of water.

YOUNG GENTLEMAN: Yes . . . now, where is . . . Oh yes.

(He draws the curtains back from the door and goes into the bedroom.
The Young Wife looks after him.

The Young Gentleman returns with a filled decanter and two glasses.)

YOUNG WIFE: Where were you?

YOUNG GENTLEMAN: In the—next room.

(*He pours a glass of water for her.*)

YOUNG WIFE: Now I'm going to ask you something, Alfred, and you must swear to tell the truth.

YOUNG GENTLEMAN: I swear . . .

YOUNG WIFE: Was there ever another woman in these rooms?

YOUNG GENTLEMAN: But, Emma, this house has been around for twenty years!

YOUNG WIFE: You know what I mean, Alfred . . . with you . . .

YOUNG GENTLEMAN: With me, here? Emma! It's not nice for you to think about such things.

YOUNG WIFE: Then you have . . . how shall I . . . ? But no, I'd better not ask you. It's better if I don't ask. It's my own fault. Everything takes its revenge.

YOUNG GENTLEMAN: But what is it? What's the matter with you? *What* takes revenge?

YOUNG WIFE: No, no, no, I mustn't return to consciousness—or I'd sink into the ground for very shame.

YOUNG GENTLEMAN (*still with the decanter in his hand, sadly shakes his head*): Emma, if only you had any idea how you hurt me!

(*The Young Wife pours herself a glass of cognac.*)

YOUNG GENTLEMAN: I'll tell you something, Emma. If you're ashamed to be here—that's to say, if I'm nothing to you—if you don't feel that you mean all the bliss in the world to me—then leave. Leave.

YOUNG WIFE: That is just what I'll do.

YOUNG GENTLEMAN (*seizing her hand*): But if you realize that I can't live without you, that to kiss your hand means more to me than all the caresses of all the women in the whole world. Emma, I'm not like the other young men who know how . . . this sort of thing is done . . . call me naïve if you wish . . . I . . .

YOUNG WIFE: But what if you *were* like the other young men?

YOUNG GENTLEMAN: Then you wouldn't be here now: you aren't like the other young women.

YOUNG WIFE: How do you know?

YOUNG GENTLEMAN (*has drawn her on to the sofa and sits down close beside her*): I've thought a lot about you. I know you're unhappy.

(*The Young Wife looks pleased.*)

YOUNG GENTLEMAN: Life is so empty, so trivial. And so short. . . . Isn't life frightfully short, Emma? There is only one happiness: to find someone who loves you.

(*The Young Wife has taken a candied pear from the table and puts it into her mouth.*)

YOUNG GENTLEMAN: Give me half!

(*She offers it to him with her lips.*
Young Wife takes the Young Gentleman's hands, which threaten to go astray.) What are you doing, Alfred? Is this your promise?

YOUNG GENTLEMAN (*swallows the candied fruit, then says more boldly*): Life is so short!

YOUNG WIFE (*feebly*): But that's no reason . . .

YOUNG GENTLEMAN (*mechanically*): Oh, but it is.

YOUNG WIFE (*more feebly*): Now look, Alfred, you promised to be good. . . . And it's so light. . . .

YOUNG GENTLEMAN: Come, come, my only one, my only. . . . (*He lifts her off the sofa.*)

YOUNG WIFE: What are you doing?

YOUNG GENTLEMAN: It's not light in there.

YOUNG WIFE: Is there another room?

YOUNG GENTLEMAN (*taking her with him*): A lovely one . . . and quite dark.

YOUNG WIFE: I'd rather stay here.

(*The Young Gentleman has already got her through the curtains and in the bedroom; he begins to unhook her dress at the waist.*)

YOUNG WIFE: You're so . . . Oh God, what are you doing to me? . . . Alfred!

YOUNG GENTLEMAN: Emma, I worship you!

YOUNG WIFE: Wait, please, at least wait . . . (*weakly*) Go, I'll call you . . .

YOUNG GENTLEMAN: Let me . . . let you help me . . . let . . . me . . . help . . . you . . .

YOUNG WIFE: But you're tearing everything!

YOUNG GENTLEMAN: Don't you wear a corset?

YOUNG WIFE: I never wear a corset. Neither does Duse, incidentally. You can unbutton my boots.

(*The Young Gentleman unbuttons her boots, kisses her feet.*)

YOUNG WIFE (*slipping into the bed*): Oooh, I'm cold.

YOUNG GENTLEMAN: It'll get warm.

YOUNG WIFE (*laughing softly*): You think so?

YOUNG GENTLEMAN (*not liking this, to himself*): She shouldn't have said that! (*He undresses in the dark.*)

YOUNG WIFE (*tenderly*): Come, come, come.

YOUNG GENTLEMAN (*in a better mood at once*): At once . . .

YOUNG WIFE: It smells of violets here.

YOUNG GENTLEMAN: It's you . . . yes (*close by her*) . . . you.

YOUNG WIFE: Alfred . . . Alfred!!!!

YOUNG GENTLEMAN: Emma . . .

* * * * *

YOUNG GENTLEMAN: I must be too much in love with you . . . that's why . . . I'm nearly out of my senses.

YOUNG WIFE: . . .

YOUNG GENTLEMAN: All these past days I've been going crazy. I felt it coming.

YOUNG WIFE: Don't worry your head about it.

YOUNG GENTLEMAN: Of course not, you can almost take it for granted when a man . . .

YOUNG WIFE: Don't . . . don't . . . You're nervous. Just relax . . .

YOUNG GENTLEMAN: You know Stendhal?

YOUNG WIFE: Stendhal?

YOUNG GENTLEMAN: His book *De l'amour*.

YOUNG WIFE: No. Why do you ask?

YOUNG GENTLEMAN: There's a story in it that's most significant.

YOUNG WIFE: What sort of story?

YOUNG GENTLEMAN: A bunch of officers have gotten together . . .

YOUNG WIFE: Oh.

YOUNG GENTLEMAN: And they talk about their love affairs. And everyone says that with the woman he loved most . . . most

passionately, you know . . . she made him . . . with her he
. . . well, the fact is, it happened to every one of them . . .
what happened to me with you.

YOUNG WIFE: I see.

YOUNG GENTLEMAN: This is very typical.

YOUNG WIFE: Yes.

YOUNG GENTLEMAN: But that's not all. One of them claims . . .
it has never happened to him in all his life. But—Stendhal adds—
this man was a notorious show-off.

YOUNG WIFE: Oh.

YOUNG GENTLEMAN: All the same, it kind of throws you, that's
the stupid thing about it, even if it doesn't really matter.

YOUNG WIFE: Naturally. Anyway . . . you promised to be good.

YOUNG GENTLEMAN: Please don't laugh! That won't improve
things.

YOUNG WIFE: I'm not laughing. This Stendhal story's very interesting. I'd always thought it happened only with older men . . .
or with very . . . well, you know, men who've been too fast.

YOUNG GENTLEMAN: What an idea! That has nothing to do with
it. By the way, I forgot the most charming story in the Stendhal.
A lieutenant of hussars even says that he spent three nights—or
was it six? I can't remember—with a woman he'd been wanting
for weeks—*désiré* and all that—and all those nights they didn't
do a thing but cry with happiness—both of them. . . .

YOUNG WIFE: Both of them?

YOUNG GENTLEMAN: Both of them. Does that surprise you? I find
it so understandable. Specially when you're in love.

YOUNG WIFE: But there must be a lot who don't cry.

YOUNG GENTLEMAN (*nervously*): Surely . . . after all, it was an
exceptional case.

YOUNG WIFE: Oh . . . I thought Stendhal says all hussars cry on
these occasions.

YOUNG GENTLEMAN: There, you're just making fun. . . .

YOUNG WIFE: Not in the least. Don't be so childish, Alfred.

YOUNG GENTLEMAN: I can't help it, it makes me nervous . . . and
I have the feeling you're thinking of it the whole time. I'm embarrassed.

YOUNG WIFE: I am not thinking about it.

YOUNG GENTLEMAN: You are. If I could only be sure you love
me!

YOUNG WIFE: Do you want better proof than . . . ?

YOUNG GENTLEMAN: You see! You're always making fun of me.

YOUNG WIFE: Not at all! Come, give me your sweet little head.

YOUNG GENTLEMAN: Oh, this is good.

YOUNG WIFE: Do you love me?

YOUNG GENTLEMAN: Oh, I'm so happy!

YOUNG WIFE: But no need to cry, too!

YOUNG GENTLEMAN (*moves away, highly irritated*): Again, again! Didn't I beg you?

YOUNG WIFE: I said you shouldn't cry, that was all . . .

YOUNG GENTLEMAN: You said "No need to cry."

YOUNG WIFE: You're nervous, my dear.

YOUNG GENTLEMAN: I know that.

YOUNG WIFE: You shouldn't be. It's rather nice that . . . that we—that we—we're . . . comrades, as you might say . . .

YOUNG GENTLEMAN: Now you're starting over.

YOUNG WIFE: Don't you remember? It was one of our very first talks: we wanted to be . . . "just comrades." . . . Oh, it was lovely that time . . . at my sister's, in January, at the great ball . . . during the quadrille. . . . For Heaven's sake, I should have left long ago! My sister will be waiting—what shall I tell her? Adieu, Alfred. . . .

YOUNG GENTLEMAN: Emma! You're going to leave me like this?

YOUNG WIFE: Yes. Like this!

YOUNG GENTLEMAN: Just another five minutes . . .

YOUNG WIFE: All right, five minutes. But you must promise me to keep quite still . . . Yes? . . . I'm going to give you a good-bye kiss . . . Ssh. . . . keep still, as I told you, or I'll get right up. My sweet . . . sweet . . .

YOUNG GENTLEMAN: Emma . . . I worsh—

* * * * *

YOUNG WIFE: Darling Alfred . . .

YOUNG GENTLEMAN: Oh, it's heaven with you!

YOUNG WIFE: But now I really must go.

YOUNG GENTLEMAN: Oh, let your sister wait.

YOUNG WIFE: I must go *home*. It's too late for my sister. What time is it now?

YOUNG GENTLEMAN: How'd I find *that* out?

YOUNG WIFE: By looking at your watch!

YOUNG GENTLEMAN: But it's in my waistcoat.

YOUNG WIFE: Well, get it.

YOUNG GENTLEMAN (*gets up with a mighty heave*): Eight.

YOUNG WIFE (*rising hastily*): For Heaven's sake! Quick, Alfred, my stockings—whatever shall I say? They'll be waiting for me . . . at home . . . eight o'clock!

YOUNG GENTLEMAN: When do I see you next?

YOUNG WIFE: Never.

YOUNG GENTLEMAN: Emma! Don't you still love me?

YOUNG WIFE: That's why. Give me my boots.

YOUNG GENTLEMAN: Never again? . . . Here are the boots.

YOUNG WIFE: There's a buttonhook in my pocket book. Please hurry . . .

YOUNG GENTLEMAN: Here's the buttonhook.

YOUNG WIFE: Alfred, this can cost us both our necks!

YOUNG GENTLEMAN (*not liking this at all*): Why?!

YOUNG WIFE: Well, what can I tell him when he asks me where I've been?

YOUNG GENTLEMAN: At your sister's.

YOUNG WIFE: Yes, if only I were a good liar.

YOUNG GENTLEMAN: You'll just have to be.

YOUNG WIFE: All this for a man like you . . . Come here. Let me give you another kiss. (*She embraces him.*) And now leave me alone, go in the other room, I can't dress with you around.

(*The Young Gentleman goes to the drawing room and gets dressed. He eats a little of the pastry, drinks a glass of cognac.*)

YOUNG WIFE (*after a while, calling out*): Alfred!

YOUNG GENTLEMAN: Yes, my treasure?

YOUNG WIFE: Maybe it's good we didn't just cry.

YOUNG GENTLEMAN *smiles, not without pride*: How can you treat it so lightly.

YOUNG WIFE: What will it be like if we meet at a party one day— by chance?

YOUNG GENTLEMAN: One day? By chance? Surely you'll be at the Lobheimers' tomorrow?

YOUNG WIFE: Yes. Will you?

YOUNG GENTLEMAN: Of course. May I ask for the cotillion?

YOUNG WIFE: Oh, I won't go. How can you think . . . ? Why . . . (*She enters the drawing room, fully dressed, and takes a chocolate pastry.*) . . . I'd sink into the ground!

YOUNG GENTLEMAN: Well, tomorrow at the Lobheimers'. That's lovely.

YOUNG WIFE: No, no, I'll send word I can't come. . . . Definitely. . . .

YOUNG GENTLEMAN: Then the day after tomorrow—here.

YOUNG WIFE: What an idea!

YOUNG GENTLEMAN: At six.

YOUNG WIFE: There are cabs at the corner, aren't there?

YOUNG GENTLEMAN: As many as you like. Then it's day after tomorrow, six o'clock, here. Say yes, my dearest treasure.

YOUNG WIFE: . . . We'll talk it over tomorrow—during the cotillion.

YOUNG GENTLEMAN (*embracing her*): Angel!

YOUNG WIFE: Don't spoil my hairdo again.

YOUNG GENTLEMAN: So it's tomorrow at the Lobheimers' and the day after—in my arms.

YOUNG WIFE: Good-bye . . .

YOUNG GENTLEMAN (*suddenly worried again*): And what are you going to tell him tonight?

YOUNG WIFE: Don't ask . . . don't ask . . . it's too dreadful. Why do I love you so? Good-bye. If I meet people on the stairs again, I shall have a stroke.

(*The Young Gentleman kisses her hand yet again.*
The Young Wife goes.
Young Gentleman left alone. He sits down on the sofa.
Then he smiles away to himself.) Well, now I'm having an affair with a respectable woman!

5 The Young Wife and the Husband

A comfortable bedroom. It is ten thirty at night. The Young Wife is lying in bed, reading. The Husband comes into the room in his bathrobe.

YOUNG WIFE (*without looking up*): You've stopped working?

HUSBAND: Yes. I'm too tired. And besides . . .

YOUNG WIFE: Yes?

HUSBAND: I suddenly felt so lonely at my desk. I began longing for you.

YOUNG WIFE (*looks up*): Really?

HUSBAND (*sits by her on her bed*): Don't read any more tonight. You'll ruin your eyes.

YOUNG WIFE (*closes the book*): What's the matter?

HUSBAND: Nothing, my child. I'm in love with you. But you know that.

YOUNG WIFE: One might almost forget it sometimes.

HUSBAND: One even has to forget it sometimes.

YOUNG WIFE: Why?

HUSBAND: Marriage would be imperfect otherwise. It would—how shall I put it? it would lose its sanctity.

YOUNG WIFE: Oh . . .

HUSBAND: Believe me—it's true. . . . If in the course of the five years we've been married we hadn't sometimes forgotten we're in love with one another, we probably wouldn't be in love any more.

YOUNG WIFE: That's over my head.

HUSBAND: The fact is simply this: we've had something like ten or twelve different love affairs with one another . . . isn't that how it seems to you?

YOUNG WIFE: I haven't kept count.

HUSBAND: If we'd pushed our first affair to the limit, if I'd blindly surrendered myself to my passion for you from the beginning, we'd have gone the way of millions of others. We'd be through by now.

YOUNG WIFE: I see what you mean.

HUSBAND: Believe me—Emma—in the first days of our marriage I was afraid it would turn out that way.

YOUNG WIFE: So was I.

HUSBAND: You see? Wasn't I right? That's why it's best—from time to time—to live together just as friends.

YOUNG WIFE: Oh, I see.

HUSBAND: That way we can always keep having new honeymoons, because I never risk letting the weeks of the honeymoon . . .

YOUNG WIFE: . . . run into months.

HUSBAND: Exactly.

YOUNG WIFE: And now it seems . . . another of those periods of friendship has come to an end?

HUSBAND (*tenderly pressing her to him*): It could be so!

YOUNG WIFE: But suppose it was different—with me?

HUSBAND: It isn't different with you. You're the cleverest creature alive—*and* the most bewitching. I'm very happy to have found you.

YOUNG WIFE: How nice that you do know how to court a woman—from time to time.

HUSBAND (*has got into bed*): For a man who's seen the world a bit—come, put your head on my shoulder—seen the world a bit, marriage means something far more mysterious than to girls from good families like you. You come to us pure and—at least to a certain degree—ignorant, and so you have in reality a much clearer view of the true nature of love than we have.

YOUNG WIFE (*laughing*): Oh!

HUSBAND: Certainly. Because we're insecure—confused by the many varied experiences we have before marriage—unavoidably. You women hear a lot, and know too much, I'm afraid you read too much too, but you can never have an accurate conception of what we men have to go through. What's commonly called love is made utterly repellent to us—because, after all, what are the poor creatures we have to resort to?

YOUNG WIFE: Yes, what *are* the poor creatures you have to resort to?

HUSBAND (*kisses her on the forehead*): Be glad, my child, that you never had a glimpse of these circles. Most of them are rather pitiable beings, incidentally. Let us not cast the first stone!

YOUNG WIFE: You pity them? That doesn't seem quite right. . . .

HUSBAND (*with fine mildness*): They deserve it. You girls from good families, who can quietly wait beneath the parental roof till a decent man proposes to you—you don't know the misery that drives those poor creatures into the arms of sin.

YOUNG WIFE: They all sell themselves, then?

HUSBAND: I wouldn't quite say *that*. And I'm not thinking merely of material misery. There is also—one might say—a moral misery: an insufficient grasp of what is . . . proper, and especially of what is noble.

YOUNG WIFE: But why should we pity them? Don't they have rather a nice time of it?

HUSBAND: You have peculiar opinions, my child. Don't forget that these creatures are destined by nature to sink forever lower and lower and lower. There is no stopping it.

YOUNG WIFE (*snuggles up to him*): Sinking sounds rather nice!

HUSBAND (*pained*): How can you say such a thing, Emma? I should have thought there could be nothing more repellent to a decent woman than the thought of . . .

YOUNG WIFE: Yes, that's true, Karl, of course. I said it without thinking. Tell me more. It's so nice when you talk like this. Tell me more.

HUSBAND: What about?

YOUNG WIFE: About—those creatures!

HUSBAND: But what an idea!

YOUNG WIFE: Look, I asked you before, didn't I, right at the beginning I kept asking you to tell me about your youth.

HUSBAND: Why does that interest you?

YOUNG WIFE: Aren't you my husband? And isn't it positively unfair that I know absolutely nothing about your past?

HUSBAND: I hope you don't think I'd . . . in such bad taste . . . No, Emma! It would be profanation!

YOUNG WIFE: And yet you've . . . held any number of other young ladies in your arms, the way you're holding me now.

HUSBAND: "Young ladies!" You're a lady . . .

YOUNG WIFE: There's one question you must answer. Or else . . . or else . . . no honeymoon.

HUSBAND: You've a way of talking . . . remember, my child, you're a mother—our little girl is sleeping in there.

YOUNG WIFE (*pressing herself to him*): But I want a boy too.

HUSBAND: Emma!

YOUNG WIFE: Oh, don't be so . . . Of course, I'm your wife, but I'd like to be—your mistress, sort of.

HUSBAND: You would?

YOUNG WIFE: First my question!

HUSBAND (*accommodating*): What is it?

YOUNG WIFE: Was there a—a married woman—among them?

HUSBAND: What? How do you mean?

YOUNG WIFE: *You* know.

HUSBAND (*somewhat disturbed*): What makes you ask?

YOUNG WIFE: I'd like to know if there . . . I mean . . . there are women like that, I know . . . But have *you* . . .

HUSBAND (*gravely*): Do you know any such woman?

YOUNG WIFE: Well, I can't tell.

HUSBAND: Is there such a woman among your friends?

YOUNG WIFE: Well, how could I say yes—or no—and be sure?

HUSBAND: Has one of your women friends . . . People talk a lot when they . . . women among themselves . . . has one of them confessed . . . ?

YOUNG WIFE (*uncertainly*): No.

HUSBAND: Do you *suspect* that one of your friends . . .

YOUNG WIFE: Suspect . . . well . . . suspect . . .

HUSBAND: It seems you do!

YOUNG WIFE: Definitely not, Karl. Most certainly not. Now I think it over, I wouldn't believe it of one of them.

HUSBAND: Not one?

YOUNG WIFE: Of friends—not one.

HUSBAND: Promise me something, Emma.

YOUNG WIFE: Well?

HUSBAND: Promise you'll never go around with a woman if you have the slightest suspicion that . . . her life is not beyond reproach.

YOUNG WIFE: You need a promise for that?

HUSBAND: I know, of course, that you would never seek contact with such women. But by chance you might . . . It frequently happens that women who don't enjoy the best reputation seek the company of respectable women, partly for contrast and partly out of a certain—how shall I put it?—out of a certain nostalgia for virtue.

YOUNG WIFE: I see.

HUSBAND: Yes, I believe it's very true, what I just said. Nostalgia for virtue! For there's one thing you can be sure of: in reality all these women are very unhappy.

YOUNG WIFE: Why?

HUSBAND: How can you ask, Emma? Only imagine what sort of existence they have to lead. Full of meanness, lies, treachery—and full of danger!

YOUNG WIFE: Oh yes. I'm sure you're right.

HUSBAND: Indeed, they pay for that bit of happiness . . . that bit of . . .

YOUNG WIFE: . . . pleasure.

HUSBAND: Pleasure? What makes you call it pleasure?

YOUNG WIFE: Well, it's something, or they wouldn't do it.

HUSBAND: It's nothing. Mere intoxication.

YOUNG WIFE (*thoughtfully*): Mere intoxication.

HUSBAND: Not even intoxication. But one thing is certain—it's bought at a price!

YOUNG WIFE: Then . . you do know what you're talking about?

HUSBAND: Yes, Emma. It's my saddest memory.

YOUNG WIFE: Who was it? Tell me. Do I know her?

HUSBAND: Emma! What are you thinking of?

YOUNG WIFE: Was it long ago? Very long before you married me?

HUSBAND: Don't ask. Please, don't ask.

YOUNG WIFE: But Karl!

HUSBAND: She is dead.

YOUNG WIFE: Honestly?

HUSBAND: Yes . . . It may sound ridiculous, but I have the feeling that all these women die young.

YOUNG WIFE: Did you love her very much?

HUSBAND: Can a man love a liar?

YOUNG WIFE: Then, why . . . ?

HUSBAND: Intoxication . . .

YOUNG WIFE: Then you did . . . ?

HUSBAND: Please, don't talk about it. All that is long past. I've only loved one woman: you. A man can only love where he finds purity and truth.

YOUNG WIFE: Karl!

HUSBAND: Oh how safe, how good a man feels in these arms! Why didn't I know you as a child? I'm sure I'd never have looked at another woman.

YOUNG WIFE: Karl!

HUSBAND: You're beautiful . . . beautiful . . . Oh!

(*He puts the light out.*)

* * * * *

YOUNG WIFE: You know what I can't help thinking of tonight?

HUSBAND: What, my treasure?

YOUNG WIFE: Of . . . of . . . of Venice.

HUSBAND: The first night . . .

YOUNG WIFE: Yes . . . Like that . . .

HUSBAND: What is it? Tell me.

YOUNG WIFE: Tonight . . . that's how you love me tonight.

HUSBAND: Yes, that's how I love you.

YOUNG WIFE: Ah . . . if you could always . . .

HUSBAND (*in her arms*): Yes?

YOUNG WIFE: Oh Karl dear!

HUSBAND: What was it you wanted to say? If I could always . . . ?

YOUNG WIFE: Well, yes.

HUSBAND: Well, what would happen if I could always . . . ?

YOUNG WIFE: Then I'd always know you love me.

HUSBAND: Yes. But you know it anyhow. A man can't always be the loving husband: "a man must go out into this hostile life, take with him high goals, and learn the meaning of strife!" * Always remember this, my child. In marriage there's a time for everything—that's the beauty of it. There aren't many who still remember their Venice after five years.

YOUNG WIFE: No, of course not!

HUSBAND: And now . . . good night, my child.

YOUNG WIFE: Good night!

6 The Husband and the Little Miss

A private room in the Riedhof Restaurant; comfortable, unobtrusive elegance; the gas stove is lit. On the table the remains of a meal: meringues with much whipped cream, fruit, cheese. White Hungarian wine in the glasses.

The Husband smokes a Havana cigar, leans back on the corner of the sofa.

The Little Miss sits on a chair beside him, scoops the whipped cream out of a meringue and sucks it up with satisfaction.

HUSBAND: It's good?

LITTLE MISS (*without letting herself be interrupted*): Mm!

HUSBAND: Like another?

LITTLE MISS: No, I've eaten too much already.

HUSBAND: You've no wine left. (*He fills up her glass.*)

LITTLE MISS: No . . . I'll only leave it, sir.

HUSBAND: You're still calling me "sir."

---

* Translator's Note: These lines are quoted from Schiller's *"Das Lied von der Glocke."* Their use underscores the husband's mediocrity.

LITTLE MISS: Well, it's hard to get out of the habit, sir.

HUSBAND: "Sir"!

LITTLE MISS: What?

HUSBAND: You said "sir" again. Come and sit by me.

LITTLE MISS: One moment—I'm not through.

(*The Husband gets up, stands behind her chair and puts his arms round her, turning her head toward him.*)

LITTLE MISS: What is it now?

HUSBAND: I'd like to have a kiss.

LITTLE MISS (*gives him a kiss*): You're pretty fresh, you are.

HUSBAND: You only just noticed it?

LITTLE MISS: Oh, I noticed before . . . in the street. You must have quite an opinion of me.

HUSBAND: How's that?

LITTLE MISS: Going straight to a private room with you.

HUSBAND: You didn't go "straight" to the private room.

LITTLE MISS: But you've such a nice way of asking.

HUSBAND: You think so?

LITTLE MISS: And after all, what's wrong about it?

HUSBAND: Precisely.

LITTLE MISS: Whether you go for a walk or—

HUSBAND: It's much too cold for a walk, isn't it?

LITTLE MISS: Of course it was much too cold.

HUSBAND: But in here it's nice and warm, don't you think? (*He has sat down again and puts his arm around the Little Miss, pulling her over to his side.*)

LITTLE MISS (*weakly*): Hey!

HUSBAND: Now tell me . . . You'd noticed me before, hadn't you?

LITTLE MISS: Sure. In the Singer Strasse.

HUSBAND: I don't mean today. The day before yesterday and the day before that. I was following you.

LITTLE MISS: There's plenty follow me!

HUSBAND: I can imagine. But did you notice me?

LITTLE MISS: Well . . . um . . . you know what happened to me the other day? My cousin's husband followed me in the dark, and didn't recognize me.

HUSBAND: Did he speak to you?

LITTLE MISS: The idea! You think everybody's as fresh as you?

HUSBAND: It happens.

LITTLE MISS: Sure it happens.

HUSBAND: Well, what do you do then?

LITTLE MISS: Me? Nothing. I just don't answer.

HUSBAND: Hm . . . you answered me.

LITTLE MISS: Well, are you mad at me?

HUSBAND (*kisses her violently*): Your lips taste of whipped cream.

LITTLE MISS: Oh, they're sweet by nature.

HUSBAND: Many men have told you that, have they?

LITTLE MISS: Many men! The ideas you get!

HUSBAND: Be honest with me. How many have kissed these lips?

LITTLE MISS: Why ask? If I tell you, you won't believe me.

HUSBAND: Why not?

LITTLE MISS: Guess.

HUSBAND: Let's say—um—but you mustn't be angry!

LITTLE MISS: Why should I be?

HUSBAND: Well, at a guess . . . twenty.

LITTLE MISS (*breaking away from him*): Why not a hundred while you're at it?

HUSBAND: It was only a guess.

LITTLE MISS: It was a bad guess.

HUSBAND: Let's say—ten.

LITTLE MISS (*offended*): Oh sure! A girl who lets you talk to her in the street and goes straight to a private dining room!

HUSBAND: Don't be a child. Whether people run around in the streets or sit together in a room . . . Here we're in a restaurant, the waiter can come in any time—there's nothing to it.

LITTLE MISS: That's just what *I* thought.

HUSBAND: Have you ever been in a private dining room before?

LITTLE MISS: Well, if I must tell you the truth: yes.

HUSBAND: Well, I like that: you're honest.

LITTLE MISS: It wasn't like you think. I was with my girl friend and her fiancé, during the last Carnival.

HUSBAND: Well, it wouldn't be a tragedy if you'd been—with your boyfriend . . .

LITTLE MISS: Sure it wouldn't be a tragedy. But I haven't got a boyfriend.

HUSBAND: Go on!

LITTLE MISS: Cross my heart, I haven't.

HUSBAND: You don't mean to tell me I . . .

LITTLE MISS: What? . . . There hasn't been anyone—for more than six months.

HUSBAND: I see . . . And before that? Who was it?

LITTLE MISS: What are you so inquisitive for?

HUSBAND: Because . . . I'm in love with you.

LITTLE MISS: Really?

HUSBAND: Of course. Hadn't you noticed? Come on, tell me. (*He pulls her close to him.*)

LITTLE MISS: Tell you what?

HUSBAND: Don't keep me begging. I'd like to know who he was.

LITTLE MISS (*laughing*): Oh, a man, of course.

HUSBAND: Come on, come on, who was he?

LITTLE MISS: He was a little bit like you.

HUSBAND: Indeed.

LITTLE MISS: If you hadn't been so much like him . . .

HUSBAND: Well, what then?

LITTLE MISS: Now don't ask. You know what . . .

Husband: So that's why you let me speak to you!

LITTLE MISS: Well, yes.

HUSBAND: Now I don't know whether to be glad or annoyed.

LITTLE MISS: If I was you, I'd be glad.

HUSBAND: Oh well, okay.

LITTLE MISS: The way you talk reminds me of him too . . . and the way you look at a girl . . .

HUSBAND: What was he?

LITTLE MISS: Really, your eyes . . .

HUSBAND: What was his name?

LITTLE MISS: Don't look at me like that, no, please!
(*The Husband takes her in his arms. A long, hot kiss.
The Little Miss shakes herself free and tries to get up.*)

HUSBAND: What's the matter?

LITTLE MISS: Time to go home.

HUSBAND: Later.

LITTLE MISS: No, I *must* go home. Really. What do you think mother will say?

HUSBAND: You're living with your mother?

LITTLE MISS: Sure I am. What did you think?

HUSBAND: I see . . . with your mother. Just the two of you?

LITTLE MISS: Just the two . . . ?! There's five of us. Two boys and three girls.

HUSBAND: Don't sit so far away. Are you the eldest?

LITTLE MISS: No. I'm the second. First there's Kathi, she goes out to work. In a flower shop. Then there's me.

HUSBAND: What do you do?

LITTE MISS: I'm at home.

HUSBAND: All the time?

LITTLE MISS: Well, one of us has got to be at home.

HUSBAND: Naturally. Well—and what do you tell your mother when you—come home late?

LITTLE MISS: It doesn't often happen.

HUSBAND: Tonight for example. Your mother does ask you?

LITTLE MISS: Oh, sure she does. It doesn't matter how careful I am when I get home, she wakes up every time.

HUSBAND: What will you tell her tonight?

LITTLE MISS: Oh well, I guess I'll have been to the theater.

HUSBAND: Will she believe you?

LITTLE MISS: Why shouldn't she? I often go to the theater. Only last Sunday I was to the opera with my girl friend and her fiancé—and my older brother.

HUSBAND: Where do you get the tickets from?

LITTLE MISS: My brother's a barber.

HUSBAND: Of course, barbers . . . I suppose he's a theatrical barber.

LITTLE MISS: Why are you pumping me like this?

HUSBAND: I'm interested. And what's your other brother?

LITTLE MISS: He's still at school. He wants to be a teacher. Imagine!

HUSBAND: And you've a younger sister too?

LITTLE MISS: Yes, she's only a squirt, but at that you've got to keep an eye on her. You've no idea what these girls learn at school. Do you know, the other day I caught her having a date!

HUSBAND: What?

LITTLE MISS: I did. With a boy from the school opposite. She was out walking with him in the Strozzi Gasse at half-past seven. The brat!

HUSBAND: What did you do?

LITTLE MISS: Well, she got a spanking.

HUSBAND: You are as strict as all that?

LITTLE MISS: There's no one else to do it. My older sister's in the shop, Mother does nothing but grumble—and so everything falls on me.

HUSBAND: God, you're sweet! (*He kisses her and grows more tender.*) And you remind me of someone, too.

LITTLE MISS: Do I? Who is she?

HUSBAND: No one in particular . . . you remind me of the time when . . . well, my youth! Come, drink up, child.

LITTLE MISS: How old are you? . . . Um . . . I don't even know your name.

HUSBAND: Karl.

LITTLE MISS: Honest? Your name's Karl?

HUSBAND: His was Karl too?

LITTLE MISS: Really, it's a miracle . . . it's too . . . No, those eyes! . . . That look! (*She shakes her head.*)

HUSBAND: You still haven't told me who he was.

LITTLE MISS: A bad man, that's what he was, or he wouldn't have dropped me.

HUSBAND: Did you like him a lot?

LITTLE MISS: Sure I liked him a lot.

HUSBAND: I know what he was: a lieutenant.

LITTLE MISS: No, he wasn't in the army. They wouldn't take him. His father's got a house in the . . . but what do you want to know for?

HUSBAND (*kisses her*): Your eyes are gray, really. At first I thought they were black.

LITTLE MISS: Well, aren't they nice enough for you?

(*The Husband kisses her eyes.*)

LITTLE MISS: Oh, no—that's something I can't stand—please, please . . . Oh God . . . No, let me get up . . . just for a minute, oh please!

HUSBAND (*increasingly tender*): Oh, no! No!

LITTLE MISS: But, Karl, please!

HUSBAND: How old are you? Eighteen, is it?

LITTLE MISS: Nineteen now.

HUSBAND: Nineteen . . . and I . . .

LITTLE MISS: You're thirty . . .

HUSBAND: And . . . a little more . . . Don't let's talk of it.

LITTLE MISS: At that, he was thirty-two when I met him!

HUSBAND: How long ago?

LITTLE MISS: I can't remember. . . . You know what, there was something in the wine!

HUSBAND: How so?

LITTLE MISS: I'm quite . . . you know . . . everything's turning around.

HUSBAND: Hold on to me. Like this . . . (*He pulls her to him and becomes more and more tender; she scarcely defends herself.*) I'll tell you something, treasure, now we might really go.

LITTLE MISS: Yes—home.

HUSBAND: Not home exactly.

LITTLE MISS: What do you mean? . . . Oh no, no! . . . I wouldn't . . . What an idea!

HUSBAND: Now, listen to me, my child, next time we meet, you know, we'll arrange it so. . . . (*He has slipped to the floor, his head in her lap.*) That's good; oh, that's good!

LITTLE MISS: What are you doing? (*She kisses his hair.*) See, there must have been something in the wine . . . so sleepy . . . Hey, what happens if I can't get up? But . . . but look, Karl! . . . If somebody comes in . . . Please . . . the waiter!

HUSBAND: No waiter'll . . . come in here . . . not in . . . your lifetime.

* * * * *

The Little Miss leans back in a corner of the sofa, her eyes shut. The Husband walks up and down the small room, after lighting a cigar.

A longish silence.

HUSBAND (*looks at the girl for a long time, then says to himself*): Who knows what sort of person she really is—God in heaven! . . . So quickly . . . Wasn't very careful of me . . . Hm . . .

LITTLE MISS (*without opening her eyes*): There must have been something in that wine.

HUSBAND: How's that?

LITTLE MISS: Otherwise . . .

HUSBAND: Why blame everything on the wine?

LITTLE MISS: Where are you? Why are you so far away? Come
here to me.

    (*The Husband goes to her, sits down.*)

LITTLE MISS: Now, tell me if you really like me.

HUSBAND: But you know. . . . (*Interrupting himself quickly.*) Of
course I do.

LITTLE MISS: You see . . . there is . . . Come on, tell me the
truth, what was in that wine?

HUSBAND: You think I go around poisoning people?

LITTLE MISS: Look, I just don't understand. I'm not like that. . . .
We've only known each other for . . . Listen, I'm not like that,
cross my heart—if you believe that of me . . .

HUSBAND: There, there, don't fret so! I don't think anything bad
of you. I just think you like me.

LITTLE MISS: Yes . . .

HUSBAND: After all, if two young people are alone together, and
have supper, and drink wine—there doesn't have to be anything
in the wine.

LITTLE MISS: Oh, I was just gabbing.

HUSBAND: But why?

LITTLE MISS (*somewhat defiantly*): Because I was ashamed!

HUSBAND: That's ridiculous. There's no reason for it. Especially
since I remind you of your first lover.

LITTLE MISS: Yes.

HUSBAND: Your first.

LITTLE MISS: Oh sure . . .

HUSBAND: Now it would interest me to know who the others were.

LITTLE MISS: There weren't any.

HUSBAND: That isn't true. It can't be true.

LITTLE MISS: Please don't nag me!

HUSBAND: A cigarette?

LITTLE MISS: No. Thank you.

HUSBAND: Do you know what time it is?

LITTLE MISS: What?

HUSBAND: Half-past eleven.

LITTLE MISS: Really.

HUSBAND: Well . . . what about your mother? Used to it, is she?

LITTLE MISS: You want to send me home already?

HUSBAND: But you wanted—yourself . . .

LITTLE MISS: Look, you're different now. What have I done to you?

HUSBAND: My dear child, what's wrong? What are you thinking of?

LITTLE MISS: It was . . . the look in your eyes, honest, cross my heart, otherwise you could have waited a long . . . A *lot* of men have asked me to go to a private room with them!

HUSBAND: Well, would you like to . . . to come here again . . . soon? Or some other place . . . ?

LITTLE MISS: I don't know.

HUSBAND: Now what's that mean: you don't know?

LITTLE MISS: Why do you have to ask?

HUSBAND: All right—when? But first I must explain that I don't live in Vienna. I . . . just come here now and then. For a couple of days.

LITTLE MISS: Go on—you aren't Viennese?

HUSBAND: Well, yes, I'm Viennese, but I live . . . out of town.

LITTLE MISS: Where?

HUSBAND: Goodness, that doesn't matter, does it?

LITTLE MISS: Don't worry, I won't go there.

HUSBAND: Heavens, you can go there as much as you want. I live in Graz.

LITTLE MISS: Really?

HUSBAND: Yes. What's so astonishing about that?

LITTLE MISS: You're married, aren't you?

HUSBAND (*greatly surprised*): Whatever makes you think so?

LITTLE MISS: It looks that way to me.

HUSBAND: And if I were, it wouldn't bother you any?

LITTLE MISS: Oh, I'd like it better if you were single. But you're married, I know.

HUSBAND: Now tell me, what makes you think so?

LITTLE MISS: Oh, if a man says he doesn't live in town and hasn't always got time . . .

HUSBAND: That isn't so unlikely, is it?

LITTLE MISS: I don't believe it.

HUSBAND: And it wouldn't give you a guilty conscience to seduce a married man? Make him unfaithful?

LITTLE MISS: Never mind about that—I bet your wife is no different.

HUSBAND (*very indignant*): That's enough! Such observations . . .

LITTLE MISS: I thought you didn't have a wife.

HUSBAND: Whether I have a wife or not, such observations are beyond the pale! (*He has risen.*)

LITTLE MISS: But, Karl, what is it, Karl? Are you mad at me? Look, I didn't know you were married. I was just gabbing. Come on, let's be friends.

HUSBAND (*goes to her after a couple of seconds*): You really are strange creatures . . . you . . . women. (*At her side, he begins to caress her again.*)

LITTLE MISS: No . . . don't . . and it's so late . . .

HUSBAND: Now listen to me. We must have a serious talk. I want to see you again—many times.

LITTLE MISS: Honest?

HUSBAND: But if so, it's essential. . . . I must be able to rely on you. I can't be watching you all the time.

LITTLE MISS: Oh, I can look after myself.

HUSBAND: You're . . . well, not inexperienced exactly, but you're young, and—men in general are an unscrupulous bunch.

LITTLE MISS: And how!

HUSBAND: I don't mean just in morals. . . . Well, *you* know what I mean.

LITTLE MISS: Now, really, what sort of girl do you take me for?

HUSBAND: So, if you want to love me—only me—we'll be able to fix things up somehow, even if I do live in Graz. This place isn't the right thing—someone could come in at any moment!

(*The Little Miss snuggles up to him.*)

HUSBAND: Next time let's make it somewhere else, okay?

LITTLE MISS: Okay.

HUSBAND: Where we can't be disturbed.

LITTLE MISS: Right.

HUSBAND (*embraces her with fervor*): The rest we can talk over on the way home. (*He gets up, opens the door.*) Waiter . . . the check!

7 The Little Miss and the Poet

A small room, comfortably furnished, in good taste. Drapes leave it in semidarkness. Red net curtains. A big desk littered with papers and books. Against the wall, an upright piano.
The Little Miss and the Poet enter together. The Poet locks the door.

POET: Here we are, sweetheart. (*He kisses her.*)

LITTLE MISS (*in hat and cloak*): Oh, what a nice room! Only you can't see anything!

POET: Your eyes will have to get used to semidarkness. These sweet eyes! (*He kisses her eyelids.*)

LITTLE MISS: These sweet eyes won't have time to get used to it.

POET: How's that?

LITTLE MISS: Because I can't stay for more than one minute.

POET: Do take your hat off.

LITTLE MISS: For one minute?

POET (*pulls out her hatpin, takes the hat, puts it on one side*): And your cloak.

LITTLE MISS: What are you up to? I've got to go!

POET: First you must rest. We've been walking three hours.

LITTLE MISS: We were in the carriage.

POET: Coming home, yes. But in Weidling-am-Bach we were three solid hours on foot. Now do sit down, child . . . wherever you like . . . at the desk. . . . No, that isn't comfortable. Sit down on the sofa. Here. (*He puts her down on the sofa.*) If you're very tired, you can stretch out. Like this. (*He makes her lie down.*) With your little head on the cushion.

LITTLE MISS (*laughing*): But I'm not a bit tired!

POET: You *think* you aren't. Right, and now if you feel sleepy, you can go to sleep. I'll keep perfectly quiet. Or I can play you a lullaby . . . one of my own. (*He goes to the piano.*)

LITTLE MISS: Your own?

POET: Yes.

LITTLE MISS: But, Robert, I thought you were a doctor.

POET: How's that? I told you I was a writer.

LITTLE MISS: Well, writers are doctors, aren't they?

POET: Of philosophy? Not all writers. Not me, for instance. Why did you bring *that* up?

LITTLE MISS: Because you said the piece you were going to play was your own.

POET: Oh well . . . maybe it isn't. It doesn't matter. Does it? It never matters who's done a thing—just so long as it's beautiful—you agree?

LITTLE MISS: Oh sure . . . as long as it's beautiful!

POET: Do you know what I meant by that?

LITTLE MISS: By what?

POET: What I said just now.

LITTLE MISS (*drowsily*): Oh, sure.

POET (*gets up, goes to her, and strokes her hair*): You didn't understand a word.

LITTLE MISS: Now look, I'm *not* stupid.

POET: Of course you are. That's why I love you. It's a fine thing for women to be stupid. In your way, that is.

LITTLE MISS: Hey, don't be rude!

POET: Little angel! Isn't it nice just to lie there on a soft Persian rug?

LITTLE MISS: Oh yes. Won't you go on playing the piano?

POET: I'd rather stay with you. (*He strokes her.*)

LITTLE MISS: Look, can't we have the light on?

POET: Oh no . . . twilight is so comforting. Today we were bathing in sunshine all day long. Now we've come out of the bath, so to speak, and we're wrapping the twilight round us like a bathrobe. (*He laughs.*) No, it'll have to be put a little differently . . . won't it?

LITTLE MISS: I don't know.

POET (*edging away from her*): It's divine, this stupidity! (*He takes out a notebook and writes a few words in it.*)

LITTLE MISS: What are you doing? (*Turns around to look at him.*) What are you writing down?

POET (*in an undertone*): Sun—bath—twilight—robe . . . That's it. (*He puts the notebook in his pocket, laughs.*) Nothing. And now tell me, treasure, wouldn't you like something to eat or drink?

LITTLE MISS: I guess I'm not thirsty. But I am hungry.

POET: Hm . . . now, I'd rather you were thirsty. The cognac's right here, but if it's food I'll have to go out and get it.

LITTLE MISS: Can't they bring it up for you?

POET: That's the difficulty. My maid isn't around anymore. . . . Never mind. I'll go. What would you like?

LITTLE MISS: It isn't worth it, I've got to go home anyway.

POET: Oho, no you don't! I'll tell you what: when we leave, we'll go and have supper somewhere.

LITTLE MISS: I haven't got time. And—where could we go? We'd be seen.

POET: You know so many people?

LITTLE MISS: It's enough if one of them sees us, the damage would be done.

POET: What damage?

LITTLE MISS: What do you think? If Mother heard anything . . .

POET: We could go to a place where nobody could see us. There are restaurants with private rooms after all . . .

LITTLE MISS (*sings*): "Just to share a private room with you . . ."

POET: Have you ever been to a private dining room?

LITTLE MISS: As a matter of fact I have.

POET: Who was the lucky man?

LITTLE MISS: Oh, it wasn't what you think . . . I was with my girl friend and her fiancé. They took me.

POET: Really? Am I supposed to believe that?

LITTLE MISS: Suit yourself.

POET (*close to her*): Did you blush? It's gotten dark in here. I can't make out your features. (*He touches her cheek with his hand.*) Even so—I recognize you.

LITTLE MISS: Well, take care you don't mix me up with another girl.

POET: Peculiar! I can't remember what you look like.

LITTLE MISS: Thank you very much.

POET (*seriously*): Do you know, it's rather spooky—I can't visualize your face—in a certain sense I've already forgotten you. Now, if I couldn't recognize your voice either . . . what would you be? So near and yet so far—rather spooky, what?

LITTLE MISS: What are you talking about?

POET: Nothing, angel, nothing. Where are your lips? (*He kisses her.*)

LITTLE MISS: Won't you put the light on?

POET: No . . . (*He grows very tender.*) Tell me if you love me!

LITTLE MISS: Oh, I do. I do!

POET: Have you ever loved anyone else as much?

LITTLE MISS: I told you I haven't.

POET: But . . . (*He sighs.*)

LITTLE MISS: Well—he was my fiancé.

POET: I'd rather you didn't think of him.

LITTLE MISS: Oh . . . what are you doing . . . now look . . .

POET: Let's imagine we're in a castle in India.

LITTLE MISS: I'm sure people there couldn't be as badly behaved as you.

POET: How idiotic! Divine! If only you had an inkling of what you mean to me . . .

LITTLE MISS: Well, what?

POET: Don't push me away all the time. I'm not doing anything—yet.

LITTLE MISS: Listen, my corset hurts.

POET (*simply*): Take it off.

LITTLE MISS: Okay, but you mustn't be naughty.

POET: Okay.

(*Little Miss rises and takes off her corset in the dark.*)

POET (*sitting on the sofa in the meanwhile*): Tell me, doesn't it interest you at all to know my last name?

LITTLE MISS: Oh, yes—what is it?

POET: I'd better not tell you my name. I'll tell you what I call myself.

LITTLE MISS: What's the difference?

POET: Well, what I call myself—as a writer.

LITTLE MISS: You don't write under your real name?

(*Poet close to her.*)

LITTLE MISS: Ah . . . please! . . . Don't!

POET: O the sweet odor that rises from you! (*He kisses her bosom.*)

LITTLE MISS: You're tearing my chemise.

POET: Off with it all! Away with these . . . superfluities!

LITTLE MISS: Robert!

POET: Let's enter our Indian castle!

LITTLE MISS: First tell me if you really love me.

POET: I worship you! (*He kisses her hotly.*) My treasure, I worship you, my springtime . . . my . . .

LITTLE MISS: Robert . . . Robert . . .

* * * * *

POET: That was bliss supernatural . . . I call myself . . .

LITTLE MISS: Robert, oh Robert!

POET: I call myself Biebitz.

LITTLE MISS: Why do you call yourself Biebitz?

POET: Biebitz isn't my name, it's what I call myself. You know the name?

LITTLE MISS: No.

POET: You don't know the name Biebitz? How divine! Really? But you're just pretending?

LITTLE MISS: Cross my heart, I've never heard it.

POET: You never go to the theater?

LITTLE MISS: Oh, yes. Just the other day I got taken—by my girl friend's uncle—and my girl friend—and we went to the opera—*Cavalleria rusticana!*

POET: Hmm, but you don't go to the Burg Theater?

LITTLE MISS: Nobody ever gives me tickets for that.

POET: I'll send you a ticket one day soon.

LITTLE MISS: Oh please! But don't forget. Make it something funny.

POET: Yes . . . funny . . . well . . . you wouldn't like something sad?

LITTLE MISS: Not really.

POET: Even if it's by me?

LITTLE MISS: A play—by you? You write for the theater?!

POET: Excuse me, I just want to light a candle. I haven't seen you since you became mine. Angel! (*He lights a candle.*)

LITTLE MISS: Hey, don't! I feel ashamed. Give me a blanket anyway!

POET: Later! (*He walks up to her with the light and contemplates her for a long while.*)

LITTLE MISS (*covers her face with her hands*): Robert!

POET: You're beautiful. You are Beauty! You are Nature herself perhaps! You are Sacred Simplicity!

LITTLE MISS: Ouch! You're dripping wax on me! Why can't you be more careful?

POET (*puts the candlestick down*): You're what I've been looking for all this time. You love me—just me—you'd love me the same if I were a shop assistant. It does me good. I'll confess that up till now I couldn't get rid of a certain suspicion. Tell me, hadn't you the least idea I was Biebitz?

LITTLE MISS: Look, I don't know what you want with me. I don't know any Biebitz.

POET: Such is fame! Never mind, forget what I told you, forget even the name I told you. I'm Robert for you, and I want to remain Robert. I was joking! (*gaily*) I'm not a writer at all, I'm a shop assistant. In the evenings I play the piano for folksingers!

LITTLE MISS: Now you have me all mixed up . . . and the way you look at a girl! What's the matter, what's eating you?

POET: It's strange—it's hardly ever happened to me, my treasure— I feel like crying. You've got under my skin. Let's stay together, hm? We're going to love one another very much.

LITTLE MISS: Listen, is that true about the folksinging?

POET: Yes, but don't ask any more. If you love me, don't ask. Tell me, could you make yourself quite free for a couple of weeks?

LITTLE MISS: What do you mean, quite free?

POET: Well, away from home.

LITTLE MISS: What! How could I? What would Mother say? Anyway, everything would go wrong at home without me.

POET: I'd been thinking how lovely it would be to live with you for a few weeks quite alone, somewhere, in distant solitude, in the depths of Nature's forests. Nature . . . in nature. . . . And then, one day, farewell—to go who knows whither?

LITTLE MISS: Now you're talking about saying good-bye. And I thought you liked me a lot.

POET: That's just it! (*He bends down and kisses her on the forehead.*) Sweet creature!

LITTLE MISS: Hold me tight, I'm cold.

POET: It's time to get dressed. Wait, I'll light some more candles.

LITTLE MISS (*gets up*): Don't look!

POET: No. (*at the window*) Tell me, child, are you happy?

LITTLE MISS: How do you mean?

POET: In general I mean: are you happy?

LITTLE MISS: Things could be better.

POET: You don't understand me. You've told me quite enough of the state of affairs at home, I know you aren't exactly a princess. I mean, setting all that aside, when you're just feeling alive? Do you by the way feel you are really alive?

LITTLE MISS: You got a comb?

POET (*goes to the dressing table, gives her the comb, contemplates the Little Miss*): God, you're enchanting to look at!

LITTLE MISS: No . . . don't!

POET: Come, stay here with me a little longer, stay and let me get something for our supper, and . . .

LITTLE MISS: But it's much too late.

POET: It's not nine yet.

LITTLE MISS: Well, then, I've really got to hurry.

POET: When shall we meet next?

LITTLE MISS: When would you like to see me?

POET: Tomorrow?

LITTLE MISS: What's tomorrow?

POET: Saturday.

LITTLE MISS: Oh, I can't make it. I've got to go see our guardian. With my little sister.

POET: Sunday, then . . . hm . . . Sunday . . . on Sunday . . . I must explain something to you. I'm not Biebitz, Biebitz is a friend of mine. One day I'll introduce you to him. His play is on this Sunday. I'll send you a ticket, and then I'll come pick you up from the theater. You'll tell me how you like the play, won't you?

LITTLE MISS: This Biebitz thing . . . well, I may be stupid but . . .

POET: When I know how you felt about the play, I'll really know you.

LITTLE MISS: Okay . . . I'm ready.

POET: Let's go, then, my treasure.

(*They leave.*)

8 The Poet and the Actress

A room in a country inn. It is an evening in spring; meadows and hills are lit by the moon; the windows are open. All is still.

The Poet and the Actress enter; as they come in, the flame of the candle which the Poet is carrying goes out.

POET: Oh!

ACTRESS: What's the matter?

POET: The candle. But we don't need it. Look, it's quite light! Marvelous!

> (*The Actress suddenly sinks on her knees at the window, folding her hands.*)

POET: What's the matter with you?

> (*Actress remains silent.*)

POET (*goes to her*): What are you doing?

ACTRESS (*indignant*): Can't you see I'm praying?

POET: You believe in God?

ACTRESS: What do you think I am—an anarchist?

POET: Oh.

ACTRESS: Come here, kneel down beside me. You could do with some praying once in a while.

> (*The Poet kneels down beside her and puts his arms round her.*)

ACTRESS: You profligate! (*She gets up.*) And do you know to whom I was praying?

POET: To God, I presume.

ACTRESS (*with great scorn*): Oh yes? It was to you I prayed.

POET: Then why look out of the window?

ACTRESS: Tell me where you've dragged me off to, seducer.

POET: It was your own idea, my child. You wanted to go to the country. You wanted to come here.

ACTRESS: Well, wasn't I right?

POET: Yes, it's enchanting. To think it's only two hours from Vienna—and perfect solitude! What a landscape!

ACTRESS: Isn't it? You could write poetry here, if you happened to have any talent.

POET: Have you been here before?

ACTRESS: Have I been here before? I lived here for years.

POET: With whom?

ACTRESS: Oh, with Fritz, of course.

POET: I see.

ACTRESS: I worshiped that man.

POET: You've said that already.

ACTRESS: Oh, I beg your pardon—I can leave if I bore you.

POET: *You* bore me? . . . You have no idea what you mean to me.

. . . You're a world in yourself. . . . You're the Divine Spark, you're Genius. . . . You are . . . The truth is, you're Sacred Simplicity. . . . Yes, you . . . But you shouldn't talk about Fritz—now.

ACTRESS: He was an aberration, yes . . . Oh well . . .

POET: It's good you see that.

ACTRESS: Come over and kiss me.

(*The Poet kisses her.*)

ACTRESS: And now we're going to say good night. Good-bye, my treasure.

POET: What do you mean?

ACTRESS: I'm going to bed.

POET: Yes—that's all right, but this "good night" business . . . where am *I* going to sleep?

ACTRESS: I'm sure there are other rooms in this inn.

POET: For me the other rooms have singularly little attraction. By the way, I'd better light up, hadn't I?

ACTRESS: Yes.

POET (*lights the candle on the bedside table*): What a pretty room . . . They're religious here, nothing but saints' pictures. . . . Wouldn't it be interesting to spend some time among these people—another world! How little we know of our fellow men!

ACTRESS: Stop talking bosh, and give me my pocketbook, will you, it's on the table.

POET: Here, my one and only love!

(*The Actress takes from the pocket book a small framed picture and puts it on the bedside table.*)

POET: What's that?

ACTRESS: Our Lady.

POET: I beg your pardon?

ACTRESS: The Blessed Virgin.

POET: I see. You never travel without it?

ACTRESS: Never. It's my mascot. Now go, Robert.

POET: What sort of a joke is this? Don't you want me to help you?

ACTRESS: I want you to go.

POET: Will you ever take me back?

ACTRESS: Perhaps.

POET: When?

ACTRESS: Oh, in about ten minutes.

POET (*kisses her*): Darling! See you in ten minutes.

ACTRESS: Where will you be?

POET: I shall walk up and down in front of the window. I love to walk at night in the open air. I get my best ideas that way. Especially when you're nearby. Wafted by your longings, as it were, floating on your art . . .

ACTRESS: You talk like an idiot.

POET (*sorrowfully*): Some women might have said—like a poet.

ACTRESS: Now go. And don't start anything with the waitress.
(*The poet departs.*
Actress undresses. She listens to the Poet going down the wooden stairs and then to his steps beneath the open window. As soon as she is undressed, she goes to the window, looks down, sees him standing there; she calls to him in a whisper.)

ACTRESS: Come!
(*The Poet comes up in a hurry; rushes to her. In the meantime she has gone to bed and put out the light. He locks the door.*)

ACTRESS: Well, now you may sit down by me and tell me a story.

POET (*sits by her on the bed*): Shouldn't I close the window? Aren't you cold?

ACTRESS: Oh, no.

POET: What would you like me to tell you?

ACTRESS: Tell me—who are you being unfaithful to—at this moment?

POET: Unfortunately, I'm not being unfaithful—yet.

ACTRESS: Don't worry, I'm being unfaithful too.

POET: I can imagine.

ACTRESS: And who do you think it is?

POET: My dear child, I wouldn't have a notion.

ACTRESS: Guess, then.

POET: Wait a moment . . . Well, your producer.

ACTRESS: My dear, I'm not a chorus girl.

POET: Oh, it was just an idea.

ACTRESS: Guess again.

POET: Your leading man—Benno.

ACTRESS: Pooh, that man doesn't like women, didn't you know? He's having an affair with the mailman.

POET: Who would have thought it?

ACTRESS: So come and kiss me.

(*The Poet embraces her.*)

ACTRESS: What are you doing?

POET: Don't torture me like this!

ACTRESS: Listen, Robert, I'll make a suggestion. Get in bed with me.

POET: I accept.

ACTRESS: Hurry up! Hurry up!

POET: Well . . . if I'd had my way, I'd have been . . . Listen!

ACTRESS: What?

POET: The crickets are chirping outside.

ACTRESS: You must be mad, my dear, there are no crickets in these parts.

POET: But you can hear them!

ACTRESS: Oh, come on!

POET: Here I am. (*He goes to her.*)

ACTRESS: And now lie still . . . Uh! . . . Don't move!

POET: What's the idea?

ACTRESS: I suppose you'd like to have an affair with me?

POET: I thought you might realize that sooner or later.

ACTRESS: A lot of men would. . . .

POET: But at this particular moment the odds are rather strongly in my favor.

ACTRESS: Come, my cricket. From now on I'm going to call you Cricket.

POET: Fine . . .

ACTRESS: Now—who am I deceiving?

POET: Huh? Me, maybe.

ACTRESS: My child, you should have your head examined.

POET: Or maybe someone . . . you've never seen . . . someone you don't know . . . He's meant for you, but you can never find him. . . .

ACTRESS: Cricket, don't talk such fantastic rot!

POET: . . . Isn't it strange . . . even you . . . and one would have thought—But no, it would just be . . . spoiling all that's best about you if one . . . Come, come, come . . .

* * * * *

ACTRESS: That's better than acting in damn silly plays. You agree?

POET: Well, I think it's good that you occasionally act in reasonable ones.

ACTRESS: Meaning yours, you conceited pup.

POET: Of course.

ACTRESS (*seriously*): It really is a wonderful play.

POET: You see!

ACTRESS: You're a genius!

POET: By the way, why did you cancel your performance two nights ago? There was nothing wrong with you.

ACTRESS: I wanted to annoy you.

POET: Why? What had I done to you?

ACTRESS: You were conceited.

POET: In what way?

ACTRESS: Everybody in the theater says so.

POET: Really.

ACTRESS: But I told them: that man has a right to be conceited.

POET: And what did they say to that?

ACTRESS: What should those people say? I never speak to them.

POET: I see.

ACTRESS: They'd like to poison me. (*Pause.*) But they won't succeed.

POET: Don't think of them. Just be happy we're here, and tell me you love me.

ACTRESS: You need further proof?

POET: Oh, that kind of thing can't be proved.

ACTRESS: Well, that's great! What more do you want?

POET: How many others did you try to prove it to this way? And did you love them all?

ACTRESS: Oh, no. I loved only one.

POET (*embracing her*): My . . .

ACTRESS: Fritz.

POET: My name is Robert. What am I to you, if it's Fritz you're thinking of?

ACTRESS: A whim.

POET: Nice to know!

ACTRESS: Tell me, aren't you proud?

POET: Why should I be proud?

ACTRESS: I think you have some reason.

POET: Oh, because of that!

ACTRESS: Yes, because of that, my pale cricket. How about the chirping? Are they still chirping?

POET: All the time. Can't you hear?

ACTRESS: I can hear. But that's frogs, my child.

POET: You're wrong: frogs croak.

ACTRESS: Certainly, they croak.

POET: But not here, my dear child. This is chirping.

ACTRESS: You're the most pigheaded creature I've ever come across. Kiss me, frog.

POET: Please don't call me that. It makes me nervous.

ACTRESS: What do you want me to call you?

POET: I've got a name: Robert.

ACTRESS: Oh, that's too dull.

POET: I must ask you to call me simply by my name.

ACTRESS: All right, Robert, kiss me . . . Ah! (*She kisses him.*) Are you content now, frog? Ha, ha, ha!

POET: May I light myself a cigarette?

ACTRESS: Give me one.

(*The Poet takes the cigarette case from the bedside table, takes out two, lights both and hands one to her.*)

ACTRESS: By the way, you never said a word about how I did last night.

POET: Doing what?

ACTRESS: Well . . . !

POET: Oh, I see. I wasn't at the theater.

ACTRESS: I guess you like to joke.

POET: Not at all. When you canceled your performance the day before yesterday, I assumed that yesterday you couldn't be in full possession of your powers. So I preferred to abstain.

ACTRESS: You missed something.

POET: Indeed?

ACTRESS: I was sensational. People turned pale.

POET: You could see them?

ACTRESS: Benno said to me, "You were a goddess, darling."

POET: Hm . . . and so sick one day earlier.

ACTRESS: Yes. And do you know why? Out of longing for you.

POET: You just told me you canceled the performance to annoy me!

ACTRESS: What do you know of my love for you? That sort of
thing leaves you cold. I was in a fever for nights on end. With
a temperature of a hundred and five.

POET: A high temperature just for a whim!

ACTRESS: A whim, you call it? I die for love of you, and you call
it a whim?

POET: What about Fritz?

ACTRESS: What about him? What about him? Don't talk to me
about that . . . that cheap crook!

9 The Actress and the Count

*The Actress's bedroom, luxuriously furnished. It is noon; the blinds
are still down; on the bedside table, a burning candle; the Actress
is lying in her four-poster. Numerous newspapers are strewn about
on the covers.*

*The Count enters, in the uniform of a captain of Dragoons. He
stops at the door.*

ACTRESS: It's you, Count!

COUNT: Your good mother gave me permission, or of course I
wouldn't . . .

ACTRESS: Please come right in.

COUNT: I kiss your hand. A thousand pardons—coming straight
in from the street—you know, I can't see a thing. Yes . . . here
we are. (*near the bed*) I kiss your hand.

ACTRESS: Sit down, my dear Count.

COUNT: Your mother said you weren't very well, Fräulein. Nothing too serious, I hope?

ACTRESS: Nothing serious? I was dying!

COUNT: Oh dear me! Not really?

ACTRESS: In any case it's very kind of you to . . . trouble to call.

COUNT: Dying! And only last night you played like a goddess!

ACTRESS: It was a great triumph, I believe.

COUNT: Colossal! People were absolutely knocked out. As for myself, well . . .

ACTRESS: Thanks for the lovely flowers.

COUNT: Not at all, Fräulein.

ACTRESS (*turning her eyes toward a large basket of flowers, which stands on a small table by the window*): There they are!

COUNT: Last night you were positively strewn with flowers and garlands!

ACTRESS: I left them all in my dressing room. Your basket was the only thing I brought home.

COUNT (*kisses her hand*): You're very kind.

(*The Actress suddenly takes his hand and kisses it.*)

COUNT: Fräulein!

ACTRESS: Don't be afraid, Count. It commits you to nothing!

COUNT: You're a strange creature . . . a puzzle, one might almost say.

(*Pause.*)

ACTRESS: Fräulein Birken is . . . easier to solve?

COUNT: Oh, little Birken is no puzzle. Though . . . I know her only superficially.

ACTRESS: Indeed?

COUNT: Oh, believe me. But you are a problem. And I've always longed for one. As a matter of fact, last night I realized what a great pleasure I'd been missing. You see, it was the first time I've seen you act.

ACTRESS: Is that true?

COUNT: Oh, yes. You see, Fräulein, it's a big problem with the theater. I'm used to dining late. By the time I get there, the best part of the play is over, isn't it?

ACTRESS: You'll have to dine earlier from now on.

COUNT: I'd thought of that. Or of not dining at all. There's not much pleasure in it, is there—dining?

ACTRESS: What do you still find pleasure in, young fogey?

COUNT: I sometimes ask myself. But I'm no fogey. There must be another reason.

ACTRESS: You think so?

COUNT: Yes. For instance, Lulu always says I'm a philosopher. What he means is: I think too much.

ACTRESS: Lulu?

COUNT: Friend of mine.

ACTRESS: He's right . . . it is a misfortune, all that thinking.

COUNT: I've time on my hands, that's why I think. You see, Fräulein, when they transferred me to Vienna, I thought it would be better. It'd be amusing, stimulating, the city. But it's really much the same here as up there.

ACTRESS: And where is "up there"?

COUNT: Well, down there, Fräulein, in Hungary. The small towns I used to be stationed in.

ACTRESS: What were you doing in Hungary?

COUNT: I'm telling you, dear lady—the army.

ACTRESS: But why did you stay so long in Hungary?

COUNT: It happened, that's all.

ACTRESS: Enough to drive anyone mad, I should think!

COUNT: Oh, I don't know. In a way you have more to do there than here. You know, Fräulein, training recruits, exercising horses . . . and the surroundings aren't as bad as people say. It's really rather lovely, the big plain there. Such a sunset! It's a pity I'm not a painter. I often thought I'd paint one, if I were a painter. We had a man in our regiment, young Splany, and he could do it. Why I tell you this boring stuff I don't know, Fräulein.

ACTRESS: Please, Count! I'm highly amused.

COUNT: You know, Fräulein, it's so easy to talk to you. Lulu told me it would be. It's a thing one doesn't often meet.

ACTRESS: In Hungary!

COUNT: Or in Vienna! People are the same everywhere. Where there are more, it gets overcrowded but that's the only difference. Tell me, Fräulein, do you like people, really?

ACTRESS: Like them? I hate them! I don't want to see them. I never do see them. I'm always alone. This house is deserted!

COUNT: Just as I imagined: you're a misanthropist. It's bound to happen with artists. Moving in that more exalted sphere . . . Well, it's all right for you, at least you know why you're alive.

ACTRESS: Who told you that? I haven't the remotest idea why I'm alive!

COUNT: Not really, Fräulein . . . famous . . . celebrated . . .

ACTRESS: Is that—happiness?

COUNT: Happiness? Happiness doesn't exist. None of the things people chatter about really exist. . . . Love, for instance. It's the same with love.

ACTRESS: You may be right there.

COUNT: Enjoyment . . . intoxication . . . there's nothing wrong with them, they're real. I enjoy something, all right, and I know I enjoy it. Or I'm intoxicated, all right. That's real too. And when it's over, it's over, that's all.

ACTRESS (*grandly*): It's over!

COUNT: But as soon as you don't—I don't quite know how to say it—as soon as you stop living for the present moment, as soon as you think of later on or earlier on . . . Well, the whole thing collapses. "Later on" is sad, and "earlier on" is uncertain, in short, you just get mixed up. Don't you think so?

ACTRESS (*nods, her eyes very wide open*): You pluck out the heart of the mystery, my dear Count.

COUNT: And you see, Fräulein, once you're clear about that, it doesn't matter if you live in Vienna or on the Hungarian plains or in the tiny town of Steinamanger. For example . . . where can I put my cap? . . . Oh, thanks. What were we talking about?

ACTRESS: The tiny town of Steinamanger.

COUNT: Oh, yes. Well, as I was saying, there isn't much difference. Whether I spend the evening at the Casino or the Club is all one.

ACTRESS: How does this tie in with love?

COUNT: If a man believes in it, there'll always be a girl around who loves him.

ACTRESS: Fräulein Birken, for example.

COUNT: Honestly, dear lady, I can't understand why you're always mentioning little Birken.

ACTRESS: She's your mistress after all.

COUNT: Who says that?

ACTRESS: Everyone knows.

COUNT: Except me. Remarkable.

ACTRESS: But you fought a duel on her behalf!

COUNT: Possibly I was shot dead and didn't notice.

ACTRESS: Count, you are a man of honor. Sit a little closer.

COUNT: If I may.

ACTRESS: Here. (*She draws him closer, and runs her fingers through his hair.*) I knew you would come today.

COUNT: Really? Why?

ACTRESS: I knew it last night. In the theater.

COUNT: Oh, could you see me from the stage?

ACTRESS: My dear man, didn't you realize I was playing for you alone?

COUNT: How could that be?

ACTRESS: After I saw you in the front row, I was walking on air.

COUNT: Because of me? I'd no idea you'd noticed me.

ACTRESS: Oh, you can drive a woman to despair with that dignity of yours!

COUNT: Fräulein!

ACTRESS: "Fräulein?" At least take your saber off!

COUNT: Permit me. (*He unbuckles the belt, leans the saber against the bed.*)

ACTRESS: And now kiss me finally.

        (*The Count kisses her. She does not let him go.*)

ACTRESS: I wish I had never set eyes on you.

COUNT: No, no, it's better as it is.

ACTRESS: Count, you're a *poseur.*

COUNT: I am? Why?

ACTRESS: Many a man'd be happy to be in your shoes right now.

COUNT: I am very happy.

ACTRESS: Oh—I thought happiness didn't exist! Why do you look at me like that? I believe you're afraid of me, Count.

COUNT: I told you, Fräulein, you're a problem.

ACTRESS: Oh, don't bother me with philosophy . . . Come here. And ask me for something. You can have whatever you like. You're too handsome.

COUNT: Well, then I beg leave (*kisses her hand*) to return tonight.

ACTRESS: Tonight? . . . But I'm playing tonight.

COUNT: After the theater.

ACTRESS: You ask for nothing else?

COUNT: I'll ask for everything else. After the theater.

ACTRESS (*offended*): Then you can ask, you wretched *poseur.*

COUNT: You see, Fräulein . . . you see, my dear . . . We've been frank with each other till now. I'd find it all very much nicer in the evening, after the theater. . . . It'll be so much more comfortable. . . . At present, you see, I've the feeling the door's going to open at any moment.

ACTRESS: This door doesn't open from the outside.

COUNT: Fräulein, wouldn't it be frivolous to spoil something at the start? When it might just possibly turn out to be beautiful?

ACTRESS: "Just possibly"!

COUNT: And to tell the truth, I find love in the morning pretty frightful.

ACTRESS: You're the craziest man I've ever come across.

COUNT: I'm not talking about ordinary females. After all, in general, it doesn't matter. But women like you, Fräulein—no, you can call me a fool as often as you like, but women like you. . . . Well, one shouldn't have them before breakfast, that's all. And so . . . well . . .

ACTRESS: God, you're sweet!

COUNT: Now you see I'm right, don't you? What I have in mind . . .

ACTRESS: Tell me what you have in mind.

COUNT: What I mean is . . . I'll wait for you after the theater, in my carriage, then we can drive off somewhere, well, and have supper and . . .

ACTRESS: I am not Fräulein Birken!

COUNT: I didn't say you were, my dear. Only, one must be in the mood! I get in the mood at supper. It's lovely to drive home after supper, and then . . .

ACTRESS: And then?

COUNT: Let events take their natural course.

ACTRESS: Come closer. Closer!

COUNT (*sits down on the bed*): I must say, the perfume that comes from these pillows—mignonette, is it?

ACTRESS: It's hot in here, don't you think?

(*The Count bends down and kisses her throat.*)

ACTRESS: Oh my dear Count, this isn't on your program.

COUNT: Who says so? I have no program.

(*The Actress draws him to her.*)

COUNT: It *is* hot.

ACTRESS: You find it so? And dark, like evening . . . (*pulling him to her*) It *is* evening, Count. It's night. . . . Shut your eyes if it's too light for you. Come! Come! (*The Count no longer defends himself.*)

* * * * *

ACTRESS: What's that about being in the mood, you *poseur*?

COUNT: You're a little devil.

ACTRESS: Count!

COUNT: All right, a little angel.

ACTRESS: And you should have been an actor. Really! You understand women. Do you know what I am going to do now?

COUNT: Well?

ACTRESS: I'm going to tell you I never want to see you again.

COUNT: Why?

ACTRESS: You're too dangerous for me. You turn a woman's head. And now you stand there as if nothing has happened.

COUNT: But . . .

ACTRESS: I beg you to remember, my dear Count, that I've just been your mistress.

COUNT: Can I ever forget it?

ACTRESS: So how about tonight?

COUNT: What do you mean exactly?

ACTRESS: You intended to meet me after the theater?

COUNT: Oh, yes, all right: let's say the day after tomorrow.

ACTRESS: The day after tomorrow? We were talking of tonight.

COUNT: There wouldn't be much sense in that.

ACTRESS: Fogey!

COUNT: You misunderstand me. I mean—how should I say—from the spiritual viewpoint.

ACTRESS: It's not your spirit that interests me.

COUNT: Believe me, it's all part of it. I don't agree that these things can be kept separate.

ACTRESS: Don't talk philosophy at me. When I want that, I read books.

COUNT: But we never learn from books.

ACTRESS: That's true. And that's why you'll be there tonight. We'll come to an agreement about the spiritual viewpoint, you . . . old rascal!

COUNT: Then—with your permission—I'll wait with my carriage.

ACTRESS: You'll wait here. In my apartment.

COUNT: . . . After the theater.

ACTRESS: Of course.

(*The Count buckles on his saber.*)

ACTRESS: What are you doing?

COUNT: I think it's time for me to go, Fräulein. I've been staying rather long as it is, for a formal visit.

ACTRESS: Well, it won't be a formal visit tonight!

COUNT: You think not?

ACTRESS: Just leave it to me. And now give me one more kiss, little philosopher. Here, you seducer . . . you . . . sweet thing, you spiritualist, you polecat, you . . . (*After several emphatic kisses she emphatically pushes him away.* My dear Count, it was a great honor.

COUNT: I kiss your hand, Fräulein. (*At the door*) Au revoir!

ACTRESS: Adieu, tiny town of Steinamanger!

10 The Count and the Whore

Morning, toward six o'clock. A mean little room, with one window; the dirty yellow blinds are down; frayed green curtains. A chest of drawers, with a few photographs on it and a cheap lady's hat in conspicuously bad taste. Several cheap Japanese fans behind the mirror. On the table, covered with a reddish cloth, stands a kerosene lamp, still feebly and odorously alight, with a yellow paper lampshade: next to the lamp, a jug with a little leftover beer, and a half-empty glass. On the floor by the bed, untidy feminine clothing, apparently thrown off in a hurry.

The Whore is asleep in the bed, breathing evenly. On the sofa lies the Count, fully dressed and in a light overcoat; his hat is on the floor by the head of the sofa.

COUNT (*moves, rubs his eyes, rises with a start, and, in a sitting position, looks round*): However did I get . . . Oh . . . So I did go home with that female. . . . (*He jumps up, sees her bed.*) Why, here she is. To think what all can still happen to a man of my age! I don't remember a thing—did they carry me up? No . . . I remember seeing . . . When I got into the room, yes, I was still awake then, or I woke up, or . . . or perhaps it's only that the room reminds me of something? . . . Upon my soul, yes, I saw it last night, that's all. . . . (*He looks at his watch.*) Last night indeed! A few hours ago. I knew something had to happen. Yesterday when I started drinking I felt that . . . And what happened? Nothing . . . Or did I . . . ? Upon my soul . . . the last time I couldn't remember was ten years ago. The thing is, I was drunk. If I only knew when it started . . . I remember exactly going into that whores' café with Lulu and . . . No, no . . . First we left the Sacher . . . and then, on the way, it started. . . . Now I've got it. I was driving in my carriage with Lulu . . . Silly to rack my brains. It's all one. I'll be on my way. (*He rises. The lamp rocks.*) Oh! (*He looks at the sleeping girl.*) She sleeps soundly, that one. I can't remember a thing, but I'll put the money on her bedside table—and good-bye. (*He stands and looks at her a long while.*) If one didn't know what she is . . . (*He again contemplates her.*) I've known quite a lot of girls who didn't look so virtuous, even in their sleep. Upon my soul . . . now Lulu would say I'm philosophizing, but it's true, sleep does make us all equal, it seems to me, like his big brother—Death. . . . Hmm, I'd like to know if . . . No, No, after all, that's something I'd remember. No, no, I dropped down on the sofa right away . . . and nothing happened. . . . It's incredible how women can all look alike. . . . Let's go. (*He goes to the door.*) . . . Oh, there's that. (*He takes out his wallet and is about to get a bill.*)

WHORE (*wakes up*): Um . . . Who's here so early? (*recognizing him*) Hiya, son!

COUNT: Good morning. Slept well?

WHORE (*stretches*): Come here. Little kiss.

COUNT (*bends down, thinks better of it, pulls up short*): I was just going. . . .

WHORE: Going?

COUNT: It's time really.

WHORE: You want to go like this?

COUNT (*almost embarrassed*): Well . . .

WHORE: So long, then. Come back and see us.

COUNT: Yes. Good-bye. Don't you want to shake hands?

(*The Whore pulls her hand from under the blanket and offers it.*)

COUNT (*takes her hand, mechanically kisses it, catches himself, and laughs*): As if she were a princess! Anyway, if one only . . .

WHORE: Why do you look at me like that?

COUNT: If one only sees the head, as now . . . when they wake up . . . they all look innocent . . . upon my soul, one really could imagine all sorts of things if the place didn't reek so of kerosene. . . .

WHORE: Yes, that lamp's a pest.

COUNT: How old are you, actually?

WHORE: Well, what do you think?

COUNT: Twenty-four.

WHORE: Oh, sure!

COUNT: Older?

WHORE: Nearly twenty.

COUNT: And how long have you been . . .

WHORE: In the business? A year.

COUNT: You did start early.

WHORE: Better too early than too late.

COUNT (*sits down on her bed*): Tell me, are you happy?

WHORE: What?

COUNT: Well, I mean—how's it going? Well?

WHORE: Oh, I'm doing all right.

COUNT: I see . . . Tell me, did it ever occur to you to do something different?

WHORE: What could I do?

COUNT: Well . . . you're a pretty girl, after all, you could have a lover, for instance.

WHORE: Think I don't?

COUNT: I know—but I mean, one, you know: one lover—who keeps you, so you don't have to go with just any man.

WHORE: I don't go with just any man. I can afford to be choosy, thank goodness.

(*The Count looks round the room.*)

WHORE (*notices this*): Next month we're moving into town. The Spiegel Gasse.

COUNT: We? Who?

WHORE: Oh, the madam and a couple of the other girls.

COUNT: There are others here?

WHORE: In the next room . . . can't you hear? That's Milli, she was at the café too.

COUNT: Somebody's snoring.

WHORE: That's Milli all right! She'll snore all day till ten in the evening, then she'll get up and go to the café.

COUNT: But that's an appalling sort of life!

WHORE: You said it. And the madam gets fed up with her. I'm always on the streets at twelve noon.

COUNT: What do you do on the streets at twelve noon?

WHORE: What do you think? I'm on my beat.

COUNT: Oh, yes, I see . . . Of course . . . (*He gets up, again takes out his wallet, and puts a bill on her bedside table.*) Goodbye.

WHORE: Going already? . . . So long . . . Come again soon. (*She turns over on her side.*)

COUNT (*stops again*): Listen, tell me something. It doesn't mean a thing to you by now?

WHORE: What?

COUNT: I mean, you don't have fun with it any more?

WHORE (*yawns*): I'm sleepy.

COUNT: It's all the same to you if a man is young or old, or if he . . .

WHORE: What are you asking all this for?

COUNT: Well . . . (*Suddenly struck by a thought.*) Upon my soul, now I know who you remind me of, it's . . .

WHORE: So I look like somebody, do I?

COUNT: Incredible, quite incredible—now, I beg you, please don't say a word for at least a minute. . . . (*He stares at her.*) exactly the same face, exactly the same face. (*He suddenly kisses her on the eyes.*)

WHORE: Hey!

COUNT: Upon my soul, it's a pity you aren't . . . something else . . . you could make your fortune.

WHORE: You're like Franz.

COUNT: Who's Franz?

WHORE: Oh, the waiter at our café.

COUNT: How am I just like Franz?

WHORE: He always says I could make my fortune. And I should marry him.

COUNT: Why don't you?

WHORE: Thank you very much . . . I don't want no marriage, not for anything. Maybe later.

COUNT: The eyes . . . exactly the same eyes . . . Lulu'd certainly say I'm a fool—but I'm going to kiss your eyes once more like this. And now good-bye. God bless you. I'm going.

WHORE: So long.

COUNT (*turning at the door*): Listen . . . tell me . . . aren't you a little bit surprised?

WHORE: Why?

COUNT: That I want nothing from you.

WHORE: There's a lot of men don't feel like it in the morning.

COUNT: Well, yes . . . (*to himself*) It's too silly that I'd like her to be surprised. . . . Good-bye, then . . . (*at the door*) Really, it annoys me. I know such girls are interested in nothing but the money. . . . Now why do I say "such girls"? . . . At least it's nice that she doesn't pretend, it's a relief, or should be. . . . Listen, I'll come again soon, you know.

WHORE (*with closed eyes*): Good.

COUNT: When are you usually in?

WHORE: I'm always in. Just ask for Leocadia.

COUNT: Leocadia . . . Right. Well, good-bye. (*at the door*) I have not got the wine out of my head yet. Isn't it the limit . . . I spend the night with one of these . . . and all I do is to kiss her eyes because she reminds me of someone. . . . (*He turns to her.*) Tell me, Leocadia, does it often happen that a man goes away like this?

WHORE: Like what?

COUNT: Like me.

WHORE: In the morning?

COUNT: No . . . I mean, has it occasionally happened that a man was with you—and didn't want anything?

WHORE: No, that's never happened.

COUNT: Well, what do you think is the matter? Do you think I don't like you?

WHORE: Why shouldn't you like me? Last night you liked me all right.

COUNT: I like you now too.

WHORE: Last night you liked me better.

COUNT: What makes you think so?

WHORE: Don't talk silly.

COUNT: Last night . . . Tell me, didn't I drop down on the sofa right away?

WHORE: Sure you did—with me.

COUNT: With you?

WHORE: Sure—you don't remember?

COUNT: I . . . we . . . well . . .

WHORE: But you went right off to sleep after.

COUNT: I went right off . . . I see . . . So that's how it was!

WHORE: Yes, son. You must've been good and drunk if you can't remember.

COUNT: I see . . . All the same, there is a faint resemblance . . . Good-bye . . . (*He listens.*) What's going on?

WHORE: The chambermaid's started work. Look, give her something as you go out. The front door's open, so you save on the janitor.

COUNT: Right. (*in the entrance hall*) So . . . it would have been beautiful if I'd only kissed her eyes. It would almost have been an adventure. . . . Well, I suppose it wasn't to be!

(*The Chambermaid stands by the door and opens it for him.*) Oh . . . here . . . Good night!

CHAMBERMAID: Good morning!

COUNT: Oh, of course . . . Good morning . . . Good morning!

(*Curtain.*)

Translated by Eric Bentley

COUNTESS MITZI
OR THE
FAMILY REUNION

A Comedy in One Act

CHARACTERS

COUNT ARPAD PAZMANDY
MITZI, *his daughter*
PRINCE EGON RAVENSTEIN
LOLO LANGHUBER
PHILIP
PROFESSOR WINDHOFER
WASNER
THE GARDENER
THE VALET

The garden of Count Arpad. In the background, tall iron fence. Near the middle of this, but a little more to the right, there is a gate. In the foreground, at the left, appears the facade of the two-storied villa, which used to be an imperial hunting lodge about 180 years ago and was remodeled about 30 years ago. A narrow terrace runs along the main floor, which is raised above the ground. Three wide stairs lead from the terrace down to the garden. French doors, which are standing open, lead from the terrace into the drawing room. The windows of the upper floor are of ordinary design. Above, a small balcony belonging to a kind of attic, decorated with flowers. In front of the villa, a large lawn with flower beds. A garden seat, a small table, and an armchair stand under a tree at the right, in the foreground.

Count enters from the right; he is an elderly man with gray mustache but still decidedly good-looking; his bearing and manners indicate the retired officer; he wears a riding suit and carries a crop.

VALET *(entering behind Count)*: At what time does Your Grace desire to have dinner today?

COUNT *(who speaks in the manner peculiar to the German-Hungarian officer and, who, at that particular moment, is engaged in lighting a huge cigar)*: At two.

VALET: And when is the carriage to be ready, Your Grace?

MITZI: *(appearing on the balcony with a palette and a bunch of brushes in one hand, calls down to her father)*: Good morning, Papa.

COUNT: Morning, Mitzi.

MITZI: You left me all alone for breakfast again, Papa. Where have you been anyhow?

COUNT: Out quite a ways. Rode out by way of Mauer and Rodaun. Perfectly splendid day. And what are you doing? At work already? Will we soon have something to look at again?

MITZI: Yes, indeed, papa. Nothing but flowers though, as usual.

COUNT: Isn't the professor coming to see you today?

MITZI: Yes, but not until one.

COUNT: Well, don't let me interrupt you.

(*Mitzi throws a kiss to him and disappears from the balcony.*)

COUNT (*to the valet*): What are you waiting for? Oh, the carriage. I'm not going out again today. Joseph can take the day off. Or wait a moment. (*He calls up to the balcony.*) Say, Mitzi . . .

(*Mitzi reappears on the balcony.*)

COUNT: Sorry to disturb you again. Do you think you'll want the carriage today?

MITZI: No, thank you, Papa. I can think of nothing. . . . No, thanks. (*She disappears again.*)

COUNT: So Joseph can do what he pleases this afternoon. That's— oh, see that Franz gives the nag a good rubbing down. We got a little excited this morning—both of us.

(*Valet goes out.*
Count sits down on the garden seat, picks up a newspaper from the table and begins to read.)

GARDENER (*enters*): Good morning, Your Grace.

COUNT: Morning, Peter. What's up?

GARDENER: With Your Grace's permission, I have just cut the tea roses.

COUNT: Why all that lot?

GARDENER: The bush is full of them. It's not wise, Your Grace, to leave 'em on the stem much longer. If maybe Your Grace could find some use. . . .

COUNT: Haven't got any. Why do you stand there looking at me? I'm not going to the city. I won't be needing any bouquets. Why don't you put them individually in some of those vases and things that are standing around inside? That's the fashion nowadays.

(*He takes the bunch of flowers from the gardener and inhales their fragrance while he seems to be pondering something.*) Wasn't that a carriage that stopped here?

GARDENER: That's His Highness's pair of blacks. I can tell by their step.

COUNT: Thanks very much then.

(*He hands back the roses.*
Prince comes in by the gate.
Count goes to meet him.)

GARDENER: Good morning, Your Highness.

PRINCE: Hello, Peter.

(*Gardener goes out toward the right.*
Prince wears a light-colored summer suit; is fifty-five but doesn't look it; tall and slender; his manner of speech suggests the diplomat, who is as much at home in French as in his native tongue.)

COUNT: Delighted, old chap. How goes it?

PRINCE: Thanks. Splendid day.

(*Count offers him one of his gigantic cigars.*)

PRINCE: No, thank you, not before lunch. Only one of my cigarettes, if you permit. (*He takes a cigarette from his case and lights it.*)

COUNT: So you've found time to drop in at last. Do you know how long you haven't been here? Three weeks.

PRINCE (*glancing toward the balcony*): Really that long?

COUNT: What is it that makes you so scarce?

PRINCE: You mustn't mind. But you are right, of course. And even today I come only to say good-bye.

COUNT: What—good-bye?

PRINCE: I shall be off tomorrow.

COUNT: You're going away? Where?

PRINCE: The seashore. And you—have you made any plans yet?

COUNT: I haven't given a thought to it yet—this year.

PRINCE: Well, of course, it's wonderful right here—with your enormous park. But you have to go somewhere later this summer?

COUNT: Don't know yet. But it doesn't make any difference.

PRINCE: What's wrong now?

COUNT: Oh, my dear old friend, it's all going downhill.

PRINCE: How? That's a funny way of talking, Arpad. What do you mean by "downhill"?

COUNT: One grows old, Egon.

PRINCE: Yes, and gets used to it.

COUNT: What do you know about it—you who are five years younger?

PRINCE: Almost six. But at fifty-five the springtime of life is pretty well over. Well—one gets resigned to it.

COUNT: You have always been something of a philosopher, old chap.

PRINCE: Anyhow, I can't see what's the matter with you. You look great. (*Seats himself; frequently during this scene he glances up at the balcony; pause.*)

COUNT (*with sudden decision*): Have you heard the latest? She's going to marry.

PRINCE: Who's going to marry?

COUNT: Do you have to ask? Can't you guess?

PRINCE: Oh, I see. Thought it might be Mitzi. And that would after all . . . So Lolo is going to marry.

COUNT: She is.

PRINCE: But that's hardly the "latest."

COUNT: Why not?

PRINCE: It's what she has promised, or threatened, or whatever you choose to call it, these last three years.

COUNT: Three, you say? May just as well say ten. Or eighteen. Yes, indeed. In fact, since the very start of this affair between her and me. She has always been set on it. "If ever a decent man asks me to marry him, I'll get off the stage instantly." It was almost the first thing she told me. You have heard it your- self a couple of times. And now he's come—the one she has been waiting for—and she's getting married.

PRINCE: Well, if at least he's decent.

COUNT: Very witty! But is that your only way of showing sym- pathy in a serious moment like this?

PRINCE: Now! (*He puts his hand on the Count's arm.*)

COUNT: Well, I assure you, it's a serious moment. It's no small matter when you have lived twenty years with somebody—in a near-marital state; when you have been spending your best years with her, and really shared her joys and sorrows—until you have come to think at last, that it's never going to end—and then she comes to you one fine day and says: "God bless you, dear, but I'm going to be married on the sixteenth. . . ." That's a pretty damn nasty story! (*He gets up and begins to walk about.*) And I can't blame her even. Because I understand perfectly. So what can you do about it?

PRINCE: You've always been much too kind, Arpad.

COUNT: Nothing kind about it. Why shouldn't I understand? The clock has struck thirty-eight for her. And she has said good-bye to her profession. So that anybody can sympathize with her feeling that there is no fun in continuing as a ballet dancer retired on half pay and mistress on active service to Count Pazmandy, who'll be nothing but an old fool either, as time goes on. Of course, I have been prepared for it. And I haven't blamed her a bit—'pon my soul!

PRINCE: So you have parted as perfect friends?

COUNT: Certainly. In fact, our leave-taking was quite cheerful. 'Pon my soul, I never suspected at first how tough it would prove. It's only by degrees that it's come home to me. It's quite a remarkable story, I must say. . . .

PRINCE: What's remarkable about it?

COUNT: I suppose I had better tell you all about it. On my way home that last time—one night last week—I had a feeling all of a sudden—I don't know how to express it . . . tremendously relieved, that's what I felt. Now you are a free man, I said to myself. Don't have to drive to Mayerhof Strasse every night God grants you, merely to dine and chatter with Lolo, or just sit there listening to her. Had come to be deathly boring at times, you know. And then the drive home in the middle of the night, and, on top of it, to be called to account when you happened to be dining with a friend in the Casino or taking your daughter to the opera or a theater. To make a long story short—I was really in high gear going home that night. My head was full of plans already. . . . No, not what you think! But plans for traveling, as I have long wanted to do—to Africa, or India, like a free man. . . . That is, I should have brought my little girl along, of course. . . . Yes, you may well laugh at my calling her a little girl still.

PRINCE: Nothing of the kind. Mitzi looks exactly like a young girl. Like quite a young one. Especially in that Florentine strawhat she was wearing a while ago.

COUNT: Like a young girl, you say! And yet she's exactly the same age as Lolo. You know, of course! Yes, we're growing old, Egon. Every one of us. Oh, yes . . . And lonely. But really, I didn't notice it at first. It was only by degrees it got hold of me. The first days after that farewell feast weren't so bad yet. But the day before yesterday, and yesterday, as the time approached when I used to start for Mayerhof Strasse . . . And when Peter brought in those roses a moment ago—for Lolo, of course— why, then it seemed pretty plain to me that I had become a widower for the second time in my life. Yes, my dear fellow. And this time forever. Now comes the loneliness. It has come already.

PRINCE: But that's nonsense—loneliness!

COUNT: Pardon me, but you can't understand. Your way of living has been so different from mine. You have not let yourself be dragged into anything new since your poor wife died ten years ago. Into nothing of a serious nature, I mean. And besides, you have a profession, in a sense.

PRINCE: Have I?

COUNT: Well, as a member of the Upper House.

PRINCE: Oh, I see.

COUNT: And twice you have almost been put into the cabinet.

PRINCE: Yes, almost . . .

COUNT: Who knows? Perhaps it'll happen to you one of these days. And I'm all finished. Even had myself retired three years ago—like a fool.

PRINCE (*with a smile*): That's why you are a free man now. Perfectly free. With the world open before you.

COUNT: And no desire to do a thing, old man. That's the whole story. Since that time I haven't gone to the Casino even. Do you know what I have been doing the last few nights? I have sat under that tree with Mitzi—playing dominoes.

PRINCE: Well, don't you see? That's not being lonely. When you have a daughter, and particularly such a sensible one, with whom you have always got on so well . . . what does she say about your staying at home nights anyhow?

COUNT: Nothing. Besides, it has happened before, quite frequently. She says nothing at all. And what could she say? It seems to me she has never noticed anything. Do you think she can have known about Lolo?

PRINCE (*laughing*): Man alive!

COUNT: Of course. Yes, I know. Of course, she must have known. But then, I was still almost a young man when her mother died. She can't have held it against me.

PRINCE: No, *that* she wouldn't have. (*casually*) But being left so much alone may have troubled her at times, I should think.

COUNT: Has she complained of me? There's no reason why you shouldn't tell me.

PRINCE: I am not in her confidence. She has never complained to me. And, heavens, it may never have troubled her at all. She has so long been accustomed to this quiet, retired life.

COUNT: Yes, and she seems to have a taste for it, too. And then she used to go out a good deal until a few years ago. Between you and me, Egon, as late as three years ago—no, two years ago—I still thought she might make the plunge after all.

PRINCE: What plunge? Oh, I see. . . .

COUNT: If you could only guess what kind of men have been paying attention to her quite recently . . .

PRINCE: That's only natural.

COUNT: But she won't. She absolutely won't. What I mean is, that she can't be feeling so very lonely . . . otherwise she would . . . as she has had plenty of opportunity . . .

PRINCE: Certainly. It's her own choice. And then Mitzi has an additional resource in her painting. It's a case like that of my blessed aunt, the late Fanny Hohenstein, who went on writing books to a venerable old age and never wanted to hear a word about marriage.

COUNT: True, it may have something to do with her artistic aspirations. At times I'm inclined to look for some psychological connection between all these eccentricities.

PRINCE: "Eccentricities," you say? But you can't possibly call Mitzi eccentric.

COUNT: Oh, it's all over now. But there was a time. . . .

PRINCE: I have always found Mitzi very sensible and very well balanced. After all, painting roses and violets doesn't prove a person eccentric by any means.

COUNT: You can't think me fool enough to mean it's because of the violets and roses. . . . But if you remember when she was still a young girl . . .

PRINCE: What then?

COUNT: Oh, that story at the time Fedor Wangenheim wanted to marry her.

PRINCE: O Lord, are you still thinking of that? Besides, there was no truth in it. And that was eighteen or twenty years ago almost.

COUNT: Her wanting to join the Ursuline Sisters rather than marry that nice young fellow, to whom she was as good as engaged already—and then up and away from home all at once—you might call that extravagant, don't you think?

PRINCE: What has put you in mind of that ancient story today?

COUNT: Ancient, you say? I feel as if it happened last year only. It was at the very time when my own affair with Lolo had just begun. Ah, harking back like that . . . ! And if anybody had foretold me at the time . . . ! You know, it really began like any ordinary adventure. In the same reckless, crazy way. Yes, crazy—that's it. Not that I want to make myself out worse than I am, but it was lucky for all of us that my poor wife had already been dead a couple of years. Lolo seemed . . . my fate. Mistress and wife at the same time. Because she's such a wonderful cook, you know. And the way she makes you comfortable. And always in good humor—never a cross word . . . Well, it's all over. Let's not talk about it anymore. (*Pause*) Tell me, won't you stay for lunch? And I must call Mitzi.

PRINCE (*checking him*): Wait—I have something to tell you. (*casually, almost facetiously*) I want you to be prepared.

COUNT: Why? For what?

PRINCE: There is a young man coming here to be introduced.

COUNT (*astonished*): What? A young man?

PRINCE: If you have no objection.

COUNT: Why should I object? But who is he?

PRINCE: Dear Arpad—he's my son.

COUNT (*greatly surprised*): What?

PRINCE: Yes, my son. You see, I didn't want—as I'm going away. . . .

COUNT: Your son? You've got a son?

PRINCE: I have.

COUNT: Well, did you ever . . . ! You have got a young man who is your son—or rather, you have got a son who is a young man. How old?

PRINCE: Seventeen.

COUNT: Seventeen! And you haven't told me before! No, Egon . . . Egon! And tell me . . . seventeen . . . ? My dear chap, then your wife was still alive. . . .

PRINCE: Yes, my wife was still alive at the time. You see, Arpad, one gets mixed up in all sorts of strange affairs.

COUNT: 'Pon my soul, so it seems!

PRINCE: And thus, one fine day, you find yourself having a son of seventeen with whom you go traveling.

COUNT: So it's with him you are going away?

PRINCE: I am taking that liberty.

COUNT: No, I couldn't possibly tell you. . . . Why, he has got a son of seventeen! . . . (*Suddenly he grasps the hand of the Prince and then puts his arms about him.*) And if I may ask . . . the mother of that young gentleman, your son . . . how . . . now that you've said as much . . .

PRINCE: She's been dead for years. Died a couple of weeks after he was born. A mere slip of a girl.

COUNT: Of the common people?

PRINCE: Oh, of course. But a charming creature. I may as well tell you everything about it. That is, as far as I can recall it myself. The whole story seems like a dream. And if it were not for the boy . . .

COUNT: And all that you tell me only now! Today only—just before the boy comes to visit!

PRINCE: You never can tell how a thing like that may be received.

COUNT: Tut, tut! Received, you say . . . ? Did you believe perhaps . . . I'm something of a philosopher myself, after all. . . . And you call yourself a friend of mine!

PRINCE: Not a soul has known it—not a single soul in the whole world.

COUNT: But you might have told me. Really, I don't see how you could. . . . Come now, that wasn't very nice.

PRINCE: I wanted to wait and see how the boy developed. You never can tell. . . .

COUNT: Of course, with a mixed pedigree like that . . . But you seem reassured now?

PRINCE: Oh, yes, he's a fine fellow.

COUNT (*embracing him again*): And where has he been living until now?

PRINCE: His earliest years were spent a good way from Vienna— in the Tirol.

COUNT: With peasants?

PRINCE: No, with a small landowner. Then he went to school for some time at Innsbruck. And during the last few years I have been sending him to the preparatory school at Krems.

COUNT: So you've visited him every now and then?

PRINCE: Of course.

COUNT: And what's *his* idea of it anyhow?

PRINCE: Up to a few days ago he thought that he had lost both his parents—his father as well—and that I was a friend of his dead father.

MITZI: (*appearing on the balcony*): Good morning, Prince Egon.

PRINCE: Good morning, Mitzi.

COUNT: Well, won't you come down awhile?

MITZI: Oh, if I am not in the way . . . (*She disappears.*)

COUNT: And what are we going to say to Mitzi?

PRINCE: I prefer to leave that to you, of course. But as I am adopting the boy anyhow, and as a special decree by His Majesty will probably enable him to assume my name in a few days . . .

COUNT (*surprised*): What?

PRINCE: . . . I think it would be wiser to tell Mitzi the truth at once.

COUNT: Certainly, certainly—and why shouldn't we? Seeing that you are adopting him . . . It's really funny—but, you see, a daughter, even when she gets to be an old maid, is nothing but a little girl to her father.

MITZI (*Appears; she is thirty-seven, but still very attractive; wears a Florentine straw hat and a white dress; she gives the Count a kiss before holding out her hand to the Prince.*): Well, how do you do, Prince Egon? We don't see much of you these days.

PRINCE: Thank you.—Have you been very industrious?

MITZI: Painting a few flowers.

COUNT: Why so modest, Mitzi? (*to the Prince*) Professor Windhofer told her recently that she could safely exhibit. Won't have to fear comparison with Mrs. Wisinger-Florian herself.*

MITZI: That's so, perhaps. But I have no ambition of that kind.

PRINCE: I'm rather against exhibiting, too. It puts you at the mercy of any newspaper scribbler.

MITZI: Well, how about the members of the Upper House—at least when they make speeches?

COUNT: And how about all of us? Is there anything into which they don't poke their noses?

PRINCE: Yes, thanks to prevailing tendencies, there are people who would blackguard your pictures merely because you happen to be a countess, Mitzi.

COUNT: Yes, you're right indeed.

VALET (*entering*): Your Grace is wanted on the telephone.

COUNT: Who is it? What is it about?

VALET: There is somebody who wishes to speak to Your Grace personally.

COUNT: You'll have to excuse me a moment. (*to the Prince, in a lowered voice*) Tell her now—while I am away. I prefer it. (*He goes out followed by the valet.*)

MITZI: Somebody on the telephone—do you think Papa can have fallen into new ties already? (*She seats herself.*)

PRINCE: Into new ties, you say?

MITZI: Lolo used always to telephone around this time. But it's all over with her now. You know about it, don't you?

PRINCE: I heard just now.

MITZI: And what do you think of it, Prince Egon. I am rather sorry, to tell the truth. If he tries anything new now, I'm sure he'll burn his fingers. And I do fear there is something in the air. You see, he's still too young for his years.

PRINCE: Yes, that's so.

MITZI (*turning so that she faces the Prince*): And by the way, you haven't been here for ever so long.

---

* Refers to Mrs. Olga Wisinger-Florian, a well-known Viennese painter of floral pieces. (Trans.)

PRINCE: You haven't missed me very much . . . I fear . . . Your art . . . and heaven knows what else . . .

MITZI (*without affectation*): Nevertheless . . .

PRINCE: Awfully kind of you . . . (*Pause.*)

MITZI: What makes you silent today? Say something. Isn't there anything new happening in the world?

PRINCE (*as if he had thought of it only that moment*): Our son has just passed his examinations for the university.

MITZI (*slightly perturbed*): I hope you have more interesting news to relate.

PRINCE: More interesting . . .

MITZI: Or news, at least, that concerns me more closely than the career of a strange young man.

PRINCE: I have felt obliged, however, to keep you informed about the more important stages in the career of this young man. When he was about to be confirmed, I took the liberty to report the fact to you. But, of course, we don't have to talk any more about it.

MITZI: He pulled through, I hope?

PRINCE: With honors.

MITZI: The stock seems to be improving.

PRINCE: Let us hope so.

MITZI: And now the great moment is approaching, I suppose.

PRINCE: What moment?

MITZI: Have you forgotten already? As soon as he had passed his examinations, you meant to reveal yourself as his father.

PRINCE: So I have done already.

MITZI: You—have told him already?

PRINCE: I have.

MITZI (*after a pause, without looking at him*): And his mother— is dead . . . ?

PRINCE: She is—so far.

MITZI: And forever. (*rising*)

PRINCE: As you please.

(*The Count enters, followed by the valet.*)

VALET: But it was Your Grace who said that Joseph could take the day off.

COUNT: Yes, yes, it's all right.

(*Valet goes out.*)

MITZI: What's the matter, Papa?

COUNT: Nothing, my girl, nothing. I wanted to get somewhere quick—and that infernal Joseph . . . If you don't mind, Mitzi, I want to have a few words with Egon. . . . (*to the Prince*) Do you know, she tried to get in touch with me earlier. I mean Lolo. But she couldn't get through. And now Laura telephones—oh, well, that's her maid, you know—that she has just started on her way here.

PRINCE: Here? To see you?

COUNT: Yes.

PRINCE: But why?

COUNT: Oh, I think I can guess. You see, she has never put her foot in this place, of course, and I have been promising her all the time that she could come here once to have a look at the house and the park before she married. Her standing grievance has always been that I couldn't receive her here. On account of Mitzi, you know. Which she has understood perfectly well. And to sneak her in here some time when Mitzi was not at home— well, for that kind of thing I have never had any taste. And so she sends me a telephone message that the marriage is set for the day after tomorrow and that she is on her way here now.

PRINCE: Well, what of it? She is not coming here as your mistress, and so I can't see that you have any reason for embarrassment.

COUNT: But today of all days—and with your son due at any moment.

PRINCE: You can leave him to me.

COUNT: But I don't want it. I'm going to meet the carriage and see if I can stop her. It makes me nervous. You'll have to ask your son to excuse me for a little while. Good-bye, Mitzi. I'll be back right away. (*He goes out.*)

PRINCE: Miss Lolo has sent word that she's coming to call, and your papa doesn't like it.

MITZI: What's that? Has Lolo sent word? Is she coming here?

PRINCE: Your father has been promising her a chance to look over the place before she was married. And now he has gone to meet the carriage in order to steer her off.

MITZI: How childish! And how pathetic, when you come to think of it! I should really like to make her acquaintance. Don't you think it's too silly? There is my father, spending half his lifetime with a person who is probably very likeable—and I don't get a chance—don't have the right—to shake hands with her even. Why does he object to it anyhow? He ought to understand that I know all about it.

PRINCE: Oh, heavens, that's the way he is. And perhaps he might not have minded so much, if he were not expecting another visit at this very moment. . . .

MITZI: Another visit, you say?

PRINCE: Which I took the liberty of announcing to him.

MITZI: Who is it?

PRINCE: Our son.

MITZI: Are you—your son is coming here?

PRINCE: He'll be here in half an hour at the most.

MITZI: I say, Prince . . . this is not a joke you're trying to spring on me?

PRINCE: By no means. On a departed . . . what an idea!

MITZI: Is it really true? He's coming here?

PRINCE: Yes.

MITZI: Apparently you still think that nothing but a whim keeps me from having anything to do with the boy?

PRINCE: A whim . . . ? No. Seeing how consistent you have been in this matter, it would hardly be safe for me to call it that. And when I bear in mind how you have had the strength all these years not even to ask any questions about him . . .

MITZI: There has been nothing admirable about that. I have had the strength to do what was worse . . . when I had to let him be taken away . . . a week after he was born. . . .

PRINCE: Yes, what else could you—could we have done at the time? The arrangements made by me at the time, and approved by you in the end, represented absolutely the most expedient thing we could do under the circumstances.

MITZI: I have never questioned their expediency.

PRINCE: It was more than expedient, Mitzi. More than our own fate was at stake. Others might have come to grief if the truth had been revealed at the time. My wife, with her weak heart, would probably never have survived.

MITZI: Oh, that weak heart . . .

PRINCE: And your father, Mitzi . . . Think of your father!

MITZI: You may be sure he would have accepted the inevitable. That was the very time when he began his affair with Lolo.

Otherwise everything might not have come off so smoothly. Otherwise he might have been more concerned about me. I could never have stayed away several months if he hadn't found it very convenient at that particular moment. And there was only one danger connected with the whole story—that you might be shot dead by Fedor Wangenheim, my dear Prince.

PRINCE: Why I by him? It might have taken another turn. You are not a believer in trial by ordeal, are you? And the outcome might have proved questionable from such a point of view even. You see, we poor mortals can never be sure how things of that kind are regarded up above.

MITZI: You would never talk like that in the Upper House—supposing you ever opened your mouth during one of its sessions.

PRINCE: Possibly not. But the fundamental thing remains, that no amount of honesty or daring could have availed in the least at the time. It would have been nothing but useless cruelty toward those nearest to us. It's doubtful whether a dispensation could have been obtained—and besides, the Princess would never have agreed to a divorce—which you know as well as I do.

MITZI: As though I had in the least needed to be formally married!

PRINCE: Oh . . .

MITZI: Not in the least. That's not new to you? Didn't I tell you so at the time? Oh, you'll never guess what might . . . (*her words emphasized by her glance*) what I . . . of what I might have been capable at that time. I would have followed you anywhere—everywhere—even as your mistress. I and the child. To Switzerland, to America. After all, we could have lived wherever it happened to suit us. And perhaps, if you had gone away, they might never even have noticed your absence in the Upper House.

PRINCE: Yes, of course, we might have run away and settled down somewhere abroad. . . . But do you still believe that a situation like that would have proved agreeable in the long run, or even bearable?

MITZI: No, I don't nowadays. Because, you see, I know you now. But at that time I was in love with you. And it is possible that I—might have gone on loving you for a long time, had you not proved too cowardly to assume the responsibility for what had happened. . . . Yes, too much of a coward, Prince Egon.

PRINCE: Whether that be the proper word . . .

MITZI: Well, I don't know of any other. There was no hesitation on my part. I was ready to face everything—with joy and pride. I was ready to be a mother, and to confess myself the mother of our child. And you knew it, Egon. I told you so seventeen years ago, in that little house in the woods where you kept me hidden. But half measures have never appealed to me. I wanted to be a mother in every respect or not at all. The day I had to let the boy be taken away from me, I made up my mind never more to trouble myself about him. And for that reason I find it ridiculous of you to bring him here all of a sudden. If you'll allow me to give you a piece of good advice, you'll go and meet him, as papa has gone to meet Lolo—and take him back home again.

PRINCE: I wouldn't dream of doing so. After what I have just had to hear from you again, I guess it's settled that his mother is dead. All the more reason for me to take charge of him. He is my son in the eyes of the world too. I have adopted him.

MITZI: You've . . . ?

PRINCE: Tomorrow he will probably be able to assume my name. I shall introduce him wherever it suits me. And of course, first of all to my old friend—your father. If you should find it disagreeable to see him, there will be nothing left for you but to stay in your room while he is here.

MITZI: If you believe that I think your tone very appropriate . . .

PRINCE: Oh, just as appropriate as your bad temper.

MITZI: My bad temper . . . ? Do I look it? Really, if you please . . . I have simply permitted myself to find this fancy of yours in rather poor taste. Otherwise my temper is just as good as ever.

PRINCE: I have no doubt of your good humor under ordinary circumstances. . . . I am perfectly aware, for that matter, that you have managed to become reconciled to your fate. I, too, have managed to submit to a fate which, in its own way, has been no less painful than yours.

MITZI: In what way? To what fate have you had to submit . . . ? Everybody can't become a Cabinet minister. Oh, I see . . . that remark must refer to the fact that His Highness did me the honor ten years ago, after the blissful departure of his noble spouse, to apply for my hand.

PRINCE: And again seven years ago, if you'll be kind enough to remember.

MITZI: Oh, yes, I do remember. Nor have I ever given you any cause to question my good memory.

PRINCE: And I hope you have never ascribed my proposals to anything like a desire to expiate some kind of guilt. I asked you to become my wife simply because of my conviction that true happiness was to be found only by your side.

MITZI: True happiness! . . . Oh, what a mistake!

PRINCE: Yes, I do believe that it was a mistake at that moment. Ten years ago it was probably still too early. And so it was, perhaps, seven years ago. But not today.

MITZI: Yes, today too, my dear Prince. Your fate has been never to know me, never to understand me at all—no more when I loved you than when I hated you, and not even during the long time when I have been completely indifferent toward you.

PRINCE: I have always known you, Mitzi. I know more about you than you seem able to guess. Thus, for instance, I am not unfamiliar with the fact that you have spent the last seventeen years in more profitable pursuits than weeping over a man who, in all likelihood, was not worthy of you at the time in question. I am even aware that you have chosen to expose yourself to several disillusionments subsequent to the one suffered at my hands.

MITZI: Disillusionments, you say? Well, for your consolation, my dear Prince, I can assure you that some of them proved very enjoyable.

PRINCE: I know that, too. Otherwise I should hardly have dared to call myself familiar with the history of your life.

MITZI: And do you think that I am not familiar with yours? Do you want me to present you with a list of your mistresses? From the wife of the Bulgarian attaché in 1887 down to Mademoiselle Therese Grédun—if that be her real name—who retained the honors of her office up to last spring at least. It seems likely that I know more than you even, for I can give you a practically complete list of those with whom she has deceived you.

PRINCE: Oh, don't, if you please. There is no real pleasure in knowledge of that kind when you don't uncover it yourself.

(*A carriage is heard stopping in front of the house.*)

PRINCE: That's he. Do you want to disappear before he comes out here? I can detain him that long.

MITZI: Don't trouble yourself, please. I prefer to stay. But don't imagine that there is anything astir within me. . . . This is nothing but a young man coming to call on my father. There he is now. . . . As to blood being thicker than water—I think it's nothing but a fairy tale. I can't feel anything at all, my dear Prince.

PHILIP (*comes quickly through the main entrance; he is seventeen, slender, handsome, elegant, but not foppish; shows a charming, though somewhat boyish, forwardness, not quite free from embarrassment*): Good morning. (*He bows to Mitzi.*)

PRINCE: Good morning, Philip.—Countess, will you permit me to introduce my son? This is Countess Mitzi, daughter of the old friend of mine in whose house you are now.

(*Philip kisses the hand offered him by Mitzi; brief pause.*)

MITZI: Won't you be seated, please?

PHILIP: Thank you, Countess.

(*All remain standing.*)

PRINCE: You came in the carriage? Might just as well send it back, as mine is here already.

PHILIP: Won't you come back with me instead, Papa? You see, I think Wasner does a great deal better than your Franz with his team of ancients.

MITZI: So Wasner has been driving you?

PHILIP: Yes.

MITZI: The old man himself? Do you know that's a great honor? Wasner won't take the box for everybody. Up to about two years ago he used to drive my father.

PHILIP: Oh . . .

PRINCE: You're a little late, by the way, Philip.

PHILIP: Yes, I have to beg your pardon. Overslept, you know. (*to Mitzi*) I was out with some of my colleagues last night. You may have heard that I passed my examinations a couple of weeks ago, Countess. That's why we rather made a night of it.

MITZI: You seem to have caught on to our Viennese ways pretty quickly, Mister—

PRINCE: Oh, dear Mitzi, call him Philip, please.

MITZI: But I think we must sit down first of all, Philip. (*with a glance at the Prince*) Papa should be here any moment now. (*She and the Prince sit down.*)

PHILIP (*still standing*): If you permit me to say so—I think the park is magnificent. It is much finer than ours.

MITZI: You are familiar with the Ravenstein park?

PHILIP: Certainly, Countess. I have been living at Ravenstein House three days already.

MITZI: Is that so?

PRINCE: Of course, gardens cannot do as well in the city as out here. Ours was probably a great deal more beautiful a hundred years ago. But then our place was still practically outside the city.

PHILIP: It's a pity that all sorts of people have been allowed to build houses around our place like that.

MITZI: We are better off in that respect. And we shall hardly live to see the town overtake us.

PHILIP (*affably*): But why not, Countess?

MITZI: A hundred years ago these grounds were still used for hunting. The place adjoins the Tiergarten, you know. Look over that wall there, Philip. And our villa was a hunting lodge once, belonging to the Empress Maria Theresa. The stone figure over there goes back to that period.

PHILIP: And how old is our place, Papa?

PRINCE (*smiling*): Our place, sonny, dates back to the seventeenth century. Didn't I show you the room in which Emperor Leopold spent a night?

PHILIP: Emperor Leopold, 1643 to 1705.

(*Mitzi laughs.*)

PHILIP: Oh, that's an echo of the examinations. When I get old enough . . . (*He interrupts himself.*) I beg your pardon! What I meant to say was simply—all that stuff will be out of my head in a year. And, of course, when I learned those dates, I didn't know Emperor Leopold had been such a good friend of the family.

MITZI: You seem to think your discovery enormously funny, Philip?

PHILIP: Discovery, you say. . . . Well, frankly speaking, it could hardly be called that. (*He looks at the Prince.*)

PRINCE: Go on, go on!

PHILIP: Well, you see, Countess, I have always had the feeling that I wasn't really born a Philip Radeiner.

MITZI: Radeiner? (*to the Prince*) Oh, that was the name . . . ?

PRINCE: Yes.

PHILIP: And, of course, it was very pleasant to find my suspicions confirmed—but I really knew it all along. I can put two and two together. And some of the other boys had also figured out— that I . . . Really, Countess, that story about Prince Ravenstein coming to Krems merely to see how the son of his late friend was getting along—don't you think it seemed a little too novel-istic. . . . dime store literature, and that sort of thing? All the clever ones felt pretty sure that I was of noble blood, and as I was one of the cleverest. . . .

MITZI: So it seems. . . . And what are your plans for the future, Philip?

PHILIP: Next October I shall begin my year as volunteer with the Sixth Dragoons, which is the regiment in which we Ravensteins always serve. And what's going to happen after that—whether I stay in the army or become an archbishop—in due time, of course. . . .

MITZI: That would probably be the best thing. The Ravensteins have always been strong in the faith.

PHILIP: Yes, it's mentioned in the world history books even. They were Catholic at first; then they turned Protestant in the Thirty Years War; and finally they became Catholic again—but they always remained strong in their faith. It was only the faith that changed.

PRINCE: Philip, Philip!

MITZI: That's the spirit of the time, Prince Egon.

PRINCE: And an inheritance from his mother.

MITZI: You have been working hard, your father tells me, and have passed your examinations with honors.

PHILIP: Well, that wasn't difficult, Countess. I seem to get hold of things quickly. That's probably another result of the common blood in me. And I had time to spare for things not in the school curriculum—such as horseback riding and . . .

MITZI: And what?

PHILIP: Playing the clarinet.

MITZI (*laughing*): Why did you hesitate to tell about that?

PHILIP: Because . . . Well, because everybody laughs when I say that I play the clarinet. And so did you, too, Countess. Isn't that queer? Did anybody ever laugh because you said that your hobby was painting?

MITZI: So you have already heard about that?

PHILIP: Yes, indeed, Countess—Papa told me. And besides, there is a floral piece in my bedroom—a Chinese vase, you know, with a laburnum branch and something purplish in color.

MITZI: That purplish stuff must be lilacs.

PHILIP: Oh, lilacs, of course. I saw that at once. But I couldn't recall the name just now.

VALET (*entering*): There is a lady who wishes to see the Count. I have showed her into the drawing room.

MITZI: A lady . . . ? You'll have to excuse me for a moment, gentlemen. (*She goes out.*)

PHILIP: That's all right, Papa—if it's up to me, I have no objection.

PRINCE: To what? Of what are you talking?

PHILIP: I have no objection to your choice.

PRINCE: Have you lost your senses, boy?

PHILIP: But really, papa, do you think you can hide anything from me? That common blood in me, you know. . . .

PRINCE: What put such an idea into your head?

PHILIP: Now look here, papa! You have been telling me how anxious you were to introduce me to your old friend, the Count. And then the Count has a daughter—which I have known all the time, by the way. . . . The one thing I feared a little was that she might be too young.

PRINCE (*offended, and yet unable to keep serious*): Too young, you say. . . .

PHILIP: It was perfectly plain that you had a certain weakness for that daughter. . . . Why, you used to be quite embarrassed when talking of her. And then you have been telling me all sorts of things about her that you would never have cared to tell otherwise. Why, for example, should I be interested in the paintings of some unknown Countess—supposing even that you *could* tell her lilacs from her laburnums by their color? And, as I said, my one fear was that she might be too young to be my mother, that is, not your wife. Of course, there is not yet anybody too young or beautiful for you. But now I can tell you, Papa, that she suits me absolutely as she is.

PRINCE: Well, if you are not the most impudent rogue I ever came across . . . ! Do you really think I would ask you, if I should ever—

PHILIP: Not exactly ask, Papa . . . but a happy family life requires that all the members like each other . . . don't you think so?

(*Mitzi and Lolo Langhuber enter.*)

MITZI: You must look around, please. I am sure my father would be very sorry to miss you. (*She starts to make the usual introductions.*) Permit me to . . .

LOLO: Oh, Your Highness.

PRINCE: Well, Miss Pallestri . . .

LOLO: Langhuber, if you please. I have come to thank the Count for the magnificent flowers he sent me at my farewell performance.

PRINCE (*introducing*): My son Philip. And this is Miss . . .

LOLO: Charlotta Langhuber.

PRINCE (*to Philip*): Better known as Miss Pallestri.

PHILIP: Oh, Miss Pallestri! Then I have already had the pleasure . . .

PRINCE: What?

PHILIP: You see, I have Miss Pallestri in my collection.

PRINCE: What . . . what sort of collection is that?

LOLO: There must be some kind of mistake here, Your Highness. I can not recall. . . .

PHILIP: Of course, you can't, for I don't suppose you could feel that I was cutting out your picture from a newspaper at Krems?

LOLO: No, thank heaven!

PHILIP: It was one of our amusements at school, you know. There was one who cut out all the crimes and disasters he could get hold of.

LOLO: What a dreadful fellow that must have been!

PHILIP: And there was one who went in for historical personalities, like North Pole explorers and composers and that kind of people. And I used to collect ladies of the theater. Much better looking, you know. I have got two hundred and thirteen—which

I'll show you sometime, Papa. Quite interesting, you know. With an operetta star from Australia among the rest.

LOLO: I didn't know Your Highness had a son—and such a big one at that.

PHILIP: Yes, I have been blossoming in the dark until now.

PRINCE: And now you are trying to make up for it, I should say.

LOLO: Oh, please let him, Your Highness. I enjoy it when young people are a little spirited.

PHILIP: So you are going to retire to private life, Miss Pallestri? That's too bad. Just when I might have the pleasure at last of seeing you on those boards that signify the world . . .

LOLO: That's awfully kind of Your Highness, but unfortunately one hasn't time to wait for the youth that's still growing. And the more mature ones are beginning to find my vintage a little out of date, I fear.

PRINCE: They say that you are about to be married.

LOLO: Yes, I am about to enter the holy state of matrimony.

PHILIP: And who is the happy man, if I may ask?

LOLO: Who is he? Why, he is waiting outside now—with that carriage.

MITZI: What—a coachman?

LOLO: But Countess—what do you mean, coachman? Only in the same manner as when your Papa himself—beg your pardon!—happens to be taking the bay out for a spin at times. Cab owner, that's what my fiancé is—and house owner, and a Viennese citizen who gets on the box himself only when it pleases him and when there is somebody of whom he holds in special esteem. Now he is driving for a certain Baron Radeiner—whom he has just brought out here to see your father, Countess. And I am having my doubts about that Baron Radeiner.

PHILIP: Permit me to introduce myself—Baron Radeiner.

LOLO: It's you, Your Highness?

PHILIP: I have let nobody but Wasner drive me since I came here.

LOLO: And under an assumed name at that, Your Highness? Well, we are finding out a lot of nice things about you!

COUNT (*appears, very hot*): Well, here I am. (*taking in the situation*) Ah!

LOLO: Your humble servant, Count! I have taken the liberty—I wanted to thank you for the magnificent flowers.

COUNT: Oh, please—it was a great pleasure. . . .

PRINCE: And here, old friend, is my son Philip.

PHILIP: I regard myself as greatly honored, Count.

COUNT (*giving his hand to Philip*): I bid you welcome to my house. Please consider yourself at home here.—I don't think any further introductions are required.

MITZI: No, Papa.

COUNT (*slightly embarrassed*): It's very charming of you, my dear lady. Of course, you know better than anybody that I have always been one of your admirers. . . . But tell me, please, how in the world did you get out here? I have just been taking a walk along the main road, where every carriage has to pass, and I didn't see you.

LOLO: What do you take me for, Count? My cab days are past now. I came by the train, which is the proper thing for me.

COUNT: I see. . . . But I hear that your fiancé himself . . .

LOLO: Oh, he has fancier passengers to look after.

PHILIP: Yes, I have just had the pleasure of being conducted here by the fiancé of Miss Pallestri.

COUNT: Is Wasner driving for you? Well, that settles it—of course—clear psychological connections! (*Offers his cigar case*) Want a smoke?

PHILIP (*accepting*): Thank you.

PRINCE: But, Philip . . . ! A monster like that before lunch!

COUNT: Excellent. Nothing better for the health. I like you already. Suppose we sit down.

(*The Count, the Prince and Philip seat themselves, while Mitzi and Lolo remain standing close to them.*)

COUNT: So you'll be off with your father tomorrow?

PHILIP: Yes, Count. And I'm looking forward to it tremendously.

COUNT: Will you be gone long?

PRINCE: That depends on several circumstances.

PHILIP: I have to report myself at the regiment on the first of October.

PRINCE: And it's possible that I may go farther south after that.

COUNT: Well, that's news. Where?

PRINCE (*with a glance at Mitzi*): Egypt, and the Sudan maybe—for a little hunting.

MITZI (*to Lolo*): Let me show you the park.

LOLO: It's a marvel. Ours doesn't compare with it, of course. (*She and Mitzi come forward.*)

MITZI: Have you a garden at your place, too?

LOLO: Certainly. As well as an ancestral palace—at Ottakring. The great-grandfather of Wasner was in the cab business in his days already.—My, but that's beautiful! The way those flowers are hanging down. I ought to try that at home.

COUNT (*disturbed*): Why are the ladies leaving us?

MITZI: Never mind, papa, I'm merely explaining the architecture of our facade.

PHILIP: Do you often get visits from ladies of the theater, Count?

COUNT: No, this is more or less a coincidence.
(*The men stroll off toward those parts of the garden that are not visible.*)

MITZI: It seems strange that this is the first time I have had the chance to speak to you. I am very glad to meet you.

LOLO (*with a grateful glance*): And I you! Of course, I have known you by sight for many years. I have so often looked up at your box.

MITZI: But not at me.

LOLO: Oh, that's all over now.

MITZI: Do you know, I really feel a little offended—on his behalf.

LOLO: Offended, you say . . . ?

MITZI: It will be a hard blow for him. Nobody knows better than I how deeply he has been attached to you. Although he has never said a word to me about it.

LOLO: Do you think it's so very easy for me either, Countess? But tell me, Countess, what else could I do? I am no longer a spring chicken, you know. And one can't help hankering for something more settled. As long as I had a profession of my own, I could allow myself—what do they call it now?—to entertain liberal ideas. In a way it went with the job. But how would that look now, when I am retiring to private life?

MITZI: Oh, I can see that perfectly. But what is he going to do now?

LOLO: Why shouldn't he marry, too? I assure you, Countess, that there are many who would give all their five fingers. . . . Don't you realize, Countess, that I, too, have found it a hard step to take?

MITZI: Do you know what I have often wondered? Whether he never thought of making you his wife?

LOLO: Oh, yes, that's just what he wanted.

MITZI: What . . . ?!

LOLO: Do you know when he asked me, the last time, Countess? Less than a month ago.

MITZI: And you said no?

LOLO: I did. It wouldn't have been good. Me a Countess! Can you imagine it? I being your stepmother, Countess . . . ! Then we could not have been chatting nicely as we are doing now.

MITZI: If you only knew how much I like you . . .

LOLO: But I don't want to appear better than I am. And who knows what I might . . .

MITZI: What might you?

LOLO: Well, this is the truth of it. I have fallen head over heels in love with Wasner. Which I hope won't make you think the worse of me. In all these eighteen years I have had nothing to blame myself with, as far as your dear papa is concerned. But you can't wonder if my feelings began to cool off a little as the years passed along. And rather than to make your dear papa—oh, no, no, Countess . . . I owe him too much gratitude for that. . . . Lord!

MITZI: What is it?

LOLO: There he is now, looking right at me.
    (*Mitzi looks in the direction indicated.*
    Wasner, who has appeared at the entrance, raises his tall hat in salute.)

LOLO: Don't you think me an awful fool, Countess? Every time I catch sight of him suddenly, my heart starts pounding. Yes, there's no fool like an old one.

MITZI: Old . . . ? Do you call yourself old? Why, there can't be much difference between us.

LOLO: Oh, mercy . . . (*with a glance at Mitzi*)

MITZI: I am thirty-seven.—No, don't look at me with any pity. There is no cause for that. None whatever.

LOLO (*apparently relieved*): I have heard some whispers, Countess—of course, I didn't believe anything. But I thank heaven it was true.

(*They shake hands.*)

MITZI: I should like to congratulate your fiancé right now, if you'll permit me.

LOLO: That's too sweet of you—but what about the Count—perhaps he wouldn't like . . . ?

MITZI: My dear, I have always been accustomed to do as I pleased.

(*They go together toward the entrance.*)

WASNER: You're too kind, Countess. . . .

(*The Count, the Prince, and Philip have reappeared in the meantime.*)

COUNT: Look at that, will you!

WASNER: Good morning, Count. Good morning, Highness.

PRINCE: I say, Wasner, you may just as well take your bride home in that trap of yours. My son is coming with me.

WASNER: Your son . . . ?

PHILIP: Why haven't you told me that you were engaged, Wasner?

WASNER: Well, there are things you haven't told either . . . Mr. von Radeiner!

COUNT (*to Lolo*): Thank you very much for your friendly visit, and please accept my very best wishes.

LOLO: The same to you, Count. And I must say, that when one has such a daughter . . .

MITZI: It's too bad I haven't come to know you before.

LOLO: Oh, really, Countess . . .

MITZI: Once more, my dear Miss Lolo, good luck to you!

(*Mitzi embraces Lolo. Count looks on with surprise and some genuine emotion.*)

LOLO: I thank you for the kind reception, Count—and good-bye!

COUNT: Good-bye, Miss Langhuber. I trust you'll be happy . . . indeed I do, Lolo.

(*Lolo gets into the carriage which has driven up to the gate in the meantime.*

Wasner is on the box, hat in hand; they drive off. Mitzi waves her hand at them as they disappear.)

PHILIP (*who has been standing in the foreground with the Prince*): Oh, my dear papa, I can see through the whole story.

PRINCE: You can?

PHILIP: This Miss Lolo must be the natural daughter of the Count, and a sister of the Countess—her foster-sister, as they say.

PRINCE: No, you would call that a stepsister. But go on, Mr. Diplomat.

PHILIP: And of course, both are in love with you—both the Countess and the ballet dancer. And this marriage between the dancer and Wasner is your work.

PRINCE: Go on.

PHILIP: You know—there's something I never thought of until just now!

PRINCE: What?

PHILIP: I don't know if I dare?

PRINCE: Why so timid all at once?

PHILIP: Supposing my mother was not dead . . .

PRINCE: H'm . . .

PHILIP: And, through a remarkable combination of circumstances, she should now be going back to the city in the very carriage that brought me out here . . . ? And suppose it should be my own mother, whose picture I cut out of that newspaper . . . ?

PRINCE: My lad, you'll certainly end as a cabinet minister—Secretary of Agriculture, if nothing better.—But now it's time for us to say good-bye.

(*The Count and Mitzi are coming forward again.*)

PRINCE: Well, my dear friend, this must be our farewell call, I am sorry to say.

COUNT: But why don't you stay. . . . That would be delightful . . . if you could take lunch with us. . . .

PRINCE: Unfortunately, it isn't possible. We have an appointment at Sacher's.

COUNT: That's really too bad. And shall I not see you at all during the summer?

PRINCE: Oh, we shall not be entirely out of touch.

COUNT: And are you starting tomorrow already?

PRINCE: Yes.

COUNT: Where are you going?

PRINCE: To the seashore—Ostend.

COUNT: Oh, you are bound for Ostend. I have long wanted to go there.

PRINCE: But that would be fine. . . .

COUNT: What do you think, Mitzi? Let's be fashionable. Let's go to Ostend, too.

MITZI: I can't answer yet. But there's no reason why you shouldn't go, Papa.

PHILIP: That would be delightful, Countess. It would please me awfully.

MITZI (*smiling*): That's very kind of you, Philip. (*She holds out her hand to him. Philip kisses her hand.*)

COUNT (*to the Prince*): The children seem to get along beautifully.

PRINCE: Yes, that's what I have been thinking. Good-bye, then. Good-bye, my dear Mitzi. And good-bye to you, my dear old fellow. I hope at least to see you again at Ostend.

COUNT: Oh, she'll come along. Won't you, Mitzi? After all, you can get studios by the seashore, too. Or how about it, Mitzi?

(*Mitzi remains silent.*)

PRINCE: Well, until we meet again! (*He shakes hands with the Count and Mitzi. Philip kisses the hand of Mitzi once more.*)

COUNT (*giving his hand to Philip*): It has been a great pleasure. (*The Prince and Philip go out through the gate and step into the carriage which has been driving up in the meantime and which now carries them off. The Count and Mitzi come forward again and seat themselves at the table under the tree. Pause.*)

COUNT: Hasn't this been a strange day?

MITZI: Life in general is strange—only we forget it most of the time.

COUNT: I suppose you're right.

(*Pause.*)

MITZI: You know, Papa, you might just as well have brought us together a little earlier.

COUNT: Who? Oh, you and . . .

MITZI: Me and Miss Lolo. She's a dear.

COUNT: So you like her? Well, if it were only possible to know in advance . . . But what's the use? Now it's all over.

(*Mitzi takes hold of his hand.*)

COUNT (*rises and kisses her on the forehead; strolls about aimlessly for a few seconds*): Tell me, Mitzi, what you think . . . How do you like the boy?

MITZI: Philip? Oh, he's a little fresh.

COUNT: Fresh, perhaps, but smart. I hope he'll stay in the army. That's a much more sensible career than the diplomatic service.

Slow, but sure. All you need is to live long enough in order to become a general. But a political career . . . Now look at Egon . . . he almost became minister three times. . . . And suppose he had succeeded? (*walking back and forth*) Yes, yes . . . we shall be rather lonely this summer.

MITZI: But why shouldn't you go to Ostend, Papa?

COUNT: Yes, why not . . . ? Really, won't you come along? It would be rather . . . without you, you know. . . . It's no use looking at me like that. I know! I haven't paid as much attention to you in the past as I should have . . .

MITZI (*taking his hand again*): Oh, Papa, you're not going to apologize, are you? I understand perfectly.

COUNT: Oh, well. But, you see, I shall not get much joy out of that trip without you. And what would you be doing here, all by yourself? You can't paint all day long.

MITZI: The only trouble is . . . the Prince has asked me to marry him.

COUNT: What? Is it possible? No, you don't mean . . . And . . . and you said no?

MITZI: Practically.

COUNT: You did . . . ? Oh, well . . . After all, I have never tried to persuade you. It must be as you. . . . But I can't understand why. I have noticed for a long time, that he . . . As far as age is concerned, you wouldn't be badly matched. And as for the rest . . . sixty millions are not to be despised exactly. But just as you say.

(*Mitzi remains silent.*)

COUNT: Or could it possibly be on account of the boy? That would be to exaggerate the matter, I assure you. Things of that kind occur in the very best families. And especially when you consider that she was always having problems with her heart. . . . All of a sudden you get dragged into an affair of that kind without exactly knowing how.

MITZI: And some poor girl of the people is thrown aside and allowed to go to the dogs.

COUNT: Oh, please, that's only in the books. And how could he help it? Those women unfortunately almost always die young. And who knows what he might have done, if she hadn't died. . . . I really think that his action in regard to the boy has been pretty decent. That took courage, you know. I could tell you more than one case. . . . But don't let us talk of it. If that should be the only thing against him, however . . . And besides, our being together at Ostend wouldn't commit you in any way.

MITZI: No, that's true.

COUNT: Well, then . . . I tell you what. You make the trip with me. And if you like it there, you can stay. If not, you can go on to London for a visit with Aunt Lora. I mean simply, that there is no sense in your letting me go away alone.

MITZI: All right.

COUNT: What do you mean?

MITZI: I'll go with you. But without any obligation—absolutely free.

COUNT: You'll come with me, you say?

MITZI: I will, papa.

COUNT: Oh, I'm so glad. Thank you, Mitzi.

MITZI: Why should you thank me? It's a pleasure to me.

COUNT: You can't imagine, of course . . . without you, Mitzi . . . There would be so much to remember—this time in particular. . . . You know, of course, that I took Lolo to Normandy last year?

MITZI: Of course, I know. . . .

COUNT: And as far as Egon is concerned . . . not that I want to persuade you by any means . . . but in a strange place like that you often get more acquainted with a person in a couple of days than during many years at home.

MITZI: It's settled now that I go with you, Papa. And as for the rest, don't let us talk of it—for the time being.

COUNT: Then, you know, I'm going to telephone to the ticket office at once and reserve sleeping car compartments for the day after tomorrow—or for tomorrow.

MITZI: Are you in such a hurry?

COUNT: What's the use of sitting about here, once we have made up our minds? So I'll telephone. . . . Does that suit you?

MITZI: Yes.

(*Count puts his arms about her. Professor Windhofer appears at the garden gate.*)

COUNT: Why, there's the professor. Do you have a lesson today?

MITZI: I had forgotten it, too.

PROFESSOR (*handsome; about thirty-five; his beard is blond and trimmed to a point; he is very carefully dressed and wears a gray overcoat; he takes off his hat as he enters the garden and comes forward*): Good morning, Countess. How do you do, Count?

COUNT: Good morning, my dear Professor, and how are you? You have to pardon me. I was just about to go to the telephone— we are going away, you know.

PROFESSOR: Oh, are you going away? Please, don't let me detain you.

COUNT: I suppose I shall see you later, Professor. (*He goes into the house.*)

PROFESSOR: So you are going away, Countess?

MITZI: Yes, to Ostend.

PROFESSOR: That's rather a sudden decision.

MITZI: Yes, rather. But that's my way.

PROFESSOR: That means an end to the lessons for the present, I suppose? Too bad.

MITZI: I don't think I shall be able today even. . . . I am feeling a little upset.

PROFESSOR: Do you?—Well, you look rather pale, Maria.

MITZI: Oh, you think so?

PROFESSOR: And how long will you be gone?

MITZI: Until the fall probably—perhaps until very late in the fall even.

PROFESSOR: Then we can resume our lessons next November at the earliest, I suppose?

MITZI (*smiling*): I don't think we shall. . . .

PROFESSOR: Oh, you don't think so?

(*They look hard at each other.*)

MITZI: No, I don't.

PROFESSOR: Which means, Maria—that I am discharged.

MITZI: How can you put it that way, Rudolph? That is not quite fair.

PROFESSOR: Pardon me. But it really came a little more suddenly than I had expected.

MITZI: Better that than have it come too slow. Don't you think so?

PROFESSOR: Well, my child, I don't have the slightest intention of reproaching you.

MITZI: Well, you have no reason. Wasn't it beautiful? (*She holds out her hand to him.*)

PROFESSOR (*takes her hand and kisses it*): Will you please excuse me to the Count?

MITZI: Are you going already . . . ?

PROFESSOR (*lightly*): Isn't that better?

MITZI (*after a pause, during which she looks straight into his eyes*): Yes, I think so.

(*They shake hands.*)

PROFESSOR: Good luck, Maria.

MITZI: Same to you. . . . And remember me to your wife and the children.

PROFESSOR: I'll tell them, Countess.

(*He goes out.*
Mitzi remains on the same spot for a little while, following him with her eyes.)

COUNT (*on the terrace*): Everything is ready. We'll leave at nine-thirty tomorrow night.—But what has become of the professor?

MITZI: I sent him away.

COUNT: Oh, you did?—And can you guess who has the compartment between yours and mine? . . . Egon and his young gentleman. Won't they be surprised though?

MITZI: Yes . . . won't they?

(*She goes into the house.*)

(*Curtain.*)

Translated by Edwin Bjorkman
and revised by Caroline Wellbery

CASANOVA's
HOMECOMING

In his fifty-third year, when Casanova was no longer driven through the thold by the adventurousness of youth but by the restlessness of age, he felt grow in his soul an intense homesickness for Venice, the city of his birth; and so, like a bird who slowly descends from the lofty heights to die, he began to approach the city in ever-narrowing circles. Again and again, during the last ten years of his exile, he had implored the Supreme Council for leave to return home. At first, in the drafting of these petitions—a work in which he was a past master—a defiant, willful spirit and even a grim pleasure seemed to have guided his pen; but recently his almost humbly beseeching words seemed to give voice ever more apparently to a painful yearning and to genuine repentance.

The sins of his earlier years (the most unpardonable to the Venetian councillors was his freethinking, not his dissoluteness, quarrelsomeness, or swindles, which were usually of a spirited nature) were by degrees passing into oblivion, and so Casanova had a certain amount of confidence that he would receive a hearing. The history of his marvelous escape from The Leads of Venice, which he had recounted on innumerable occasions at the courts of princes, in the palaces of nobles, at the supper tables of burghers, and in houses of ill fame, was beginning to make people forget any disrepute which had attached to his name. Moreover, in letters to Mantua, where he had been staying for two months, persons of influence had conveyed hope to the adventurer, whose inward and outward luster were gradually beginning to fade, that before long there would come a favorable turn in his fortunes.

Since his means were now extremely slender, Casanova had decided to await the expected pardon in the modest but respectable inn where he had stayed in happier years. To make only passing mention of less spiritual amusements, with which he could not wholly dispense—he spent most of his time in writing a polemic against the slanderer Voltaire, hoping that the publication of this document would, upon his return to Venice, secure his unchallenged position and prestige in the eyes of all well-disposed citizens.

One morning he went out for a walk beyond the town limits, trying to think up the final formulation of some sentences that were to annihilate the infidel Frenchman, when suddenly he fell prey to a disquiet that almost amounted to physical distress. He turned over in his mind the life he had been leading for the last three months. It had grown wearisomely familiar—the morning walks into the country, the evenings spent in gambling for petty stakes with the reputed Baron Perotti and the latter's pockmarked mistress; the affection lavished on him by his hostess, a woman ardent but no longer very young; yes even the time he spent over the writings of Voltaire and over the composition of an audacious rejoinder which until that moment had seemed to him by no means inadequate. Yet now, in the gentle and almost too sweet atmosphere of this morning in late summer, all these things appeared stupid and repulsive. Muttering a curse without really knowing against whom or what it was directed, gripping the hilt of his sword, darting angry glances in all directions as if invisible scornful eyes were watching him in the surrounding solitude, he turned on his heel and retraced his steps back to the town, determined to make arrangements that very hour for immediate departure. He felt convinced that he would immediately feel better were he to diminish even by a few miles the distance that separated him from the home for which he longed. He hastened his steps so that he might be sure of booking a place in the diligence, which was leaving before sundown by the eastward road. There was little else to do, for he really need not bother to pay a farewell visit to Baron Perotti. Half an hour would suffice for the packing of all his possessions. He thought of the two suits, both somewhat worn, the shabbier of which he was wearing at that moment; of the much darned, though once elegant, underlinen. With two or three snuff-boxes, a gold watch and chain, and a few books, these comprised his whole worldly wealth. He called to mind past splendors, when he had traveled as a man of distinction, driving in a fine carriage; when he had been well furnished both with necessaries and with superfluities; when he had even had his own servant—who had usually, of course, been a rogue—and impotent anger brought tears to his eyes. A young woman drove toward him, whip in hand. In her little cart, amid sacks and various odds and ends, lay her husband, drunk and snoring. Casanova strode by beneath the chestnut trees that lined the highway, his face working with wrath, unintelligible phrases hissing from between his clenched teeth. The woman glanced at him inquisitively and mockingly at first, then, on encountering an angry glare, with some alarm, and finally, after she had passed, there was amorous invitation in the look she gave him over her shoulder. Casanova, who was well aware that rage and hatred can assume the semblance of youth more readily than can gentleness and amiability, was prompt to realize that a bold response on his part would bring the cart to a standstill, and that he could then do with the young woman whatever he pleased. Nevertheless, although the recognition of this fact improved his mood for the moment, it seemed hardly worthwhile to waste even a few minutes upon so trivial an adventure. He was content, therefore, to allow the peasant woman to drive her cart and all its contents unimpeded through the dust of the roadway.

The sun now stood high, and the shade of the trees hardly tempered the searing heat. Casanova was soon compelled to slow his pace. Under the thick powder of dust the shabbiness of his garments was no longer apparent, so that by his dress and bearing he might easily have been taken for a gentleman of station who had been pleased for once in a way to walk instead of drive. He had almost reached the arched gateway near his inn when he met a heavy country carriage lumbering along the road. In it was seated a stoutish man, well dressed and still fairly young. His hands were clasped across his stomach, his eyelids drooped, and he seemed about to doze off, when accidentally catching sight of Casanova, he suddenly brightened with animation. His whole aspect betrayed great excitement. He sprang to his feet, but too quickly, and fell back into his seat. Rising again, he gave the driver a punch in the back, to make the fellow pull up. But since the carriage did not stop instantly, the passenger turned around so as not to lose sight of Casanova, signaled with both hands, and finally called to him thrice by name, in a thin, clear voice. Not till he heard the voice did Casanova recognize who it was. By now the carriage had stopped, and Casanova smilingly seized the two hands stretched out toward him, saying:

"Olivo, is it really you?"

"Yes, Signor Casanova, it is I. You recognize me, then?"

"Why not? Since I last saw you, on your wedding day, you've put on flesh; but very likely I've changed a good deal, too, in these fifteen years, though not perhaps in the same fashion."

"Not a bit of it," exclaimed Olivo. "Why, Signor Casanova, you have hardly changed at all! And it is more than fifteen years; the sixteen years were up a few days ago. As you can imagine, Amalia and I had a good talk about you on the anniversary of our wedding."

"Indeed?" said Casanova cordially. "You both think of me at times?"

The tears came to Olivo's eyes. He was still holding Casanova's hands, and he pressed them fondly.

"We have so much to thank you for, Signor Casanova. How could we ever forget our benefactor? Should we do so . . ."

"Don't speak of it," interrupted Casanova. "How is Signora Amalia? Do you know, I have been living in Mantua three months, very quietly to be sure, but taking plenty of walks as I always have done. How is it, Olivo, that I haven't run into the two of you once?"

"The matter is simple, Signor Casanova. Both Amalia and I detest the town, and we gave up living there a long time ago. Would you do me the favor to jump in? We shall be at home in an hour."

Casanova tried to excuse himself, but Olivo insisted.

"I will take no denial. How delighted Amalia will be to see you once more, and how proud to show you our three children. Yes, we have three, Signor Casanova. All girls. Thirteen, ten, and eight— not one of them old enough yet—you'll excuse me, won't you— to have her head turned by Casanova."

He laughed good-humoredly and made as if to help Casanova into the carriage. The latter shook his head. He had been tempted for a moment by natural curiosity to accept Olivo's invitation. Then his impatience returned in full force, and he assured his would-be host that unfortunately urgent business called him away from Mantua that very afternoon.

What could he expect to find in Olivo's house? Sixteen years was a long time! Amalia would be no younger and no prettier. A girl of thirteen would hardly find him interesting at his age. Olivo, too, whom he had known in old days as a lean and eager student, was now a portly, countrified paterfamilias. The proposed visit did not offer sufficient attractions to induce Casanova to abandon a journey that was to bring him thirty or forty miles nearer to Venice. Olivo, however, was disinclined to take no for an answer. Casanova must at least accept a lift back to the inn, a kindly suggestion that could not decently be refused. Within a few minutes they had arrived. The hostess, a buxom woman in the middle thirties, welcomed Casanova with a glance that did not fail to disclose to Olivo the tender relationship between the pair. She shook hands with Olivo as an old acquaintance. She was a customer of Signor Olivo's, she explained to Casanova, for an excellent medium-dry wine grown on his estate. Olivo hastened to announce that the Chevalier de Seingalt (the hostess had addressed Casanova by this title, and Olivo promptly followed suit) was so cruel as to refuse the invitation of an old friend, on the ridiculous plea that today of all days he had to leave Mantua. The woman's look of gloom convinced Olivo that this was the first she had heard of Casanova's intended departure, and the latter felt it desirable to explain that his mention of the journey had been a mere pretext, lest he should incommode his friend's household by an unexpected visit, and that he had, in fact, an important piece of writing to finish during the next few days, and no place was better suited for the work than the inn, where his room was agreeably cool and quiet.

Olivo protested that the Chevalier de Seingalt would do his modest home the greatest possible honor by finishing the work in question there. The retired country atmosphere could not but be helpful in such an undertaking. If Casanova should need learned treatises and works of reference, there would be no lack of them, for Olivo's niece, the daughter of a deceased half brother, a girl who though young was extremely erudite, had arrived a few weeks before with a whole trunkful of books. Should any guests drop in at times of an evening, the chevalier need not disturb himself—

unless, indeed, after the labors of the day, cheerful conversation or a game of cards might offer welcome distraction. Hardly had Casanova heard of the niece, when he decided he would like to make her acquaintance, and after a show of further reluctance he yielded to Olivo's solicitation, declaring, however, that on no account would he be able to leave Mantua for more than a day or two. He begged the hostess to forward promptly by messenger any letters that should arrive during his absence, since they might be of the first importance. Matters having thus been arranged to Olivo's complete satisfaction, Casanova went to his room, made ready for the journey, and returned to the parlor in a quarter of an hour. Olivo, meanwhile, had been having a lively business talk with the hostess. He now rose, drank off his glass of wine, and with a significant wink promised to bring the chevalier back, not perhaps tomorrow or the day after, but in any case in good order and condition. Casanova, however, suddenly distracted and restless, gave such a cool good-bye to the fond hostess that, at the carriage door, she whispered a parting word in his ear which was anything but amiable.

During the drive along the dusty road beneath the glare of the noonday sun, Olivo gave a garrulous and somewhat incoherent account of his life since the friends' last meeting. Shortly after his marriage he had bought a plot of land near the town, and had started in a small way as market gardener. Doing well at this trade, he had gradually been able to undertake more ambitious farming ventures. At length, under God's favor, and thanks to his own and his wife's efficiency, he had been able three years earlier to buy from the pecuniarily embarrassed Count Marazzani the latter's old and somewhat dilapidated country seat with a vineyard attached. He, his wife, and his children were comfortably settled upon this patrician estate, though with no pretense to patrician splendor. All these successes were ultimately due to the hundred and fifty gold pieces that Casanova had presented to Amalia, or rather to her mother. But for this magical aid, Olivo's lot would still have been the same. He would still have been giving instruction in reading and writing to ill-behaved youngsters. Most likely, he would have been an old bachelor and Amalia an old maid.

Casanova let him ramble on without paying much heed. The incident was one among many of the date to which it belonged.

As he turned it over in his mind, it seemed to him the most trivial of them all, it had hardly even troubled the waters of memory. He had been traveling from Rome to Turin or Paris—he had forgotten which. During a brief stay in Mantua, he caught sight of Amalia in church one morning. Pleased with her appearance, with her handsome but pale and somewhat woebegone face, he gallantly addressed her a friendly question. In those days everyone had been complaisant to Casanova. Gladly opening her heart to him, the girl told him that she was not well off; that she was in love with a schoolteacher who was likewise poor; that his father and her own mother were both unwilling to give their consent to so inauspicious a union. Casanova promptly declared himself ready to help matters on. He sought an introduction to Amalia's mother, a good-looking widow of thirty-six who was still quite worthy of being courted. Before long Casanova was on such intimate terms with her that his word was law. When her consent to the match had been won, Olivo's father, a merchant in reduced circumstances, was no longer adverse, being specially influenced by the fact that Casanova (presented to him as a distant relative of the bride's mother) undertook to defray the expenses of the wedding and to provide part of the dowry. To Amalia, her generous patron seemed like a messenger from a higher world. She couldn't help showing her gratitude in the manner prompted by her own heart. When, the evening before her wedding, she withdrew with glowing cheeks from Casanova's last embrace, she was far from thinking that she had done any wrong to her future husband, who after all owed his happiness solely to the amiability and openhandedness of this marvelous friend. Casanova had never troubled himself as to whether Amalia had confessed to Olivo the length to which she had gone in gratitude to her benefactor; whether, perchance, Olivo had taken her sacrifice as a matter of course and had not considered it any reason for retrospective jealousy; or whether Olivo had to this day remained in ignorance of the matter. Nor did Casanova allow these questions to trouble his mind today.

The heat continued to increase. The carriage, with bad springs and hard cushions, jolted the occupants abominably. Olivo went on chattering in his high, thin voice; talking incessantly of the fertility of his land, the excellencies of his wife, the good behavior of his children, and the innocent pleasures of intercourse with his neighbors—farmers and landed gentry. Casanova began to be bored and asked himself irritably why on earth he had accepted an invitation which could bring nothing but petty vexations, and even ultimately disappointments. He thought longingly of the cool parlor in Mantua, where at this very hour he might have been working unhindered at his polemic against Voltaire. He had already made up his mind to get out at an inn now in sight, hire whatever conveyance might be available, and drive back to the town, when Olivo uttered a loud "Hullo!" waved his hands in his own peculiar manner and, grabbing Casanova by the arm, pointed to a pony trap which had suddenly pulled up and come to a halt next to their own carriage, as if by mutual understanding. Three young girls sprang out, moving with such activity that the knifeboard on which they had been sitting flew into the air and was overturned.

"My daughters," said Olivo, turning to Casanova, not without pride.

Casanova promptly moved as if to relinquish his seat in the carriage.

"Stay where you are, my dear Chevalier," said Olivo. "We shall be at home in a quarter of an hour, and for that little while we can all make shift together. Maria, Nanetta, Teresina, this is the Chevalier de Seingalt, an old friend of mine. Shake hands with him. But for him you would—"

He broke off, and whispered to Casanova, "I was just going to say something foolish."

Amending his phrase, he said, "But for him, things would have been very different!"

Like Olivo, the girls had black hair and dark eyes. All of them including Teresina, the eldest, who was still quite the child, looked at the stranger with frank rustic curiosity, and the youngest, Maria, obeying an instruction from her father, set about in all earnestness to kiss his hand. Casanova, however, did not allow this, instead kissing each of the girls upon both cheeks. Olivo said a word or two to the lad who was driving the trap in which the children had come, whereupon the fellow whipped up the pony and continued on along the road toward Mantua.

Laughing and joking, the girls took possession of the seat opposite Olivo and Casanova. They were closely packed; they all spoke at once; and since their father likewise went on talking,

Casanova found it far from easy at first to follow the conversation. One name caught his ear, that of Lieutenant Lorenzi. Teresina explained that the Lieutenant had passed them on horseback not long before, had said he intended to call in the evening, and had sent his respects to Father. Mother had at first meant to come with them to meet Father, but as it was so frightfully hot, she had thought it better to stay at home with Marcolina. As for Marcolina, she was still in bed when they left home. When they came along the garden path, they had pelted her with berries and hazelnuts through the open window, or she would still be asleep.

"That's not Marcolina's way," said Olivo to his guest. "Generally she is at work in the garden at six or even earlier and sits over her books till dinner time. Of course, we had visitors yesterday, and were up later than usual. We had a mild game of cards—not the sort of game you are used to, for we are innocent folk and don't want to win money from one another. Besides, since our good abbot usually participates, you can imagine, Chevalier, that there's nothing very sinful about our game."

At the mention of the abbot, the three girls laughed again, had an anecdote to tell, and this made them laugh more than ever. Casanova nodded amicably, without paying much attention. In imagination he saw Marcolina, as yet unknown to him, lying in her white bed, opposite the window. She had thrown off the bedclothes; her body half naked; her hands sleepily warding off the hail of berries and nuts. His senses flamed. He was as certain that Marcolina and Lieutenant Lorenzi were in love with one another as if he had seen them himself in a passionate embrace. He was just as ready to detest the unknown Lorenzi as to long for the never seen Marcolina.

Through the shimmering haze of noon, a small, square tower now became visible, thrusting upward through the grayish-green foliage. The carriage turned into a byroad. To the left were vineyards rising on a gentle slope; to the right the crests of ancient trees showed above the wall of a garden. The carriage halted at an archway whose weatherworn door stood wide. The passengers alighted, and at the master's nod the coachman drove away to the stable. A broad avenue lined with chestnut trees led to the house, which at first sight had an almost bare, even neglected appearance. Casanova's attention was especially attracted by a broken window in the first story. Nor did it escape his notice that the battlements of the squat tower were crumbling in places. But the house door was gracefully carved; and directly he entered the hall it was plain that the interior was carefully kept and was certainly in far better condition than might have been supposed from the outward aspect.

"Amalia," shouted Olivo, so loudly that the vaulted ceiling rang. "Come down as quickly as you can! I have brought a friend home with me, Amalia, and such a friend!"

Amalia had already appeared on the stairs, although to most of those who had just come out of the glaring sunlight she was invisible in the twilit interior. Casanova, whose keen eyes had retained the ability to see well even in the dark, had noted her presence sooner than Olivo. He smiled and was aware that the smile made him look younger. Amalia had not grown fat, as he had feared. She was still slim and youthful. She recognized him instantly.

"What a pleasant surprise!" she exclaimed without the slightest embarrassment, hastening down the stairs, and offering her cheek to Casanova, whereupon the latter did not hesitate to give her a friendly hug.

"Am I really to believe," said he, "that Maria, Nanetta, and Teresina are your very own daughters, Amalia? No doubt the passage of the years makes it possible. . . ."

"And all the other evidence is in keeping," supplemented Olivo. "You can count on that, Chevalier!"

Amalia let her eyes dwell reminiscently upon the guest. "I suppose," she said, "it was your meeting with the Chevalier that has made you so late, Olivo?"

"Indeed it was. But I hope there is still something to eat?"

"Marcolina and I were frightfully hungry, but of course we didn't sit down to eat alone."

"Can you manage to wait a few minutes longer," asked Casanova, "while I get rid of the dust of the drive?"

"I will show you your room immediately," answered Olivo. "I do hope, Chevalier, you will find it to your taste; almost as much to your taste," he winked, and added in a low tone, "as your room in the inn at Mantua—though here one or two little things may be lacking."

He led the way upstairs into the gallery surrounding the hall.

From one of the corners a narrow wooden stairway led into the tower. At the top, Olivo opened the door into the turret chamber, and stopping on the threshold politely invited Casanova to occupy the modest guestroom. A maidservant brought up the travel bag, and Olivo withdrew. Casanova stood left alone in a medium-sized room, simply furnished, but equipped with all necessaries. It had four tall and narrow baywindows, each offering a broad view in every direction, across the sunlit plain with its green vineyards, bright meadows, golden fields, white roads, light-colored houses, and dusky gardens. Casanova concerned himself little about the view and hastened to make ready, being impelled less by hunger than by an eager curiosity to see Marcolina face to face. He did not change, for he wished to reserve his best suit for evening wear.

When Casanova entered the dining hall, a paneled chamber on the ground floor, he saw seated at the amply laden table, in addition to his host and hostess and their three daughters, a young woman wearing a simple gray dress of some shimmering material. She had a graceful figure. Her gaze rested on him as frankly and indifferently as if he were a member of the household, or had been a guest a hundred times before. Her face did not light up in the way to which he had grown accustomed in earlier years, when, even a stranger, he appeared in the breathtaking splendor of his youth or in the dangerous beauty of his handsome prime. But for a good while now Casanova had ceased to expect this from a new acquaintance. Nevertheless, even of late the mention of his name had usually sufficed to arouse on a woman's face an expression of tardy admiration, or at least some trace of regret, which was an admission that the hearer would have loved to have met him a few years earlier. Yet now, when Olivo introduced him to Marcolina as Signor Casanova, Chevalier de Seingalt, she smiled as she would have smiled at some utterly indifferent name that carried with it no suggestion of adventure and mystery. Even when he took his seat by her side, kissed her hand, and allowed his eyes as they dwelt on her to gleam with delight and desire, her manner betrayed nothing of the demure gratification that might have seemed an appropriate answer to so ardent a wooing.

After a few polite commonplaces, Casanova told his neighbor that he had been informed of her intellectual endeavors and asked what was her chosen subject of study. Her chief interest, she rejoined, was in the higher mathematics, to which she had been introduced by Professor Morgagni, the renowned teacher at the university of Bologna. Casanova expressed his surprise that so charming a young lady should have an interest, certainly exceptional, in such a sober and difficult subject. Marcolina replied that in her view the higher mathematics was the most imaginative of all the sciences; one might even say that its nature made it akin to the divine. When Casanova asked for further enlightenment upon a view so novel to him, Marcolina modestly declined to continue the topic, declaring that the others at table, and above all her uncle, would much rather hear more about the experiences of a widely traveled friend, whom he had not seen for such a long time, than listen to a philosophical disquisition. Amalia eagerly took up the proposal; and Casanova, always willing to oblige in this matter, said in easygoing fashion that during recent years he had been mainly engaged in secret diplomatic missions. To mention only places of importance, he had continually been going to and fro between Madrid, Paris, London, Amsterdam, and St. Petersburg. He gave an account of meetings and conversations, some grave and some gay, with men and women of all classes, and did not forget to speak of his friendly reception at the court of Catherine of Russia. He jestingly related how Frederick the Great had nearly appointed him instructor at a cadet school for Pomeranian barons—a danger from which he had escaped by a precipitous flight. Of these and many other things he spoke as recent happenings, although in reality they had occurred years or decades before. Romancing freely, he was hardly conscious when he was lying either on a small scale or on a large, being equally delighted with his own conceits and with the pleasure he was giving to his listeners.

While thus recounting real and imaginary incidents, he could almost delude himself into the belief that he was still the bold, radiant Casanova, the favorite of fortune and of beautiful women, the honored guest of secular and spiritual princes, the man whose spendings and gamblings and gifts must be reckoned in thousands. It was possible for him to forget that he was a decayed starveling, supported by pitiful remittances from former friends in England and Spain—sums which often failed to arrive, so that he was reduced to the few and paltry gold pieces which he could win from

Baron Perotti or from the baron's guests. He could even forget that his highest aim now was to return to his natal city where he had been cast into prison and from which, since his escape, he had been banned; to return as one of the lowest of its citizens, as writer, as beggar, as nonentity; to accept so inglorious a close to a once brilliant career.

Marcolina listened attentively like the others, but with the same expression as if she had been listening to someone reading aloud from an amusing narrative. Her face did not betray the remotest realization of the fact that the speaker was Casanova; that she was listening to the person who had had all these experiences and many more; that she was sitting beside the lover of a thousand women. Very different was the fire in Amalia's eyes. To her, Casanova was the same as ever. To her, his voice was no less seductive than it had been sixteen years earlier. He could not but be aware that at a word or a sign, and as soon as he pleased, he could revive this old adventure. But what was Amalia to him at this hour, when he longed for Marcolina as he had never longed for any woman before? Beneath the shimmering folds of her dress he seemed to see her naked body; her firm young breasts allured him; once when she stooped to pick up her handkerchief, Casanova's inflamed fancy made him attach so ardent a significance to her movement that he felt near to swooning. Marcolina did not fail to notice the involuntary pause in the flow of his conversation; she perceived that his gaze had begun to flicker strangely. In her countenance he could read a sudden hostility, a protest, a trace of disgust. Casanova speedily recovered his self-command, and was about to continue his reminiscences with renewed vigor, when a portly priest entered. Olivo introduced him as Abbot Rossi, and Casanova at once recognized him as the man he had met twenty-seven years earlier upon a market boat plying between Venice and Chioggia.

"You had one eye bandaged," said Casanova, who rarely missed a chance of showing off his excellent memory. "A young peasant woman wearing a yellow kerchief around her head advised you to use a healing unguent which an apothecary with an exceedingly hoarse voice happened to have with him."

The abbot nodded, and smiled, well pleased. Then, with a sly expression, he came quite close to Casanova, as if about to tell him a secret. But he spoke out loud.

"As for you, Signor Casanova, you were with a wedding party.

I don't know whether you were one of the ordinary guests or whether you were best man, but I remember that the bride looked at you far more languishingly than at the bridegroom. The wind rose; there was half a gale; and you began to read a highly audacious poem."

"No doubt the chevalier only did so in order to allay the storm," said Marcolina.

"I never claim the powers of a wizard," rejoined Casanova. "But I will not deny that after I had begun to read, no one bothered any more about the storm."

The three girls had encircled the abbot. They had their reasons. From his capacious pockets he produced quantities of luscious sweets and popped them into the children's mouths with his stumpy fingers. Meanwhile Olivo gave the newcomer a circumstantial account of how he had just now met Casanova once again. Dreamily Amalia continued to direct her bright gaze at the beloved guest's masterful brown forehead. The children ran out into the garden; Marcolina had risen from the table and was watching them through the open window. The abbot had brought a message from the Marchese Celsi, who proposed to call that evening, his health permitting, with his wife, upon his worthy friend Olivo.

"Excellent," said Olivo. "We shall have a pleasant game of cards in honor of the chevalier. I am expecting the two Ricardis; and Lorenzi is also coming—the girls met him while he was out riding."

"Is he still here?" asked the abbot. "A week ago I was told he had to rejoin his regiment."

"I expect the Marchesa got him an extension of leave from the colonel."

"I am surprised," interjected Casanova, "that any Mantuese officers can get leave at present." He invented as he spoke: "Two friends of mine, one from Mantua and the other from Cremona, left last night with their regiments, marching toward Milan."

"Has war broken out?" inquired Marcolina from the window. She had turned around; the expression on her face was concealed by shadows, but there was a slight quaver in her voice which probably no one but Casanova noticed.

"It may come to nothing," he said lightly. "But since the Spaniards seem to adopt a threatening attitude, it is necessary to be on the alert."

"Does anyone know," Olivo asked with importance, wrinkling his brow, "whether we shall side with Spain or with France?"

"I don't think Lieutenant Lorenzi will care a straw about that," suggested the abbot. "All he wants is a chance to put his military prowess to the test."

"He has done so already," said Amalia. "He was in the battle at Pavia three years ago."

Marcolina said not a word.

Casanova knew enough. He went to the window beside Marcolina and looked out into the garden. He saw nothing but the expansive wild meadow where the children were playing. It was surrounded by a close-set row of stately trees within the encompassing wall.

"What lovely grounds," he said, turning to Olivo. "I should so like to have a look at them."

"Nothing would please me better, Chevalier," answered Olivo, "than to show you my vineyards and the rest of my estate. You need only ask Amalia, and she will tell you that during the years since I bought this little place, I have had no keener desire than to welcome you as guest upon my own land and under my own roof. Ten times at least I was on the point of writing you an invitation, but how could I know whether my letter would reach you. If I did happen to hear from someone that he had recently seen you in Lisbon, I could be quite sure that in the interval you would have left for Warsaw or Vienna. Now, when as if by miracle I have caught you on the point of quitting Mantua, and when—I can assure you, Amalia, it was no easy matter—I have succeeded in enticing you here, you are so miserly with your time that—would you believe it, Signor Abbot, he refuses to spare us more than a couple of days!"

"Perhaps the chevalier will allow himself to be persuaded to prolong his visit," said the abbot, who was contentedly allowing a slice of peach to dissolve in his mouth. As he spoke, he glanced at Amalia in a way that led Cassanova to infer that his hostess had told the abbot more than she had told her husband.

"I fear that will be quite impossible," said Casanova with decision. "I need not conceal from friends who are so keenly interested in my fortunes, that my Venetian fellow citizens are on the point of atoning for the injustice of earlier years. The atonement comes rather late but is all the more honorable. I should seem ungrateful, or even resentful, were I to resist their urging any longer." With a wave of his hand he warded off an eager but respectful inquiry which he saw taking shape upon his host's lips and hastened to remark, "Well, Olivo, I am ready. Show me your little kingdom."

"Would it not be wiser," interposed Amalia, "to wait until it is cooler? I am sure the chevalier would prefer to rest for a while or to stroll in the shade." Her eyes sought Casanova's with shy entreaty, as if she thought her fate would be decided once again during such a walk in the garden.

No one had anything to say against Amalia's suggestion, and they all went out of doors. Marcolina, who led the way, ran across the sunlit meadow to join the children in their game of battledore and shuttlecock. She was hardly taller than the eldest of the three girls; and when her hair came loose in the exercise and floated over her shoulders she too looked like a child. Olivo and the abbot seated themselves on a stone bench beneath the trees, not far from the house. Amalia sauntered on with Casanova. As soon as the two were out of hearing, she began to converse with Casanova in the old tone, as though she had never used a different one with him.

"So we meet again, Casanova! How I have longed for this day. I never doubted its coming."

"A mere chance has brought me," said Casanova coldly.

Amalia smiled. "Have it your own way," she said. "Anyhow, you are here! All these sixteen years I have done nothing but dream of this day!"

"I can't help thinking," countered Casanova, "that throughout the long interval you must have dreamed of many other things—and must have done more than dream."

Amalia shook her head. "You know better, Casanova. Nor had you forgotten me, for were it otherwise, in your eagerness to get to Venice, you would never have accepted Olivo's invitation."

"What do you mean, Amalia? Can you imagine I have come here to make a cuckold of your husband?"

"How can you use such a phrase, Casanova? Were I to be yours once again, there would be neither betrayal nor sin."

Casanova laughed. "No sin? Why not a sin? Because I'm an old man?"

"You are not old. For me you can never be an old man. In your arms I had my first taste of bliss, and I doubt not it is my destiny that my last bliss shall be shared with you!"

"Your last?" Casanova echoed cynically, though he was not altogether unmoved. "I think my friend Olivo would have a word to say about that."

"What you speak of," said Amalia reddening, "is duty, and even pleasure; but it is not and never has been bliss."

They did not walk to the end of the grass alley. Both seemed to shun the neighborhood of the meadow, where Marcolina and the children were playing. As if by common consent they retraced their steps, and, silent now, approached the house again. One of the ground-floor windows at the gable end of the house was open. Through this Casanova glimpsed in the dark interior a half-drawn curtain, from behind which the foot of a bed projected. Over an adjoining chair was hanging a light, gauzy dress.

"Is that Marcolina's room?" enquired Casanova.

Amalia nodded. "Do you like her?" she said—nonchalantly, as it seemed to Casanova.

"Of course, since she is good looking."

"Good looking and virtuous."

Casanova shrugged, as if that hadn't been the point. Then: "Tell me, Amalia, if today had been the first time you had ever seen me, would you still have found me handsome?"

"I do not know if your looks have changed. To me you seem just the same as of old. You are as I have always seen you, as I have seen you in my dreams."

"Look well, Amalia. See the wrinkles on my forehead; the loose folds of my neck; the crow's-feet round my eyes. And look," he grinned, "I have lost one of my eye teeth. Look at these hands, too, Amalia. My fingers are like claws; there are yellow spots on the fingernails; the blue veins stand out. They are the hands of an old man, Amalia!"

She clasped both his hands as he held them out for her to see, and reverently kissed them one after the other in the shaded walk. "Tonight, I will kiss you on the lips," she said, with a mingling of humility and tenderness, which roused his gall.

Close by, where the alley opened on to the greensward, Marcolina was stretched on the grass, her hands clasped beneath her head, looking skyward while the shuttlecocks flew to and fro. Suddenly reaching upward, she seized one of them in midair and laughed triumphantly. The girls flung themselves upon her, she couldn't defend herself, their curls were tossing.

Casanova trembled. "Neither my lips nor my hands are yours to kiss. Your waiting for me and your dreams of me will prove to have been vain—unless I should first have made Marcolina mine."

"Are you mad, Casanova?" exclaimed Amalia, with distress in her voice.

"If I am, we have nothing to reproach each other with," replied Casanova. "You are mad because in me, an old man, you think that you can rediscover the beloved of your youth; I am mad because I have taken it into my head that I wish to possess Marcolina. But perhaps we shall both be restored to reason. Marcolina shall restore me to youth—for you. So help me to my wishes, Amalia!"

"You are really beside yourself, Casanova. What you ask is impossible. She will have nothing to do with any man."

Casanova laughed. "What about Lieutenant Lorenzi?"

"Lorenzi? What do you mean?"

"He is her lover. I am sure of it."

"You are utterly mistaken. He asked for her hand, and she rejected his proposal. Yet he is young and handsome. I almost think him handsomer than you ever were, Casanova!"

"He was a suitor for her hand?"

"Ask Olivo if you don't believe me."

"Well, what do I care about that? What care I whether she be virgin or strumpet, wife or widow—I want to make her mine!"

"I can't give her to you, my friend!" And he sensed from her tone that she pitied him.

"You see for yourself," he said, "what a disgraceful creature I have become. Ten years ago, five years ago, I should have needed neither helper nor advocate, even though Marcolina had been the very goddess of virtue. And now I am trying to make you play the go-between. If I were only a rich man. Had I but ten thousand ducats. But I have not even ten. I am a beggar, Amalia."

"Had you a hundred thousand, you could not buy Marcolina. What does she care about money? She loves books, the sky, the meadows, butterflies, playing with children. She has inherited a small competence which more than suffices for her needs."

"Were I but a sovereign prince," cried Casanova, somewhat theatrically, as was his wont just when he was in the grip of a genuine passion. "Had I but the power to commit men to prison, to send them to the scaffold. But I am nothing. A beggar, and a liar into the bargain. I importune the Supreme Council for a post, a crust of bread, a home! What has become of me? Don't I disgust you, Amalia?"

"I love you, Casanova!"

"Then give her to me, Amalia. It rests with you, I am confident. Tell her what you please. Say I have threatened you. Say you think I am capable of setting fire to the house. Say I am a fool, a dangerous lunatic escaped from an asylum, but that the embraces of a virgin will restore me to sanity. Yes, tell her that."

"She does not believe in miracles."

"Does not believe in miracles? Then she does not believe in God either. So much the better! I have influence with the Archbishop of Milan. Tell her so. I can ruin her. I can destroy you all. It is true, Amalia. What books does she read? Doubtless some of them are on the Index. Let me see them. I will compile a list. A hint from me. . . ."

"Not a word more, Casanova! Here she comes. Keep yourself well in hand; do not let your eyes betray you. Listen, Casanova; I have never known a more pure-minded girl. Did she suspect what I have heard from you, she would feel herself soiled, and for the rest of your stay she would not so much as look at you. Talk to her; talk to her. You will soon ask her pardon and mine."

Marcolina came up with the girls, who ran on into the house. She paused, as if out of courtesy to the guest, standing before him, while Amalia deliberately withdrew. Indeed, it actually seemed to Casanova that from those pale, half-parted lips, from the smooth brow crowned with light-brown hair now restored to order, there emanated an aroma of aloofness and purity. Rarely had he had this feeling with regard to any woman; nor had he had it in the case of Marcolina when they were within four walls. A kind of reverence, of surrender unqualified by even the slightest desire, seemed to take possession of his soul. Discreetly, in a respectful tone such as at that day was customary toward persons of rank, in a manner which she could not but regard as flattering, he inquired whether it was her purpose to resume her studies that evening. She answered that in the country her work was somewhat irregular. Nevertheless, she couldn't prevent mathematical problems upon which she had recently been pondering from at times preoccupying her even during free hours. This had just happened while she was lying on the meadow gazing up into the sky.

Casanova, emboldened by the friendliness of her demeanor, asked jestingly what was the nature of this lofty, urgent problem. She replied, in much the same tone, that it had nothing whatever to do with the Kabbalah, with which, so rumor ran, the Chevalier de Seingalt achieved significant results. He would therefore not know what to make of her problem.

Casanova was piqued that she should speak of the Kabbalah with such unconcealed contempt. In his rare hours of heart searching he was well aware that the mystical system of numbers which passed by that name had neither sense nor purpose. He knew it had no correspondence with any natural reality; that it was no more than an instrument whereby cheats and jesters—Casanova assumed these roles by turn and was a master player in both capacities—could lead credulous fools by the nose. Nevertheless, in defiance of his own better judgment, he now undertook to defend the Kabbalah as a serious and perfectly valid science. He spoke of the divine nature of the number seven, to which there are so many references in Holy Writ; of the deep prophetic significance of pyramids of figures, for the construction of which he had himself invented a new system; and of the frequent fulfillment of the forecasts he had based upon this system. In Amsterdam a few years ago, through the use of numerology, he had induced Hope the banker to take over the insurance of a ship which was thought a lost cause, whereby the banker had made two hundred thousand gold guilders. He held forth so eloquently in defense of his preposterous theories that, as often happened, he began to believe all the nonsense he was talking. At length he went so far as to maintain that the Kabbalah was not so much a branch of mathematics as the metaphysical perfectionment of mathematics.

At this point, Marcolina, who had been listening attentively and with apparent seriousness, suddenly assumed a half-commiserating, half-mischievous expression, and said, "You are trying, Signor Casanova"—she now seemed deliberately to avoid addressing him as chevalier—"to give me an elaborate proof of your renowned talent as entertainer, and I am extremely grateful to you.

But, of course, you know as well as I do that the Kabbalah has not merely nothing to do with mathematics but is in conflict with the very essence of mathematics. The Kabbalah bears to mathematics the same sort of relationship that the confused or fallacious chatter of the Sophists bore to the clear, lofty doctrines of Plato and of Aristotle."

"Nevertheless, beautiful and learned Marcolina, you will admit," answered Casanova promptly, "that even the Sophists were far from being such contemptible, foolish apprentices as your harsh criticism would have us assume. Let me give you a contemporary example. Monsieur Voltaire's whole technique of thought and writing entitles us to describe him as an arch-Sophist. Yet no one will refuse the honor due his extraordinary talent. I would not myself refuse it, though I am at this moment engaged in composing a polemic against him. Let me add that I am not allowing myself to be influenced in his favor by recollection of the extreme civility he was good enough to show me when I visited him at Ferney ten years ago."

"It is really most considerate of you to be so lenient in your criticism of the greatest mind of the century!" Marcolina smilingly retorted.

"A great mind—the greatest of the century!" exclaimed Casanova. "To give him such a designation seems to me inadmissible, were it only because, for all his genius, he is an ungodly man— nay positively an atheist. No atheist can be a man of great mind."

"As I see the matter, there is no such incompatibility. But the first thing you have to prove is your title to describe Voltaire as an atheist."

Casanova was now in his element. In the opening chapter of his polemic he had cited from Voltaire's works, especially from the famous *Pucelle,* a number of passages that seemed peculiarly well fitted to justify the charge of atheism. Thanks to his unfailing memory, he was able to repeat these citations verbatim, and to marshal his own counter arguments. But in Marcolina he had to cope with an opponent who was little inferior to himself in extent of knowledge and mental acumen; and who, moreover, excelled him, not perhaps in fluency of speech, but at any rate in artistry of presentation and clarity of expression. The passages Casanova had selected as demonstrating Voltaire's spirit of mockery, his skepticism, and his atheism, were adroitly interpreted by Marcolina as testifying to the Frenchman's scientific genius, to his skill as an author, and to his indefatigable ardor in the search for truth. She boldly contended that doubt, mockery, nay unbelief itself, if associated with such a wealth of knowledge, such absolute honesty, and such high courage, must be more pleasing to God than the humility of the pious, which was apt to mask the inability to think logically, and often enough—there were plenty of examples—to mask cowardice and hypocrisy.

Casanova listened with growing astonishment. He felt quite incompetent to convert Marcolina to his own way of thinking; all the more as he increasingly realized that her counter strokes were threatening to demolish the tottering intellectual edifice which, of late years, he had been accustomed to mistake for faith. He took refuge in the trite assertion that such views as Marcolina's were a menace, not only to the ecclesiastical ordering of society, but to the very foundations of the State. This enabled him to make a clever change of front, to pass into the field of politics, where he hoped that his wide experience and his knowledge of the world would render it possible for him to get the better of his adversary. But although she lacked acquaintance with the notable personalities of the age; although she was without inside knowledge of courtly and diplomatic intrigues; although, therefore, she had to renounce any attempt to answer Casanova in detail, even when she felt an inclination to distrust the accuracy of his assertions— nevertheless, it was clear to him from the tenor of her remarks, that she had little respect for the princes of the earth or for the institutions of state; and she made no secret of her conviction that, alike in small things and in great, selfishness and lust for power not so much ruled the world as brought it to a state of hopeless confusion. Rarely had Casanova encountered such freedom of thought in women; not to mention in a girl who was certainly not yet twenty years old. It was painful to him to remember that in earlier and better days his own mind had with deliberate, self-complacent boldness moved along the paths whereon Marcolina was now advancing—although in her case she did not seem to be at all aware of her exceptional courage. Fascinated by the uniqueness of her methods of thought and expression, he almost forgot that he was walking beside a young, beautiful, desirable woman, a forgetfulness all the more remarkable as the two were alone in the leafy alley, and at a considerable distance from the house.

Suddenly, breaking off in the middle of a sentence, Marcolina joyfully exclaimed, "Here comes my uncle!"

Casanova, as if he had to rectify an omission, whispered to her, "What a nuisance. I should have liked to go on talking to you for hours, Marcolina." He was aware that his eyes were again lighting up with desire.

At this Marcolina, who in the spirited exchange of their recent conversation had for all her scoffing taken on an almost trusting attitude, immediately displayed a renewed reserve. Her expression manifested the same protest, the same repulsion, which had wounded Casanova earlier in the day.

"Am I really so repulsive?" he anxiously asked himself. Then, replying in thought to his own question: "No, that is not the reason. Marcolina is not really a woman. She is a professor, a philosopher, one of the wonders of the world perhaps—but not a woman."

Yet even as he mused, he knew he was merely attempting to deceive himself, console himself, save himself; and all his endeavors were vain.

Olivo, who had now come up, addressed Marcolina. "Have I not done well to invite some one here with whom you can converse as learnedly as with your professors at Bologna?"

"Indeed, Uncle," answered Marcolina, "there was not one of them who would have ventured to challenge Voltaire to a duel!"

"What, Voltaire? The chevalier has called him out?" cried Olivo, not understanding.

"Your witty niece, Olivo, refers to the polemic on which I have been at work for the last few days, the pastime of leisure hours. I used to have more sensible things to do."

Marcolina, ignoring this remark, said, "You will find it pleasantly cool now for your walk. Good-bye then." She nodded a farewell and moved briskly across the meadow to the house.

Casanova, repressing an impulse to follow her with his eyes, inquired, "Is Signora Amalia coming with us?"

"No, Chevalier," answered Olivo. "She has a number of things to attend to in the house; and besides, this is the girls' lesson time."

"What an excellent housewife and mother! You're a lucky fellow, Olivo!"

"I tell myself the same thing every day," responded Olivo, his eyes moistening with tears.

They passed by the gable end of the house. Marcolina's window was still open; the pale, diaphanous gown showed up against the dark background of the room. Along the wide chestnut avenue they made their way on to the road, now completely in the shade. Leisurely, they walked up the slope skirting the garden wall. Where it ended, the vineyard began. Between tall poles, from which purple clusters hung, Olivo led his guest to the summit. With a complaisant air of ownership, he waved toward the house, lying at the foot of the hill. Casanova fancied he could detect a female figure flitting to and fro in the turret chamber.

The sun was near to setting, but the heat was still considerable. Beads of perspiration coursed down Olivo's cheeks, but Casanova's brow showed no trace of moisture. Strolling down the farther slope, they reached a sumptuous meadow. From tree to tree vines were trained trellis-wise, while between the rows of olive trees golden ears of wheat swayed in the breeze.

"In a thousand ways," said Casanova appreciatively, "the sun brings increase."

With even greater wealth of detail than before, Olivo recounted how he had acquired this fine estate, and how a few prosperous vintage years and harvests had made him a well-to-do, in fact a wealthy, man. Casanova pursued the train of his own thoughts, attending to Olivo's narrative only in so far as was requisite to enable him from time to time to interpose a polite question or to make an appropriate comment. Nothing claimed his interest until Olivo, after talking of all and sundry, came back to the topic of his family, and finally to Marcolina. But Casanova learned little that was new. She had lost her mother early. Her father, Olivo's half brother, had been a physician in Bologna. Marcolina, while still a child, had astonished everyone by her precocious intelligence; but the marvel was soon staled by custom. A few years later her father died. Since then she had been living in the household of a distinguished professor at the university of Bologna, Morgagni to wit, who hoped that his pupil would become a woman of great learning. She always spent the summer with her uncle.

There had been several proposals for her hand; one from a Bolognese merchant; one from a neighboring landowner; and lastly the proposal of Leiutenant Lorenzi. She had refused them all, and it seemed to be her design to devote her whole life to the service of knowledge. As Olivo rambled on with his story, Casanova's desires grew beyond measure, while the recognition that these desires were utterly foolish and futile reduced him almost to despair.

Casanova and Olivo regained the highroad. In a cloud of dust, a carriage drove up, and as they drew near the occupants shouted greetings. The newcomers were an elderly gentleman in elegant attire and a lady who was somewhat younger, of generous proportions, and conspicuously rouged.

"The marchese," whispered Olivo to his companion.

The carriage halted.

"Good evening, my dear Olivo," said the marchese. "Will you be so good as to introduce me to the Chevalier de Seingalt? I have no doubt that it is the Chevalier whom I have the pleasure of seeing."

Casanova bowed slightly, saying, "Yes, I am he."

"I am the Marchese Celsi. Let me present the marchesa, my spouse." The lady offered her fingertips. Casanova touched them with his lips. The marchese had a narrow face, of a yellow, waxy tint; his greenish eyes were piercing; his thick eyebrows were of reddish color, and met across the root of the nose. These characteristics gave him a somewhat less than friendly aspect. "My good Olivo," he said, "we are all going to the same destination. Since it is little more than half a mile to your house, I shall get out and walk with you. You won't mind driving the rest of the way alone," he added, turning to the marchesa, who had meanwhile been gazing at Casanova with searching, passionate eyes. Without awaiting his wife's answer, the marchese nodded to the coachman, who promptly lashed the horses furiously, as if he had some reason for driving his mistress away at top speed. In an instant the carriage vanished in a whirl of dust.

"The whole neighborhood," said the marchese, who was two or three inches taller than Casanova, and unnaturally lean, "is already aware that the Chevalier de Seingalt has come to spend a few days with his friend Olivo. It must be glorious to bear so renowned a name."

"You are very kind, Signor Marchese," replied Casanova. "I have not yet abandoned the hope of winning such a name, but I am still far from having done so. It may be that a work on which I am now engaged will bring me nearer to the goal."

"We can take a shortcut here," said Olivo, turning into a path which led straight to the wall of his garden.

"Work?" echoed the marchese with a doubtful air. "May I inquire to what sort of work you refer, Chevalier?"

"If you ask me that question, Signor Marchese, I shall in my turn feel impelled to inquire what you meant just now when you referred to my renown."

Arrogantly, he faced the marchese's piercing eyes. He knew perfectly well that neither his romance *Icosameron* nor yet his three-volume work, *Confutazione della storia del governo veneto d'Amelot de la Houssaie,* had brought him any notable reputation as an author. Nevertheless it was his pose to imply that for him no other sort of reputation was desirable. He therefore deliberately misunderstood the marchese's tentative observations and cautious allusions, which implied that Casanova was a celebrated seducer, gamester, man of affairs, political emissary, or what not. Celsi made no reference to authorship, for he had never heard of either the *Refutation of Amelot* or the *Icosameron*. At length, therefore, in polite embarrassment, he said, "After all, there is only one Casanova."

"There, likewise, you are mistaken, Signor Marchese," said Casanova coldly. "I have relatives, and a connoisseur like yourself must surely be acquainted with the name of one of my brothers, Francesco Casanova, the painter."

It seemed that the marchese had no claim to connoisseurship in this field either, and he turned the conversation to acquaintances living in Naples, Rome, Milan, or Mantua, persons whom Casanova was not unlikely to have met. In this connection he also mentioned the name of Baron Perotti, but somewhat contemptuously.

Casanova was constrained to admit that he often played cards at the baron's house. "For distraction," he explained; "for half an hour's relaxation before bedtime. In general, I have given up this way of wasting my time."

"I am sorry," said the marchese, "for I must own it has been one of the dreams of my life to compete with you. Not only, indeed, at the card table; for when I was younger I would gladly have been your rival in other fields. Would you believe it—I forget how long ago it was—I once entered Spa on the very day, at the very hour, when you left the place. Our carriages must have passed one another on the road. In Ratisbon, too, I had the same piece of ill luck. There I actually occupied the room which you had left just an hour before."

"It is indeed unfortunate," said Casanova, flattered in spite of himself, "that people's paths so often cross too late in life."

"Not yet too late!" exclaimed the marchese with spirit. "There are certain respects in which I will gladly admit to being vanquished before the fight beings, and it bothers me little. But as regards games of chance, my dear Chevalier, we are perhaps both of us precisely at the age—"

Casanova cut him short. "At the age—very likely. Unfortunately, however, I can no longer look forward to the pleasure of measuring myself at the card table with a partner of your rank. The reason is simple." He spoke in the tone of a dethroned sovereign. "Despite my renown, my dear Marchese, I am now practically reduced to the condition of a beggar."

The marchese involuntarily lowered his eyes before Casanova's haughty gaze. He shook his head incredulously, as if he had been listening to a strange jest. Olivo, who had followed the conversation with the keenest attention, and had accompanied the skillful parries of his marvelous friend with approving nods, could hardly repress a gesture of alarm. They had just reached a narrow wooden door in the garden wall. Olivo produced a key, and turned the creaking lock. Giving the marchese precedence into the garden, he grasped Casanova by the arm, whispering, "You must take back those last words, Chevalier, before you set foot in my house again. The money I have been owing you these sixteen years awaits you. I was only afraid to speak of it. Amalia will tell you. It is counted out and ready. I had proposed to hand it over to you on your departure. . . ."

Casanova gently interrupted him. "You owe me nothing, Olivo. You know perfectly well that those paltry gold pieces were a wedding present from the friend of Amalia's mother. Please drop the subject. What are a few ducats to me?" He raised his voice as he spoke, so that the marchese, who had paused at a few paces' distance, could hear the concluding words. "I stand at a turning point in my fortunes."

Olivo exchanged glances with Casanova, as if asking permission, and then explained to the marchese, "You must know that the Chevalier has been summoned to Venice, and will set out for home in a few days."

"I would rather put it," remarked Casanova as they approached the house, "that summonses, growing ever more urgent, have been reaching me for a considerable while. But it seems to me that the senators took long enough to make up their minds, and may in their turn practice the virtue of patience."

"Unquestionably," said the marchese, "you are entitled to stand upon your dignity, Chevalier."

They emerged from the avenue on to the meadow, across which the shadow of the house had now lengthened. Close to the dwelling, the rest of the little company was awaiting them. All rose and came to meet them. The abbot led the way, with Marcolina and Amalia on either side.

They were followed by the marchesa, with whom came a tall, young officer, clad in a red uniform trimmed with silver lace, and wearing jackboots—evidently Lorenzi. As he spoke to the marchesa, he scanned her powdered shoulders as if they were well-known samples of other pretty objects with which he was equally familiar. The marchesa smiled up at him beneath half-closed lids. Even a novice in such matters could hardly fail to realize the nature of their relationship, or to perceive that they were quite unconcerned at its disclosure. They were conversing in animated fashion, but in low tones; and they ceased talking only when they caught up with the others.

Olivo introduced Casanova and Lorenzi to one another. They exchanged glances with a cold aloofness that seemed to offer mutual assurances of dislike; then, with a forced smile, both bowed quickly without offering to shake hands. Lorenzi was handsome, with a narrow visage and features sharply cut for his age. At the back of his eyes something difficult to grasp seemed to lurk, something likely to suggest caution to an experienced person. For only a moment, Casanova was in doubt as to who it was that Lorenzi reminded him of. Then he realized that his own image stood before him, the image of himself as he had been thirty years before.

"Have I been reincarnated in his form?" Casanova asked himself. "But I must have died before that could happen." It flashed through his mind: "Have I not been dead for a long time? What is there left of the Casanova who was young, handsome, and happy?"

Amalia broke in upon his musings. As if from a distance, though she stood close at hand, she asked him how he had enjoyed his walk. Raising his voice so that all could hear, he expressed his admiration for the fertile, well-managed estate. Meanwhile upon the meadow the maidservant was laying the table for supper. The two elder girls were helping. With much fuss and giggling, they brought out of the house the silver, the wine glasses, and other requisites. Gradually the dusk fell; a cool breeze stirred through the garden. Marcolina hurried to the table, to put the finishing touches to the work of the maidservant and the girls. The others wandered about the meadow and along the alleys. The marchesa was extremely polite to Casanova. She said that she wished to hear the story of his remarkable escape from The Leads in Venice, although, as she added with a significant smile, it was not unknown to her that he had had far more dangerous adventures, which he might perhaps be less inclined to recount. Casanova rejoined that he had indeed had a number of lively experiences, but had never made serious acquaintance with that mode of existence whose meaning and very essence were danger. Although, many years before, during troubled times, he had for a few months been a soldier upon the island of Corfu (was there any profession on earth into which the current of fate had not drifted him?), he had never had the good fortune to go through a real campaign, such as that which, he understood, Lieutenant Lorenzi was about to experience—a piece of luck for which he was inclined to envy the Leiutenant.

"Then you know more than I do, Signor Casanova," said Lorenzi in a challenging tone. "Indeed, you are better informed than the colonel himself, for he has just given me an indefinite extension of leave."

"Is that so?" exclaimed the marchese, unable to master his rage. He added spitefully, "Do you know, Lorenzi, we, or rather my wife, had counted so definitely on your leaving, that we had invited one of our friends, Baldi the singer, to stay with us next week."

"No matter," rejoined Lorenzi, unperturbed. "Baldi and I are the best of friends. We shall get on famously together. You think so, don't you?" he said, turning to the marchesa and flashing his teeth.

"You'd better!" said the marchesa, laughing gaily.

As she spoke she seated herself at the table, beside Olivo, with Lorenzi on the other hand. Opposite sat Amalia, between the marchese and Casanova. Next to Casanova, at one end of the long, narrow table, was Marcolina; next to Olivo, at the other end, sat the Abbot. Supper, like dinner, was a simple but tasteful meal. The two elder girls, Teresina and Nanetta, waited on the guests, and served the excellent wine grown on Olivo's hillsides. Both the marchese and the abbot paid their thanks to the young waitresses with playful and somewhat equivocal caresses to which a stricter parent than Olivo would probably have objected. Amalia seemed to be unaware of all this. She was pale, dejected, and looked like a woman determined to be old, since her own youth had ceased to interest her.

"Is this all that remains of my empire?" thought Casanova bitterly, contemplating her in profile. Yet perhaps it was the illumination which gave so gloomy a cast to Amalia's features. From the interior of the house no more than one broad bream of light fell upon the guests. Otherwise the glimmer in the sky sufficed them. The dark crests of the trees closed off all views; Casanova was reminded of a mysterious garden in which, late one evening many years before, he had awaited the coming of his mistress.

"Murano!" he whispered to himself, and trembled. Then he spoke aloud: "On an island near Venice there is a convent garden where I last set foot several decades ago. At night, there, the scent is just like this."

"I guess you were once also a monk," remarked the marchesa, sportively.

"Nearly," replied Casanova with a smile, explaining, truthfully enough, that when he was a lad of fifteen he had been given minor orders by the archbishop of Venice, but that before attaining full manhood he had decided to lay aside the cassock.

The abbot mentioned that there was a nunnery close at hand and strongly recommended Casanova visit the place if he had never seen it. Olivo heartily endorsed the recommendation, singing the praises of the picturesque old building, the attractive setting, and the rich diversity of the road leading there.

"The lady abbess, Sister Serafina," continued the abbot, "is an extremely learned woman, a duchess by birth. She has told me—by letter, of course, for the inmates are under a vow of perpetual silence—that she has heard of Marcolina's erudition, and would like to meet her face to face."

"I hope, Marcolina," said Lorenzi, speaking to her for the first time, "that you will not attempt to imitate the noble abbess in other respects as well as learning."

"Why should I?" rejoined Marcolina brightly. "We can maintain our freedom without vows. Better without than with, for a vow is a form of coercion."

Casanova was sitting next to her. He did not dare to let his foot touch hers lightly, or to press his knee against hers. He was certain that should she for the third time look at him with that expression of horror and loathing, he would be driven to some act of folly. As the meal progressed, as the number of emptied glasses grew and the conversation waxed livelier and more general, Casanova heard, once more as from afar, Amalia's voice.

"I have spoken to Marcolina."

"You have spoken to her?" A mad hope flamed up in him.

"Calm yourself, Casanova. We did not speak of you, but only of her and her plans for the future. I say to you again, she will never give herself to any man."

Olivo, who had been drinking freely, suddenly rose, glass in hand, and delivered himself of a few stumbling phrases concerning the great honor conferred upon his humble home by the visit of his dear friend, the Chevalier de Seingalt.

"But where, my dear Olivo, is the Chevalier de Seingalt of whom you speak?" inquired Lorenzi in his clear, insolent voice.

Casanova's first impulse was to throw the contents of his glass in Lorenzi's face.

Amalia touched his arm lightly, to restrain him, and said, "Many people today, Chevalier, still know you best by the old and more widely renowned name of Casanova."

"I was not aware," said Lorenzi, with offensive gravity, "that the King of France had ennobled Signor Casanova."

"I was able to save the King that trouble," answered Casanova quietly. "I trust, Lieutenant Lorenzi, that you will be satisfied with an explanation to which the Burgomaster of Nuremberg offered no objection when I gave it to him in circumstances with which I need not weary the company." There was a moment of silent expectation. Casanova continued, "The alphabet is our common heritage. I chose a collocation of letters which pleased my taste, and ennobled myself without being indebted to any prince, who might perhaps have been disinclined to allow my claim. I style myself Casanova, Chevalier de Seingalt. I am indeed sorry, Lieutenant Lorenzi, if this name fails to meet with your approval."

"Seingalt! It is a splendid name," said the abbot, repeating it several times, as if he were tasting it.

"There is not a man in the world," exclaimed Olivo, "who has a better right to name himself Chevalier than my distinguished friend Casanova!"

"As for you, Lorenzi," added the marchese, "when your reputation has reached as far as that of Signor Casanova, Chevalier de Seingalt, we will not hesitate, should you so desire, to give you also the title of Chevalier."

Casanova, somewhat nettled at not being allowed to fight his own battle, was about to resume the defense in person, when out of the dusk of the garden two elderly gentlemen, shabbily dressed, put in an appearance beside the table. Olivo greeted them with effusive cordiality, being delighted to turn the conversation and to put an end to a dispute that threatened to destroy the harmony of the evening. The newcomers were the brothers Ricardi. As Casanova had learned from Olivo, they were old bachelors. At one time members of the great world, they had been unfortunate in various undertakings. At length they had returned to their birthplace, the neighboring village, to lead a retired life in a wretched little house they had rented. They were eccentric fellows, but quite harmless.

The Ricardis expressed their delight at renewing their acquaintance with the chevalier, whom, they said, they had met in Paris a good many years ago.

Casanova could not recall the meeting.

"Perhaps it was in Madrid?" said the Ricardis.

"Maybe," replied Casanova, though he was absolutely certain that he had never seen either of them before.

The younger of the two was spokesman. The elder, who looked as if he might be ninety at least, accompanied his brother's words with incessant nods and grimaces.

By now everyone had left the table. The children had already disappeared earlier. Lorenzi and the marchesa were strolling in the dusk across the meadow, Marcolina and Amalia were in the hall, setting out the table for cards.

"What is the aim of all this?" said Casanova to himself, as he stood alone in the garden. "Do they imagine me to be rich? Are they on the lookout for plunder?"

These preparations, the ingratiating manners of the marchese, the sedulous attentions of the abbot, the appearance of the brothers Ricardi on the scene, were arousing his suspicions. Was it not possible that Lorenzi might be a party to the intrigue? Or Marcolina? Or even Amalia? For a moment it flashed through his mind that his enemies might be at work upon some scheme of the eleventh hour to make his return to Venice difficult or impossible. But a moment's reflection convinced him the notion was absurd—were it only because he no longer had any enemies. He was merely an old fellow in reduced circumstances. Who was likely to take any trouble to hinder his return to Venice? Glancing through the open window, he saw the company assembling around the table, where the cards lay ready, and the filled wineglasses were standing. It seemed to him clear beyond all possibility of doubt that there was nothing afoot except an ordinary, innocent game of cards, in which the coming of a new player is always an agreeable change.

Marcolina passed him and wished him good luck.

"Aren't you going to take a hand?" he said. "At least you will look on?"

"What point would there be? Good night, Chevalier."

From the interior, voices called out into the night: "Lorenzi."—"Chevalier."—"We are waiting for you."

Casanova, standing in the darkness, could see that the marchesa was trying to draw Lorenzi away from the open meadow into the greater darkness under the trees. There she began to press herself against him, but Lorenzi roughly tore himself away and strode toward the house. Meeting Casanova in the entry, he gave him precedence with mock politeness. Casanova accepted the precedence without a word of thanks.

The marchese was the first banker. Olivo, the brothers Ricardi, and the abbot staked such trifling amounts that to Casanova— even today when his whole worldly wealth consisted of no more than a few ducats—the game seemed ludicrous. All the more was this the case since the marchese raked in his winnings and paid out his losses with a ceremonious air, as if he were handling enormous sums. Suddenly Lorenzi, who had hitherto taken no part in the game, staked a ducat, won, let the doubled stake stand; won again and again, and continued to have the same luck with but occasional interruptions. The other men, however, went on staking petty coins, and the two Ricardis in particular appeared quite annoyed when the marchese seemed to treat them with less consideration than he treated Lieutenant Lorenzi. The two brothers played together upon the same hazard. Beads of perspiration formed upon the brow of the elder, who handled the cards. The younger, standing behind his brother, talked unceasingly, with the air of giving infallible counsel. When the silent brother won, the loquacious brother's eyes gleamed; but at a loss, he raised despairing eyes heavenward. The abbot, impassive for the most part, occasionally enunciated some scrap of proverbial wisdom. For instance: "Luck and women cannot be constrained." Or, "The earth is round, and heaven is far away." At times he looked at Casanova with an air of sly encouragement, his eyes moving on from Casanova to rest upon Amalia where she sat beside her husband. It seemed as if his chief concern must be to bring the erstwhile lovers together once again. As for Casanova, all he could think of was that Marcolina was in her room, undressing in leisurely fashion, and that if the window were open, her white skin must be gleaming into the night. Seized with desire so intense as almost to put him beside himself, he moved to rise from his place by the marchese and to leave the room. The marchese, however, interpreting this movement as a resolve to take a hand in the game, said, "At last! We were sure you would not be content to play the part of spectator, Chevalier."

The marchese dealt him a card. Casanova staked all he had on his person, about ten ducats, which was nearly the whole of his entire wealth. Without counting the amount, he emptied his purse on the table, hoping to lose it at a single cast. That would be a sign of luck. He had not troubled to think precisely what sort of luck it would signify, whether his speedy return to Venice, or the desired sight of Marcolina's nudity. But before he had made up his mind upon this point, the marchese had lost the venture. Like

Lorenzi, Casanova let the double stake lie; and just as in Lorenzi's case, fortune stood by him. The marchese no longer troubled himself to deal to the others. The silent Ricardi rose somewhat mortified; the other Ricardi wrung his hands. Then the two withdrew, dumbfounded, to a corner of the room. The abbot and Olivo took matters more phlegmatically. The former ate sweets and repeated his proverbial tags. The latter watched the turn of the cards with eager attention. At length the marchese had lost five hundred ducats to Casanova and Lorenzi. The marchesa moved to depart and looked significantly at the lieutenant on her way out of the room. Amalia accompanied her guest. The marchesa swung her hips in a manner that was extremely distasteful to Casanova. Amalia walked along beside her looking humble and aged. Now that the marchese had lost all his ready cash, Casanova became banker, and, considerably to the marchese's annoyance, he insisted that the others should return to the game. The brothers Ricardi took their places right away, eagerly and greedily. The abbot shook his head, saying he had had enough. Olivo played merely because he did not wish to be discourteous to his distinguished guest.

Lorenzi's luck held. When he had won four hundred ducats in all, he rose from the table, saying, "Tomorrow I shall be happy to give you your revenge. But now, by your leave, I shall ride home."

"Home!" cried the marchese with a scornful laugh—he had won back a few ducats by this time. "That is a strange way to phrase it!" He turned to the others: "The lieutenant is staying with me. My wife has already driven home. I hope you'll have a pleasant time, Lorenzi!"

"You know perfectly well," rejoined Lorenzi imperturbably, "that I shall ride straight to Mantua, and not to your place, to which you were so good as to invite me yesterday."

"You can ride to hell for all I care!" said the other.

Lorenzi politely took his leave of the rest of the company, and, to Casanova's astonishment, departed without making any suitable retort to the marchese. Casanova went on with the game, still winning, so that the marchese ere long was several hundred ducats in his debt. "What's the use of it all?" thought Casanova at first. But by degrees he was once more ensnared by the lure of the gaming table. "After all," he mused, "this is not going too badly. I shall soon be a thousand to the good, perhaps even two thousand.

The marchese will not fail to pay his debt. It would be pleasant to take a modest fortune with me to Venice. But why Venice? Who regains wealth, regains youth. Wealth is everything. At any rate, I shall now be able to buy her. Whom? The only woman I want. . . . She is standing naked at the window. . . . I am sure she is waiting there, expecting me to come. . . . She is standing at the window to drive me mad! And I am here."

All the same, with unruffled brow he continued dealing the cards, not only to the marchese, but also to Olivo and to the brothers Ricardi. To the latter from time to time he pushed over a gold piece to which they had no claim, but which they accepted without comment. The noise of a trotting horse came from the road. "Lorenzi," thought Casanova. The hoofbeats echoed for a time from the garden wall, until sound and echo gradually died away. At length, however, Casanova's luck turned. The marchese staked more and more boldly. By midnight Casanova was as poor as at the beginning; nay, poorer, for he had lost the few ducats with which he had made his first venture. Pushing the cards away, he stood up with a smile, saying, "Thank you, gentlemen, for a pleasant game."

Olivo stretched out both hands toward Casanova. "Dear friend, let us go on with the game. . . . You have a hundred and fifty ducats. Have you forgotten them? Not only a hundred and fifty ducats, but all that I have, everything, everything." His speech was thick, for he had been drinking throughout the evening.

Casanova signified his refusal with an exaggerated but courtly gesture. "Luck and women cannot be constrained," he said, bowing toward the abbot, who nodded contentedly and clapped his hands.

"Till tomorrow, then, my dear Chevalier," said the marchese. "We will join forces to win the money back from Lieutenant Lorenzi."

The brothers Ricardi insistently demanded that the game should continue. The marchese, who was in a jovial mood, opened a bank for them. They staked the gold pieces which Casanova had allowed them to win. In a couple of minutes they had lost them all to the marchese, who declined to go on playing unless they could produce cash. They wrung their hands. The elder began to cry like a child. The younger, to comfort his brother, kissed him on both cheeks. The marchese inquired whether the carriage had returned, and the abbot said he had heard it drive up half an hour earlier. Thereupon the marchese offered the abbot and the two Ricardis a lift, promising to set them down at their doors. All four left the house together.

When they had gone, Olivo took Casanova by the arm and assured his guest repeatedly, with tears in his voice, that everything in the house was at Casanova's absolute disposal. They walked past Marcolina's window. Not merely was the window closed, but the iron grating had been fastened; within, the window was curtained. There had been times, thought Casanova, when all these precautions had been unavailing, or had been without significance. They reentered the house. Olivo would not be dissuaded from accompanying the guest up the creaking staircase into the turret chamber. He embraced Casanova as he bade him good night.

"Tomorrow," he said, "you shall see the nunnery. But sleep as late as you please. We are not early risers here; anyhow we shall adapt the hours to your convenience. Good night!" He closed the door quietly behind him, but his heavy tread resounded through the house.

The room in which Casanova was now left to his own devices was dimly lighted by two candles. His gaze roamed successively to the four windows, looking to the four quarters of heaven. The prospect was much the same from them all. The landscape had a bluish sheen. He saw broad plains with no more than trifling elevations, except to the northward where the mountains were faintly visible. A few isolated houses, farms, and larger buildings, could be made out. Among these latter was one which stood higher than the rest. Here there was still a light in one of the windows, and Casanova imagined it must be the marchese's mansion. The furniture of the room was simple. The double bed stood straight out into the room. The two candles were on a long table. There were a few chairs and a chest of drawers bearing a gilt-framed mirror. Everything was in perfect order, and the valise had been unpacked. On the table, locked, lay the shabby portfolio containing Casanova's papers. There were also some books which he was using in his work and which he had therefore taken along; writing materials had been provided. He did not feel sleepy. Taking his manuscript out of the portfolio, he reread what he had last written. Since he had broken off in the middle of a paragraph, it was easy for him to continue. He took up the pen, wrote a nasty sentence or two, then paused.

"To what purpose?" he demanded of himself, as if in a cruel flash of inner illumination. "Even if I knew that what I am writing, what I am going to write, would be considered incomparably fine; even if I could really succeed in annihilating Voltaire, and in making my renown greater than his—would I not gladly commit these papers to the flames could I but have Marcolina in my arms? For that boon, should I not be willing to vow never to set foot in Venice again, even though the Venetians should wish to escort me back to the city in triumph?"

"Venice!" . . . He breathed the word once more. Its splendor captivated his imagination, and in a moment its old power over him had been restored. The city of his youth rose before his eyes, enveloped by all the magic of memory. His heart ached with a yearning more intense and painful than anything he thought ever to have felt before. To renounce the idea of returning home seemed to him the most incredible of the sacrifices which his destiny might demand. How could he go on living in this poor and faded world without the hope, without the certainty, of ever seeing the beloved city again? After the years and decades of wanderings and adventures, after all the happiness and unhappiness he had experienced, after all the honor and all the shame, after so many triumphs and so many humiliations—he must at length find a resting place, must at length find a home. Was there any other home for him than Venice? Was there any good fortune reserved for him other than this, that he should have a home once more? It was long since he had been able to command enduring happiness anywhere outside. He could still at times grasp happiness, but for a moment only; he could no longer hold it fast. His power over his fellows, over women no less than over men, had vanished. Only where he evoked memories could his words, his voice, his glance, still be arresting; apart from this, his presence was void of effect. His day was done! He was willing to admit what he had hitherto been especially eager to conceal from himself, that even his literary labors, including the polemic against Voltaire upon which his last hopes reposed, would never secure any notable success. Here, likewise, he was too late. Had he in youth but had leisure and patience to devote himself seriously to the work of the pen, he was confident he could have ranked with the leading members of the profession of authorship, with the greatest imaginative writers and philosophers. He was as sure of this as he was sure that, granted more perseverance and foresight than he actually possessed, he could have risen to supreme eminence as financier or as diplomat. But what happened to his patience and his foresight, what became of all his plans in life, when the lure of a new love adventure summoned? Women, always women. For them he had again and again cast everything to the winds; sometimes for women who were refined, sometimes for women who were vulgar; for passionate women and for frigid women; for maidens and for harlots. All the honors of this world and all of the bliss of the next had ever seemed cheap to him in comparison with a successful night upon a new love quest. Did he regret what he had lost through his perpetual seeking and never or forever finding, through this earthly and superearthly flitting from desire to pleasure and from pleasure back again to desire? No, he had no regrets. He had lived such a life as none other before him; and could he not still live it after his own fashion? Everywhere there remained women upon his path, even though they might no longer be quite so crazy about him as of old. Amalia? He could have her for the asking, at this very hour, in her drunken husband's bed. The hostess in Mantua; was she not in love with him, fired with affection and jealousy as if he were a handsome lad? Perotti's mistress, pockmarked, but a woman with a fine figure? The very name of Casanova had intoxicated her with its aroma of a thousand conquests. Had she not implored him to grant her but a single night of love; and had he not spurned her as one who could still choose where he pleased? But Marcolina—such as Marcolina were no longer at his disposal. Had such as Marcolina ever been at his disposal? Doubtless there were women of that kind. Maybe he had met such women before. Always, however, some more willing than she had been available, and he had never been the man to waste so much as a day in vain sighing. Since not even Lorenzi had succeeded with Marcolina, since she had rejected the hand of this comely officer who was as handsome and as bold as he, Casanova, had been in youth, Marcolina might well prove to be that wonder of the world in the existence of which he had hitherto disbelieved—the virtuous woman. At this point he laughed so freely that the walls echoed. "The bungler, the fool!" he exclaimed out loud, as so often in such self-communings. "He did not know how to make a good use of his opportunities. Or the marchesa was hanging round his neck all the time. Or perhaps he took her as a next-best, when Marcolina, the philosopher, the woman of learning, proved unattainable!"

Suddenly a thought struck him. "Tomorrow I will read her my polemic against Voltaire. I can think of no one else who would be a competent critic. I shall convince her. She will admire me. She will say: 'Excellent, Signor Casanova. Your style is magnificent, old fellow!' God! . . . 'You have positively annihilated Voltaire, you brilliant senior!'"

He paced the chamber like a beast in a cage, hissing out the words. A terrible wrath possessed him, against Marcolina, against Voltaire, against himself, against the whole world. It was all he could do to restrain himself from roaring aloud. At length he threw himself upon the bed without undressing, and lay with eyes wide open, looking up at the rafters among which silvery spiders' webs were visible, glistening in the candlelight. Then, as often happened to him after playing cards late at night, pictures of cards chased one another swiftly through his brain, until he sank into a dreamless sleep, which, however, lasted only briefly. When he awakened, he listened to the mysterious silence. The southern and the eastern windows of the turret chamber were open. Through them from the garden and the fields entered sweet odors of all kinds. Gradually the silence was broken by the vague noises from near and from far which usually herald the dawn. Casanova could no longer lie quiet; a vigorous impulse toward movement gripped him and lured him into the open. The song of the birds called to him; the cool breeze of early morning played upon his brow. Softly he opened the door and moved cautiously down the stairs. Cunning, from long experience, he was able to avoid making the old staircase creak. The lower flight, leading to the ground floor, was of stone. Through the hall, where half-emptied glasses were still standing on the table, he made his way into the garden. Since it was impossible to walk silently on the gravel, he promptly stepped on to the meadow which now, in the early twilight, seemed to extend limitlessly. He slipped into the side alley, from which he could see Marcolina's window. It was closed, barred, and curtained, just as it had been overnight. Barely fifty paces from the house, Casanova seated himself upon a stone bench. He heard a cart roll by on the other side of the wall, and then everything was quiet again. A fine gray haze was floating over the meadow, giving it the aspect of a partly transparent pond with hazy outlines. Once again Casanova thought of that night long ago in the convent garden at Murano; he thought of another garden on another night; he hardly knew what memories he was recalling; perchance it was a composite reminiscence of a hundred nights, just as at times a hundred women whom he had loved would fuse in memory into one figure that loomed enigmatically before his questioning senses. After all, was not one night just like another? Was not one woman just like another? Especially when the affair was past and gone? The phrase "past and gone" continued to hammer upon his temples, as if destined henceforth to become the pulse of his forlorn existence.

It seemed to him that something was rattling behind him along the wall. Or was it only an echo that he heard? Yes, the noise had really come from the house. Marcolina's window had suddenly been opened, the iron grating had been pushed back, the curtain drawn. A shadowy form was visible against the dark interior. Marcolina, clad in a white nightdress, was standing at the window, as if to breathe the fragrance of morning. In an instant, Casanova slipped behind the bench. Peeping over the top of it, through the foliage in the avenue, he watched Marcolina as if spellbound. She stood unthinking, it seemed, her gaze vaguely piercing the twilight. Not until several seconds had elapsed did she appear to collect herself, to grow fully awake and aware, directing her eyes slowly, now to right and now to left. Then she leaned forward, as if seeking for something on the gravel, and next she turned her head, from which her hair was hanging loosely, and looked up toward the windows in the upper story. Thereafter, she stood motionless for a while, supporting herself with a hand on either side of the window frame as though she were fastened to an invisible cross. Now at length, suddenly illumined as it were from within, her features grew plain to Casanova's vision. A smile flitted across her face. Her arms fell to her sides; her lips moved strangely, as if whispering a prayer; once more she looked searchingly across the garden, then nodded almost imperceptibly, and at the instant someone who must hitherto have been crouching at her feet swung across the sill into the open. It was Lorenzi. He flew rather than walked across the gravel into the alley, which he crossed barely ten yards from Casanova, who held his breath as he lay behind the bench. Lorenzi, hastening on, made his way down a narrow strip of grass running along the wall, and disappeared from view. Casanova heard a door groan on its hinges—the very door doubtless through which he, Olivo, and the marchese had reentered the garden on the previous day—and then all was still. Marcolina had remained motionless. As soon as she knew that Lorenzi was safely away, she drew a deep breath, and closed grating and window. The curtain fell back into its place, and all was as it had been. Except for one thing; for now, as if there were no longer any reason for delay, day dawned over house and garden.

Casanova was still lying behind the bench, his arms outstretched before him. After a while he crept on all fours to the middle of the alley, and thence onward till he reached a place where he could not be seen from Marcolina's window or from any of the others. Rising to his feet with an aching back, he stretched body and limbs and felt himself restored to his senses, as though retransformed from a whipped hound into a human being— doomed to feel the chastisement, not as bodily pain, but as profound humiliation.

"Why," he asked himself, "did I not go to the window while it was still open? Why did I not leap over the sill? Could she have offered any resistance; would she have dared to do so; hypocrite, liar, strumpet?"

He continued to rail at her as though he had a right to do so, as though he had been her lover to whom she had pledged faithfulness and whom she had betrayed. He swore to question her face to face; to denounce her before Olivo, Amalia, the marchese, the abbot, the servants, as nothing better than a lustful little whore. As if for practice, he recounted to himself in detail what he had just witnessed, delighting in the invention of incidents which would degrade her yet further. He would say that she had stood naked at the window; that she had permitted the unchaste caresses of her lover while the morning wind played upon them both. After thus allaying the first vehemence of his anger, he turned to consider whether he might not make a better use of his present knowledge. Was she not in his power? Could he not now exact by threats the favors which she had not been willing to grant him for love? But this infamous design was speedily abandoned; not so much because Casanova realized its infamy, as because, even while the plan crossed his mind, he was aware of its futility. Why should Marcolina, accountable to no one but herself, be concerned at his threats? In the last resort she was astute enough, if needs must, to have him driven from the house as a slanderer and blackmailer. Even if, for one reason or another, she were willing to give herself to him in order to preserve the secret of her amours with Lorenzi (he was aware that he was speculating on something beyond the bounds of possibility), a pleasure thus extorted would become for him a nameless torment. Casanova knew himself to be one whose rapture in a love relationship was a thousandfold greater when conferring pleasure than when receiving it. Such a victory as he was contemplating would drive him to frenzy and despair. Suddenly he found himself at the door in the garden wall. It was locked. Then Lorenzi had a master key! But who, it now occurred to him to ask, had ridden the horse he had heard trotting away after Lorenzi had left the card table? A servant hired for the purpose, obviously. Involuntarily Casanova smiled his approval. They were worthy of one another, these two, Marcolina and Lorenzi, the woman philosopher and the officer. A splendid career lay before them.

"Who will be Marcolina's next lover?" he thought questioningly. "The professor in Bologna in whose house she lives? Fool, fool! That is doubtless an old story. Who next? Olivo? The abbot? Wherefore not? Or the serving lad who stood gaping at the door yesterday when we drove up? She has given herself to all of them. I am sure of it. But Lorenzi does not know. There at least I have the edge over him."

Yet all the while he was inwardly convinced that Lorenzi was Marcolina's first lover. Nay, he even suspected that the previous night was the first on which she had given herself to Lorenzi. Nevertheless, as he made the circuit in the garden within the wall, he continued to indulge these spiteful, lascivious fantasies. At length he reached the hall door, which he had left open, and saw that for the moment there was nothing left for him to do but to regain the turret chamber unseen and unheard. With all possible caution he crept upstairs and sank into the armchair which stood in front of the table. The loose leaves of the manuscript seemed to have been awaiting his return. Involuntarily his eyes fell upon the sentence in the middle of which he had broken off. He read, "Voltaire will doubtless prove immortal. But this immortality will have been purchased at the price of his immortal part. Wit has consumed his heart just as doubt has consumed his soul, and therefore . . ."

At this moment the morning sun flooded the chamber with red light, so that the page in his hand glowed. As if vanquished, he laid it on the table beside the others. Suddenly aware that his lips were dry, he poured himself a glass of water from the carafe on the table; the drink was lukewarm and sweetish to the taste. Nauseated, he turned his head away from the glass and found himself facing his image in the mirror upon the chest of drawers. A wan, aging countenance with disheveled hair stared back at him. In a self-tormenting mood he allowed the corners of his mouth to droop even more, as if he were playing a cheap role on the stage; disarranged his hair yet more wildly; put out his tongue at his own image in the mirror; croaked a string of inane invectives against himself; and finally, like a naughty child, blew the leaves of his manuscript from the table on to the floor. Then he began to rail against Marcolina again. He loaded her with obscene epithets. "Do you imagine," he hissed between his teeth, "that your pleasure will last? You will become fat and wrinkled and old just like the other women who were young when you were young. You will be an old woman with flaccid breasts; your hair will be dry and grizzled; you will be toothless, you will have a bad smell. Last of all you will die. Perhaps you will die while you are still quite young. You will become a mass of corruption, food for worms."

To wreak final vengeance upon her, he endeavored to picture her as dead. He saw her lying in an open coffin, wrapped in a white shroud. But he was unable to attach to her image any sign of decay, and her unearthly beauty aroused him to renewed frenzy. Through his closed eyelids he saw the coffin transform itself into a nuptial bed. Marcolina lay laughing there with lambent eyes. As if in mockery, with her small, white hands she tore open the white garment covering her firm little breasts. But as he stretched forth his arms toward her, in the moment when he was about to clasp her in his passionate embrace, the vision faded.

Someone was knocking at the door. Casanova awoke from a heavy sleep to find Olivo standing before him.

"At your writing so early?"

Casanova promptly collected his wits. "It is my custom," he said, "to devote the early morning hours to my work. What time is it?"

"Eight o'clock," answered Olivo. "Breakfast is ready in the garden. We will start on our drive to the nunnery as early as you please, Chevalier. How the wind has blown your papers about!"

He stooped to pick up the fallen sheets. Casanova did not interfere. He had moved to the window, and was looking down upon the breakfast table which had been set on the meadow in the shade of the house. Amalia, Marcolina, and the three young girls, all dressed in white, were at breakfast. They called up a good morning. He had no eyes for anyone but Marcolina, who smiled at him frankly and in the friendliest fashion. In her lap was a plateful of early-ripe grapes, and she popped them into her mouth one after the other. Contempt, anger, and hatred vanished from Casanova's heart. All he knew was that he loved her. Made drunken by the very sight of her, he turned away from the window to find Olivo on hands and knees still assembling the scattered pages of manuscript from under the table and chest of drawers. "Don't trouble any further," he said to his host. "Leave me to myself for a moment while I get ready for the drive."

"No hurry," answered Olivo, rising, and brushing the dust from his knees. "We shall easily be home in time for lunch. We want to get back early, anyhow, for the marchese would like us to begin cards early in the afternoon. I suppose he wants to leave before sunset."

"It doesn't matter to me what time you begin cards," said Casanova, as he arranged his manuscript in the portfolio. "Whatever happens, I shall not take a hand in the game."

"Yes you will," explained Olivo with a decision foreign to his usual manner. Laying a roll of gold pieces on the table, he continued, "Thus do I pay my debt, Chevalier. A belated settlement, but it comes from a grateful heart."

Casanova made a gesture of refusal.

"I insist," said Olivo. "If you do not take the money, you will wound us deeply. Besides, last night Amalia had a dream which will certainly induce you—but I will let her tell the story herself."

He turned and left the room precipitately. Casanova counted the money. Yes, there were one hundred and fifty gold pieces, the very sum that fifteen years earlier he had presented to the bridegroom, the bride, or the bride's mother—he had forgotten which.

"The most sensible thing I could do," he mused, "would be to pack up the money, say farewell to Olivo and Amalia, and leave the place at once, if possible without seeing Marcolina again. Yet when was I ever guided by reason?—I wonder if news has reached Mantua from Venice? But my good hostess promised to forward without fail anything that might arrive."

The maid meanwhile had brought a large earthenware pitcher filled with water freshly drawn from the spring. Casanova sponged himself all over. Greatly refreshed, he dressed in his best suit, the one he had intended to wear the previous evening had there been time to change. Now, however, he was delighted that he would be able to appear before Marcolina better clad than on the previous day, to present himself in a new form as it were.

So he sauntered into the garden wearing a coat of gray satin richly embroidered and trimmed with Spanish lace; a yellow waistcoat; and kneebreeches of cherry-colored silk. His aspect was that of a man who was distinguished without being proud. An amiable smile played about his lips, and his eyes sparkled with the fire of inextinguishable youth. To his disappointment, he found no one but Olivo, who bade him be seated, and invited him to fall to upon the modest fare. Casanova's breakfast consisted of bread, butter, milk, and eggs, followed by peaches and grapes, which seemed to him the finest he had ever eaten. Now the three girls came running across the lawn. Casanova kissed them in turn, bestowing on the thirteen-year-old Teresina such caresses as the abbot had been free with on the previous day. Her eyes gleamed in a way with which Casanova was familiar. He was convinced this meant something more to her than childish amusement. Olivo was delighted to see how well the chevalier got on with the girls. "Must you really leave us tomorrow morning?" he inquired shyly and gently.

"This very evening," rejoined Casanova jovially. "You know, my dear Olivo, I must consider the wishes of the Venetian senators. . . ."

"How have they earned the right to any such consideration from you?" broke in Olivo. "Let them wait. Stay here for another two days at least; or, better still, for a week."

Casanova slowly shook his head. He had seized Teresina's hands, and held her prisoner between his knees. She drew herself gently away, with a smile no longer that of a child. At this moment Amalia and Marcolina emerged from the house, the former wearing a black shawl, the latter a white one draped over their light-colored garments. Olivo besought them to second his invitation. But when neither found a word to say on the matter, Casanova's voice and expression assumed an unduly severe emphasis as he answered, "Quite out of the question."

On the way through the chestnut avenue to the road, Marcolina asked Casanova whether he had made satisfactory progress with the polemic. Olivo had told her that his guest had been at the writing table since early morning.

Casanova was half inclined to make an answer that would have been malicious in its ambiguity, and would have taken her aback without betraying himself. Reflecting, however, that premature advances could do his cause nothing but harm, he held his wit in leash and civilly rejoined that he had been content to make a few emendations, the fruit of his conversation with her yesterday. Now they all seated themselves in the lumbering carriage. Casanova sat opposite Marcolina, Olivo opposite Amalia. The vehicle was so roomy that, notwithstanding the inevitable joltings, the inmates were not unduly jostled one against the other. Casanova begged Amalia to tell him her dream. She smiled cordially, almost brightly, no longer displaying any trace of mortification or resentment.

"In my dream, Casanova, I saw you driving past a white building in a splendid carriage drawn by six chestnut horses. Or rather, the carriage pulled up in front of this building, and at first I did not know who was seated inside. Then you got out. You were wearing a magnificent white court dress embroidered with gold, so that your appearance was almost more resplendent than it is today." Her tone conveyed a spice of gentle mockery. "You were wearing, I am sure of it, the thin gold chain you are wearing to-day, and yet I had never seen it until this morning!" This chain, with the gold watch and gold snuffbox set with garnets (Casanova was fingering it as she spoke), were the only trinkets of value still left to him. "An old man, looking like a beggar, opened the carriage door. It was Lorenzi. As for you, Casanova, you were young, quite young, younger even than you seemed to me in those days." She said "in those days" quite unconcernedly, regardless of the fact that in the train of these words all her memories came attendant, winging their way like a flight of birds. "You bowed right and left, although there was not a soul within sight; then you entered the house. The door slammed to behind you. I did not know whether the storm had slammed it, or Lorenzi. So startling was the noise that the horses took fright and galloped away with the carriage. Then came a clamor from neighboring streets, as if people were trying to save themselves from being run over; but soon all was quiet again. Next I saw you at one of the windows. Now I knew it was a gaming house. Once more you bowed in all directions, though the whole time there was no one to be seen. You looked over your shoulder, as if someone were standing behind you in the room; but I knew that no one was there. Now, of a sudden, I saw you at another window, in a higher story, where the same gestures were repeated. Then higher still, and higher, and yet higher, as if the building were piled story upon story, interminably. From each window in succession, you bowed toward the street, and then turned to speak to persons behind you—who were not really there at all. Lorenzi, meanwhile, kept on running up the stairs, flight after flight, but was never able to overtake you. He wanted you because you had forgotten to give him a gratuity. . . ."

"What next?" inquired Casanova, when Amalia paused.

"There was a great deal more, but I have forgotten," said Amalia.

Casanova was disappointed. In such cases, whether he was relating a dream or giving an account of real incidents, it was his way to round off the narrative, attempting to convey a meaning. He remarked discontentedly, "How strangely everything is distorted in dreams. Fancy, that I should be wealthy; and that Lorenzi should be a beggar, and old!"

"As far as Lorenzi is concerned," interjected Olivo, "there is not much wealth about him. His father is fairly well off, but no one can say that of the son."

Casanova had no need to ask questions. He was speedily informed that it was through the marchese that they had made the lieutenant's acquaintance. The marchese had brought Lorenzi to the house only a few weeks before. A man of the chevalier's wide experience would hardly need prompting to enlighten him as to the nature of the young officer's relationship to the marchesa. After all, if the husband had no objection, the affair was nobody else's business.

"I think, Olivo," said Casanova, "that you have allowed yourself to be convinced of the marchese's complaisance too easily. Did you not notice his manner toward the young man, the mingling of contempt and ferocity? I should not like to wager that all will end well."

Marcolina remained impassive. She seemed to pay no attention to this talk about Lorenzi, but sat with unruffled countenance, and to all appearance quietly delighting in the landscape. The road led upward by a gentle ascent zigzagging through groves of olives and holly trees. Now they reached a place where the horses had to go more slowly, and Casanova alighted to stroll beside the carriage. Marcolina talked of the lovely scenery round Bologna, and of the evening walks she was in the habit of taking with Professor Morgagni's daughter. She also mentioned that she was planning a journey to France next year, in order to make the personal acquaintance of Saugrenue, the celebrated mathematician at the University of Paris, with whom she had corresponded. "Perhaps," she said with a smile, "I may look in at Ferney on the way, in order to learn from Voltaire's own lips how he has been affected by the polemic of the Chevalier de Seingalt, his most formidable adversary."

Casanova was walking with a hand on the side of the carriage, close to Marcolina's arm. Her loose sleeve was touching his fingers. He answered coolly, "It matters less what Monsieur Voltaire thinks about the matter than what posterity thinks. A final decision upon the merits of the controversy must be left to the next generation."

"Do you really think," said Marcolina earnestly, "that final decisions can be reached in questions of this sort?"

"I am surprised that you should ask such a thing, Marcolina. Though your philosophic views, and (if the term be appropriate) your religious views, seem to me by no means irrefutable, at least they must be firmly established in your soul—if you believe that there is a soul."

Marcolina, ignoring the jabs in Casanova's words, sat looking tranquilly toward the sky, its dark blue spreading over the tree crests, and replied, "Sometimes, and especially on a day like this"—to Casanova, knowing what he knew, the words conveyed the thrill of reverence in the newly awakened heart of a woman—"I feel as if all that people speak of as philosophy and religion were no more than playing with words. A game nobler perhaps than others, but still more meaningless than them all. Infinity and eternity will never be within the grasp of our understanding. Our path leads from birth to death. What else is left for us than to live a life accordant with the law that each of us bears within—or a life of rebellion against that law? For rebellion and submissiveness both issue from God."

Olivo looked at his niece with timid admiration, then turned to contemplate Casanova with some anxiety. Casanova was in search of a rejoinder which should convince Marcolina that she was in one breath affirming and denying God, or should prove to her that she was proclaiming God and the devil to be the same. He realized, however, that he had nothing but empty words to set against her feelings, and today even these did not come to him readily. His expression showed him to be somewhat at a loss, and apparently reminded Amalia of the confused menaces he had uttered on the previous day. So she hastened to remark, "Marcolina is deeply religious all the same, I can assure you, Chevalier."

Marcolina smiled dreamily.

"We are all religious in our several ways," said Casanova politely, looking straight ahead.

Now came a turn in the road, and the nunnery was in sight. The slender tops of cypresses showed above the encircling wall. At the sound of the approaching carriage, the great doors had swung open. The porter, an old man with a flowing white beard, bowed gravely and gave them admittance. Through the cloisters, between the columns of which they caught glimpses of an overgrown, dark green garden, they advanced toward the main building, from whose unadorned, gray, and prisonlike exterior an unpleasantly cool air wafted over them. Olivo pulled the bellrope; the answering sound was high-pitched, and died away in a moment. A veiled nun silently appeared and ushered the guests into the bare and spacious parlor. It contained merely a few plain wooden chairs, and the back was cut off by a heavy iron grating, beyond which nothing could be seen but a vague darkness. With bitterness in his heart, Casanova recalled the adventure which still seemed to him the most wonderful of all his experiences. It had begun in just such surroundings as the present. Before his eyes loomed the forms of the two inmates of the Murano convent who had been friends in their love for him. In conjunction they had bestowed upon him hours of incomparable sweetness. When Olivo, in a whisper, began to speak of the strict discipline imposed upon this sisterhood—once they were professed, the nuns must never show their face unveiled before a man, and furthermore they were condemned to perpetual silence—a smile flitted across Casanova's face and promptly faded.

The abbess suddenly emerged in their midst from out of the gloom. In silence she saluted her guests, and with an exaggerated reverence of her veiled head acknowledged Casanova's expressions of gratitude for the admission of himself, a stranger. But when Marcolina wished to kiss her hand, the abbess gathered the girl in her arms. Then, with a wave of the hand inviting them to follow, she led the way through a small room into a cloister surrounding a quadrangular flower garden. In contrast to the outer garden, which had run wild, this inner garden was tended with especial care. The flower beds, brilliant in the sunshine, showed a wonderful play of glowing and fading colors. The warm odors were almost intoxicating. One, intermingled with the rest, aroused no responsive echo in Casanova's memory. Puzzled, he was about to say a word on the subject to Marcolina, when he perceived that the enigmatic, stimulating fragrance emanated from herself. She had removed her shawl from her shoulders and was carrying it over her arm. From the opening of her now more loosely falling gown came a perfume at once kindred to that of the thousand flowers of the garden, and yet unique.

The abbess, still without a word, conducted the visitors between the flower beds upon narrow, winding paths which traversed the garden like a delicate labyrinth. The graceful ease of her gait showed how much she herself was enjoying the chance of showing others the motley splendors of her garden. As if she had determined to make her guests giddy, she moved on faster and ever faster like the leader of a lively folk dance. Then, quite suddenly, so that Casanova seemed to awaken from a confusing dream, they all found themselves in the parlor once more. On the other side of the grating, dim figures were moving. It was impossible to distinguish whether, behind the thick bars, three or five or twenty veiled women were flitting to and fro like startled ghosts. Indeed, none but Casanova, with eyes preternaturally acute to pierce the darkness, could discern that they were human outlines at all. The abbess attended her guests to the door, mutely gave them a sign of farewell, and vanished before they had found time to express their thanks for her courtesy. Suddenly, just as they were about to leave the parlor, a woman's voice near the grating uttered the word "Casanova." Nothing but his name, in a tone that seemed to him quite unfamiliar. From whom came this breach of a sacred vow? Was it a woman he had once loved, or a woman he had never seen before? Did the syllables convey the ecstasy of an unexpected reencounter, or the pain of something irrecoverably lost; or did they tremble with the lamentation that an ardent wish of earlier days had been so late and so fruitlessly fulfilled? Casanova could not tell. All that he knew was that his name, which had so often voiced the whispers of tender affection, the stammerings of passion, the acclamations of happiness, had today for the first time pierced his heart with the full resonance of love. But, for this very reason, any further curiosity would have seemed to him ignoble and foolish. The door closed behind the party, shutting in a secret which he was never to unriddle. Were it not that the expression on each face had shown timidly and hastily that the call to Casanova had reached the ears of all, each might have thought himself or herself a prey to illusion. No one uttered a word as they walked through the cloisters to the great doors. Casanova followed behind, with bowed head, as if on the occasion of some profoundly affecting farewell.

The porter was waiting. He received his alms. The visitors stepped into the carriage, and immediately started on the road homeward. Olivo seemed embarrassed, Amalia removed. Marcolina, however, was quite unmoved. Too pointedly, in Casanova's estimation, she attempted to engage Amalia in a discussion of household affairs, a topic upon which Olivo was compelled to come to his wife's assistance. Casanova soon joined in the discussion, which turned upon matters relating to kitchen and cellar. An expert on these topics as well, he saw no reason why he should keep his knowledge and experience to himself, and he seized the opportunity of giving a fresh proof of versatility. Amalia then roused herself from her absent mood. After their recent experience—at once incredible and haunting—everyone, but especially Casanova, derived a certain comfort from an extremely commonplace atmosphere of mundane life. When the carriage reached home, where an inviting odor of roast meat and cooking vegetables greeted them, Casanova was in the midst of an appetizing description of a Polish pasty, a description to which even Marcolina attended, as it seemed to Casanova, with a flattering air of domesticity.

In a strangely tranquilized, almost happy mood, which was a surprise to himself, Casanova sat at table with the others, and paid court to Marcolina in the joking, high-spirited manner which might seem appropriate from a distinguished elderly gentleman toward a well-bred young woman of the middle class. She accepted his attentions and returned them with perfect grace. He found it difficult to believe that his demure neighbor was the same Marcolina from whose bedroom window he had seen a young officer emerge, a man who had obviously held her in his arms but a few moments earlier. It was equally difficult for him to realize how this tender girl, who was fond of romping on the grass with other children, could conduct a learned correspondence with Saugrenue, the renowned mathematician of Paris. Yet at the same time he derided himself for the ridiculous sluggishness of his imagination. Had he not learned a thousand times that in the souls of all truly vital persons, discrepant and even apparently hostile elements may coexist in perfect harmony? He himself, who shortly before had been a profoundly disturbed, a desperate man, ready for evil deeds, was now so gentle, so kindly, in so merry a mood, that Olivo's little daughters were shaking their sides with laughter. Nevertheless, as was usual with him after strong excitement, his appetite was positively ferocious, and this served to warn him that order was not yet fully restored in his soul.

With the last course, the maid brought in a despatch which had just arrived for the chevalier by special messenger from Mantua. Olivo noticed that Casanova grew pale from excitement. He told the servant to provide the messenger with refreshment, then turned to his guest.

"Pray don't stand upon ceremony, Chevalier. Read your letter."

"If you will excuse me," answered Casanova. He rose with a slight bow, went to the window and opened the missive with simulated indifference. It was from Signor Bragadino, an old friend of the family and a confirmed bachelor, over eighty years of age, and for the last decade a member of the Supreme Council. He had shown more interest than other patrons in pressing Casanova's suit. The writing had an exceptionally delicate appearance, although the characters were a little shaky. The letter read as follows:

My dear Casanova:

I am delighted at last to be able to send you news which will, I hope, be substantially accordant with your wishes. The Supreme Council, at its last sitting, which took place yesterday evening, did not merely express its willingness to permit your return to Venice, but also even desires that this return of yours should be as speedy as possible, since there is an intention to turn to immediate account the active gratitude which you have pledged in so many of your letters.

Since Venice has been deprived for so long of your presence, you may perhaps be unaware, my dear Casanova, that quite recently the internal affairs of our beloved native city have taken a rather unfavorable trend both politically and morally. Secret societies have come into existence, directed against the constitution of the Venetian state, and even, it would seem, aiming at its forcible overthrow. As might be expected, the members of these societies, persons whom it would not be too harsh to call conspirators, are chiefly drawn from certain freethinking, irreligious, and in every sense lawless circles. Not to speak of what goes on in private, we learn that in the public squares and in coffeehouses, the most outrageous, the most treasonable conversations, take place. But only in exceptional instances has it been possible to catch the guilty in the act, or to secure definite proof against the offenders. A few admissions have been enforced by the rack, but these confessions have proved so untrustworthy that several members of the Council are of opinion that for the future it would be better to abstain from methods of investigation which are not only cruel but are apt to lead us astray. Of course there is no lack of individuals who stand behind public order and the welfare of the state, individuals who would be delighted to place their services at the disposal of the government; but most of them are so well known as staunch supporters of the existing constitution that when they are present, people are reserved in what they say and are most unlikely to give vent to treasonable talk.

At yesterday's sitting, one of the senators, whom I will not name, expressed the opinion that a man who had the reputation of being without moral principle and who was furthermore regarded as a freethinker—in short, Casanova, such a man as yourself—if recalled to Venice would not fail to secure prompt and sympathetic welcome in the very circles which the government regards with suspicion. If he played his cards well, such a man would soon inspire the most absolute confidence.

In my opinion, irresistibly and as if by the force of a law of nature, there would gravitate around your person the very elements which the Supreme Council, in its indefatigable zeal for the state, is most eager to render harmless and to punish in an exemplary manner. For your part, my dear Casanova, you would give us an acceptable proof of your patriotic zeal, and would furnish in addition an infallible sign of your complete conversion from all those tendencies for which, during your imprisonment in The Leads, you had to atone by punishment which, though severe, was not, as you now see for yourself (if we are to believe your epistolary assurances), altogether unmerited. Should you be prepared, immediately on your return home, to act in the way previously suggested, to seek acquaintance with the elements sufficiently specified above, to introduce yourself to them in the friendliest fashion as one who cherishes the same tendencies, and to furnish the Senate with accurate and full reports of everything which might seem to you suspicious or worthy of note.

For these services the authorities would offer you, to begin with, a salary of two hundred and fifty lire per month, apart from special payments in cases of exceptional importance. I need hardly say that you would receive in addition, without too close a scrutiny of the items, an allowance for such expenses as you might incur in the discharge of your duties (I refer, for instance, to the treating of this individual or of that, little gifts made to women, and so on).

I do not attempt to conceal from myself that you may have to fight down certain scruples before you will feel inclined to fulfill our wishes. Permit me, however, as your old and sincere friend (who is himself young once), to remind you that it can never be regarded as dishonorable for a man to perform any services that may be essential for the safety of his beloved fatherland—even if, to a shallow-minded and unpatriotic citizen, such services might seem to be of an unworthy character. Let me add, Casanova, that your knowledge of human nature will certainly enable you to draw a distinction between levity and criminality, to differentiate the jester from the heretic. Thus it will be within your power, in appropriate cases, to temper justice with mercy, and to deliver up to punishment those only who, in your honest opinion, may deserve it.

Above all I would ask you to consider that, should you reject the gracious proposal of the Supreme Council, the fulfillment of your dearest wish—your return to Venice—is likely to be postponed for a long and I fear for an indefinite period; and that I myself, if I may allude to the matter, as an old man of eighty-one, would in all human probability have to renounce the pleasing prospect of ever seeing you again.

Since, for obvious reasons, your appointment will be of a confidential and not of a public nature, I beg you to address to me personally your reply, for which I make myself responsible, and which I wish to present to the Council at its next sitting a week hence. Act with all convenient speed, for, as I have previously explained, we are daily receiving offers from for the most part thoroughly trustworthy persons who in their patriotism voluntarily place themselves at the disposal of the Supreme Council. Nevertheless, there is hardly one among them who can compare with you, my dear Casanova, in respect of experience or intelligence. If, in addition to all the arguments I have adduced, you take my affection for you into account, I find it difficult to doubt that you will gladly respond to the call which now reaches you from so exalted and so friendly a source.

Till then, receive the assurances of my undying friendship.

BRAGADINO

Postscript. Immediately upon receipt of your acceptance, it will be a pleasure to me to send you a remittance of two hundred lire through the banking firm of Valori in Mantua. The sum is to defray the cost of your journey.

B.

Long after Casanova had finished reading the letter, he stood holding the paper so as to conceal his distorted features and the deathly pallor of his countenance. From the dining table came a continuous noise, the rattle of plates and the clinking of glasses; but conversation had entirely ceased. At length Amalia ventured to say, "The food is getting cold, Chevalier; won't you go on with your meal?"

"You must excuse me," replied Casanova, letting his face be

seen once more, for by now, owing to his extraordinary ability to mask his expressions, he had regained outward composure. "I have just received excellent news from Venice, and I must reply instantly. With your leave, I will go to my room."

"Suit yourself, Chevalier," said Olivo. "But do not forget that our card game begins in an hour."

In the turret chamber Casanova sank into a chair. A cold sweat broke out over his body; chills took hold of him; he was seized with such nausea that he felt as if he were about to choke. For a time he was unable to think clearly, and he could do no more than devote his energies to the task of self-restraint without quite knowing why he did so. But there was no one in the house upon whom he could vent his extreme fury; and he was still able to recognize the utter absurdity of a half-formed idea that Marcolina must be in some way contributory to the intolerable shame which had been put upon him. As soon as he was in some degree once more master of himself, his first thought was to take revenge on the scoundrels who had believed that he could be hired as a police spy. He would steal his way to Venice in disguise and would exert his cunning to bring about the death of these wretches—or at least of whomever it was that had conceived the despicable design. Was it perhaps Bragadino himself? Why not? An old man so lost to all sense of shame that he had dared to write such a letter to Casanova; a dotard who could think that Casanova, whom he had personally known, was no better than a spy! He no longer knew Casanova! Nor did anyone know him, in Venice or elsewhere. But people should learn to know him once more. It was true that he was no longer young enough or handsome enough to seduce an honest girl. Nor did he now have the skill and the agility needed for an escape from prison, or for gymnastic feats upon the rooftops. But in spite of his age, he was still cleverer than anyone else! Once back in Venice, he could do anything he pleased. The first step, the essential step, was to get back. Perhaps it would not be necessary to kill anyone. There were other kinds of revenge, more ingenious, more devilish, than a commonplace murder. If he were to feign acceptance of the Council's proposal, it would be the easiest thing in the world to destroy those whom he wished to destroy, instead of ruining those whom the authorities had in mind, and who were doubtless the finest fellows among all the inhabi-

tants of Venice! What! Because they were the enemies of this infamous government, because they were reputed heretics, were they
to go to The Leads where he had languished twenty-five years ago,
or even to die under the executioner's axe? He detested the government a hundred times more than they did, and with better reason. He had been a lifelong heretic; was a heretic today, with even
more holy conviction than them all. What a twisted comedy he
had been playing of late years—out of boredom and disgust. He
believe in God? What sort of a God was it who was gracious only
to the young, and left the old in the lurch? A God who, when the
fancy took him, became a devil; who transformed wealth into
poverty, fortune into misfortune, happiness into despair. "You play
with us—and we are to worship you? To doubt your existence is
the only resource left open to us if we are not to blaspheme you!
You do not exist; for if you did exist, I should curse you!"

Shaking his clenched fists heavenward, he rose to his feet. Involuntarily, a detested name rose to his lips. Voltaire! Yes, now
he was in the right mood to finish his polemic against the sage of
Ferney. To finish it? No, now was the time to begin it. A new one!
A different one! One in which the ridiculous old fool should be
shown up as he deserved: for his pusillanimity, his halfheartedness, his subservience. He an unbeliever? A man of whom the latest news was that he was on excellent terms with the priests, that
he visited church, and on feast days actually went to confession!
He a heretic? He was a gossip, a boastful coward, nothing more!
But the day of reckoning was at hand, and soon there would be
nothing left of the great philosopher but a pen-pushing buffoon.
What airs he had given himself, this worthy Monsieur Voltaire!
"My dear Monsieur Casanova, I am really vexed with you. What
concern have I with the works of Merlin? It is your fault that I
have wasted four hours over such nonsense."

All a matter of taste, excellent Monsieur Voltaire! People will
continue to read Merlin long after *La Pucelle* has been forgotten.
Possibly they will continue to prize my sonnets, the sonnets you
returned to me with a shameless smile, and without saying a word
about them. But these are trifles. Do not let us spoil a great opportunity because of our touchiness as authors. We are concerned
with philosophy—with God! We shall cross swords, Monsieur
Voltaire, please just don't die before I have a chance to deal with
you.

He was already thinking of immediately beginning his new polemic, when it occurred to him that the messenger was waiting for an answer. He hastily composed a letter to the old fool Bragadino, a letter full of hypocritical humility and simulated delight. With joy and gratitude he accepted the pardon of the Council. He would expect the remittance by return of post, so that with all possible speed he might present himself before his patrons, and above all before the honored old family friend, Bragadino. When he was just sealing the letter, someone knocked gently at the door. Olivo's eldest daughter, the thirteen-year-old Teresina, entered, to tell him that the whole company was assembled below, and that the chevalier was impatiently awaited at the card table. Her eyes gleamed strangely; her cheeks were flushed; her thick, black hair lay loose upon her temples; her little mouth was half open.

"Have you been drinking wine, Teresina?" asked Casanova striding toward her.

"Yes. How did you know?" She blushed deeper, and in her embarrassment she moistened her lips with her tongue.

Casanova seized her by the shoulders, and, breathing in her face, drew her with him and threw her on the bed. She looked at him with great helpless eyes in which the light was now extinguished. But when she opened her mouth as if to scream, Casanova's aspect was so menacing that she was almost paralyzed with fear, and let him do whatever he pleased. He kissed her with a tender fierceness, whispering, "You must not tell the abbot anything about this, Teresina, not even in confession. Some day, when you have a lover or a husband, there is no reason why he should know anything about it. You should in fact always lie. Never tell the truth to your father, your mother, or your sisters, that it may be well with you on earth. Mark my words."

As he spoke thus blasphemously, Teresina seemed to regard his utterance as a kind of blessing, for she seized his hand and kissed it reverently as if it had been a priest's.

He laughed. "Come," he said, "come, little wife, we will walk arm in arm into the room downstairs!"

She seemed a little coy at first, but smiled looking not uncontented. It was high time for them to go down, for they met Olivo coming up. He was flushed and wore a frown, so that Casanova promptly inferred that the marchese or the abbot had roused his suspicions by some coarse jest concerning Teresina's prolonged absence. His brow cleared when he beheld Casanova on the threshold, standing arm in arm with the girl as if in sport.

"I'm sorry to have kept you all waiting, Olivo," said Casanova. "I had to finish my letter." He held the missive out to Olivo in proof of his words.

"Take it," said Olivo to Teresina, smoothing her rumpled hair. "Hand it to the messenger."

"Here are two gold pieces for the man," added Casanova. "He must hurry so that the letter may leave Mantua for Venice today. And ask him to tell my hostess at the inn that I shall return this evening."

"This evening?" exclaimed Olivo. "Impossible!"

"Oh, well, we'll see," observed Casanova affably. "Here, Teresina, take this, a gold piece for yourself." When Olivo demurred, Casanova added, "Put it in your money box, Teresina. That letter is worth any amount of gold pieces!"

Teresina ran off, and Casanova nodded with delight. In days gone by he had possessed the girl's mother and grandmother also, and he thought it a particularly good joke that he was paying the little wench for her favors under the very eyes of her father.

When Casanova entered the hall with Olivo, cards had already begun. He acknowledged with serene dignity the effusive greeting of the company and took his place opposite the marchese, who was banker. The windows into the garden were open. Casanova heard voices outside; Marcolina and Amalia strolled by, glanced into the room for a moment, and then disappeared from view.

While the marchese was dealing, Lorenzi turned to Casanova with ceremonious politeness, saying, "My compliments, Chevalier. You were better informed than I. My regiment is under orders to march tomorrow afternoon."

The marchese looked surprised. "Why did you not tell us sooner, Lorenzi?"

"The matter did not seem of such supreme importance."

"It is of no great importance to me," said the marchese. "But don't you think it is of considerable importance to my wife?" He laughed in a repulsively hoarse way. "As a matter of fact, I have some interest in the matter myself. You won four hundred ducats from me yesterday, and there is not much time left in which to win them back."

"The lieutenant won money from us too," said the younger Ricardi. The elder, silent as usual, looked over his shoulder at his brother, who stood behind the elder's chair as on the previous day.

"Luck and women . . ." began the abbot.

The marchese finished the sentence for him: ". . . can be constrained."

Lorenzi carelessly scattered his gold on the table. "There you are. I will stake it all upon a single card, if you like, Marchese, so that you need not wait for your money."

Casanova suddenly became aware of a feeling of compassion for Lorenzi, a feeling he was puzzled to account for. But he believed himself to be endowed with second sight, and he had a premonition that the lieutenant would fall in his first encounter. The marchese did not accept the suggestion of high stakes, nor did Lorenzi insist. They resumed the game, therefore, much as on the previous night, everyone taking a hand at first, and only moderate sums being ventured. A quarter of an hour later, however, the stakes began to rise, and ere long Lorenzi had lost his four hundred ducats to the marchese. Casanova had no constancy either in luck or ill luck. He won, lost, and won again, in an almost ludicrously regular alternation. Lorenzi drew a breath of relief when his last gold piece had gone the way of the others. Rising from the table, he said, "I thank you, gentlemen. This," he hesitated for a moment, "this will prove to have been my last game for a long time in your hospitable house. If you will allow me, Signor Olivo, I will take leave of the ladies before riding into town, where I want to be before nightfall in order to make preparations for tomorrow."

"Shameless liar," thought Casanova. "You will return here tonight, to Marcolina's arms!" Rage flamed up in him anew.

"What!" exclaimed the marchese ill-humoredly. "The evening will not come for hours. Is the game to stop so early? If you like, Lorenzi, my coachman shall drive home with a message to the marchesa to let her know that you will be late."

"I am going to ride to Mantua," replied Lorenzi impatiently.

The marchese, ignoring this statement, went on, "There is still plenty of time. Put up some of your own money, if it be but a single gold piece." He dealt Lorenzi a card.

"I have not a single gold piece left," said Lorenzi wearily.

"Really?"

"Not one," asserted Lorenzi, as if repulsed by the whole matter.

"Never mind," said the marchese, with a sudden assumption of amiability which was far from congenial. "I will trust you as far as ten ducats goes, or even for a larger sum if necessary."

"All right, a ducat, then," said Lorenzi, taking up the card dealt to him.

The marchese won. Lorenzi went on with the game, as if this were now a matter of course, and was soon in the marchese's debt to the amount of one hundred ducats. At this stage Casanova became banker, and had even better luck than the marchese. There remained only three players. Today the brothers Ricardi stood aside without complaint. Olivo and the abbot were merely admiring onlookers. No one uttered a syllable. Only the cards spoke, and they spoke in unmistakable terms. By the hazard of fortune all the cash found its way to Casanova. In an hour he had won two thousand ducats; he had won them from Lorenzi, though they came out of the pockets of the marchese, who at length sat there without a penny. Casanova offered him whatever gold pieces he might need. The marchese shook his head. "Thanks," he said, "I have had enough. The game is over as far as I am concerned."

From the garden came the laughing voices of the girls. Casanova heard Teresina's voice in particular, but he was sitting with his back to the window and did not turn round. He tried once more to persuade the marchese to resume the game—for the sake of Lorenzi, though he hardly knew what moved him. The marchese refused with a yet more decisive headshake. Lorenzi rose, saying, "I shall have the honor, Signor Marchese, of handing the amount I owe you to you personally, before noon tomorrow."

The marchese laughed drily. "I am curious to know how you will manage that, Lieutenant Lorenzi. There is not a soul, in Mantua or elsewhere, who would lend you as much as ten ducats, not to speak of two thousand, especially today. For tomorrow you will be on the march, and who can tell whether you will ever return?"

"I give you my word of honor, Signor Marchese, that you shall have the money at eight o'clock tomorrow morning."

"Your word of honor," said the marchese coldly, "is not worth a single ducat to me, let alone two thousand."

The others held their breath. Lorenzi, apparently unmoved,

merely answered, "You will give me satisfaction, Signor Marchese."

"With pleasure, Signor Lieutenant," rejoined the marchese, "as soon as you have paid your debt."

Olivo, who was profoundly distressed, here intervened, stammering slightly, "I stand surety for the amount, Signor Marchese. Unfortunately I have not sufficient ready money on the spot; but there is the house, the estate . . ." He closed the sentence with an awkward wave of the hand.

"I refuse to accept your surety, for your own sake," said the marchese. "You would lose your money."

Casanova saw that all eyes were turned toward the gold that lay on the table before him. "What if I were to stand surety for Lorenzi," he thought. "What if I were to pay the debt for him? The marchese could not refuse my offer. I almost think it is my duty. It was the marchese's money."

But he said not a word. He felt that a plan was taking shape in his mind, and that above all he needed time in which he might become clear as to its details.

"You shall have the money this evening, before nightfall," said Lorenzi. "I shall be in Mantua in an hour."

"Your horse may break its neck," replied the marchese. "You too; intentionally, perhaps."

"Anyhow," said the abbot angrily, "the lieutenant cannot get the money here by magic."

The two Ricardis laughed; but instantly broke off.

Olivo once more addressed the marchese. "It is plain that you must grant Lieutenant Lorenzi leave to depart."

"Yes, if he gives me a pledge," exclaimed the marchese with flashing eyes, as if this idea gave him peculiar delight.

"That seems rather a good plan," said Casanova, a little absentmindedly, for his scheme was ripening.

Lorenzi drew a ring from his finger and flicked it across the table.

The marchese took it up, saying, "That is good for a thousand."

"What about this one?" Lorenzi threw down another ring in front of the marchese.

The latter nodded, saying, "That is good for the same amount."

"Are you satisfied now, Signor Marchese?" inquired Lorenzi, moving as if to go.

"I am satisfied," answered the marchese, smirking; "all the more, seeing that the rings are stolen."

Lorenzi turned sharply, clenching his fist to strike the marchese. Olivo and the abbot seized Lorenzi's arm.

"I know both the stones, though they have been reset," said the marchese without moving from his place. "Look, gentlemen, the emerald is slightly flawed, or it would be worth ten times the amount. The ruby is perfect, but it is not a large one. Both the stones come from a set of jewels which I once gave my wife. And, since it is quite impossible for me to suppose that the marchesa had them reset in rings for Lieutenant Lorenzi, it is obvious that they have been stolen—that the whole set has been stolen. Well, well, the pledge suffices, Signor Lieutenant, for now."

"Lorenzi!" cried Olivo, "we all give you our word that no one shall ever hear a syllable from us about what has just happened."

"And whatever Signor Lorenzi may have done," said Casanova, "you, Signor Marchese, are the greater scoundrel of the two."

"I hope so," replied the marchese. "When anyone is as old as we are, Chevalier de Seingalt, assuredly he should not need lessons in villainy. Good evening, gentlemen."

He rose to his feet. No one responded to his farewell, and he went out. For a space the silence was so intense, that once again the girls' laughter was heard from the garden, now seeming unduly loud. Who would have ventured to utter the word that could have reached Lorenzi's soul, as he stood at the table with his arm still raised? Casanova, the only one of the company who had remained seated, derived an involuntary artistic pleasure from the contemplation of this fine, threatening gesture, meaningless now, but seemingly petrified, as if the young man had been transformed into a statue. At length Olivo turned to him with a soothing air; the Ricardis, too, drew near; and the abbot appeared to be working himself up for a speech. But a sort of shiver passed over Lorenzi's frame. With a peremptory and bitter gesture, he rejected any offers at intervention, and, politely inclining his head, he quietly left the room. Casanova, who had meanwhile wrapped up the money in a silken kerchief, instantly followed. Without looking at the others' faces, he could feel that they were convinced it was his instant intention to do what they had all the while been expecting, namely, to place his winnings at Lorenzi's disposal.

Casanova overtook Lorenzi in the chestnut avenue. Speaking lightly, he said, "May I have the pleasure of accompanying you on your walk, Lieutenant Lorenzi?"

Lorenzi, without looking at him, answered in an arrogant tone which seemed hardly in keeping with his situation, "As you please, Chevalier; but I am afraid you will not find me an amusing companion."

"Perhaps, Lieutenant, you will on the other hand find me all the more entertaining. If you have no objection, let us take the path through the vineyard, where our conversation will be undisturbed."

They turned aside from the highroad into the narrow footway running beside the garden wall, along which Casanova had walked with Olivo on the previous day.

"You are right in supposing," began Casanova, "that I have it in mind to offer you the sum of money which you owe to the marchese. Not as a loan. That, if you will excuse my saying so, seems to me rather too risky a venture. I could let you have it as a slight return for a service which I think you may be able to do me."

"Go on," said Lorenzi coldly.

"Before I say any more," answered Casanova in a similar tone, "I must make a condition upon your acceptance of which the continuance of this conversation depends."

"Name your condition."

"Give me your word of honor that you will listen to me without interruption, even though what I have to say may arouse your displeasure or even your indignation. When you have heard me to the end, it will rest entirely with yourself whether you accept a proposal which, I am well aware, is of an extremely unusual nature. But I want you to answer it with a simple yes or no. Whatever the issue, no one is to hear a word concerning what passes at this interview between two men of honor, who are perhaps no better than they should be."

"I am ready to listen to your proposal."

"You accept my condition?"

"I will not interrupt you."

"And you will answer nothing beyond yes or no?"

"Nothing beyond yes or no."

"Very well," said Casanova. They walked slowly up the hill, between the vine stocks, in the sultry heat of the late afternoon. Casanova began to speak. "We shall perhaps understand one another best if we discuss the matter logically. It is obvious that you have absolutely no chance of obtaining the money you owe the marchese within the prescribed time. There can also be no doubt that he has made up his mind to destroy you should you fail to pay. Since he knows more of you than he actually disclosed to us today"—Casanova was venturing further than he needed to, but he loved to take these little risks when following up a path decided on in advance—"you are absolutely in the power of the old scoundrel, and your fate as an officer and a gentleman would be sealed. There you have one side of the question. On the other hand, you will be saved as soon as you have paid your debt, and as soon as you get back those rings—however you may have come by them. This will mean the recovery of an existence which is otherwise practically closed, an existence which, since you are young, handsome, and bold, offers splendor, happiness, and renown. This appears to me a most attractive prospect; especially seeing that the only alternative is an inglorious, no, a shameful ruin; for such a prospect, I should be willing to sacrifice a prejudice which I had never really possessed. I am well aware, Lorenzi," he added quickly, as if expecting contradiction and desiring to forestall it, "that you have no more prejudices than I have or ever had. What I am going to ask of you is merely what I should in your place under like circumstances be willing to do, without a moment's hesitation. Indeed, I have never hesitated, at the call of destiny or for the sake of a whim, to be base, or whatever the fools of this earth may call it. Like you, Lorenzi, I have ever been ready to risk my life for less than nothing, and to call it even. I am ready to do so now, if my proposal prove unacceptable. We are made of the same stuff, you and I; we are brothers in spirit; we may therefore disclose our souls to one another without false shame, proud in our nakedness. Here are my two thousand ducats. Call them yours, if you enable me to spend tonight in your place with Marcolina.—Let us not stand still, if you please, Lorenzi. Let us continue our walk."

They walked through the fields, beneath the fruit trees, between which the vines, heavy with grape clusters, were trellised. Casanova went on without a pause. "Don't answer me yet, Lorenzi, for I have not finished. My request would naturally be, if not monstrous, at least preposterous, if it were your intention to make Marcolina your wife, or if Marcolina's own hopes or wishes turned in this direction. But just as last night was your first night spent in love together"—he uttered this guess as if he had absolute knowledge of the fact—"so also was the ensuing night predestined, according to all human calculation, according to your own expectations and Marcolina's, to be your last night together for a long period and probably for ever. I am absolutely convinced that Marcolina herself, in order to save her lover from certain destruction, and simply upon his wish, would be perfectly willing to give this one night to his savior. For she, too, is a philosopher, and is therefore just as free from prejudices as we are. Nevertheless, certain as I am that she would meet the test, I am far from intending that it should be imposed upon her. To possess a woman outwardly passive but inwardly resistant, would be far from satisfying my desires, least of all in the present case. I wish, not merely as a lover, but also as one beloved, to enjoy a happiness for which I should be prepared to pay with my life. Understand this clearly, Lorenzi. For the reason I have explained, Marcolina must not for an instant suspect that I am the man whom she is clasping to her sweet bosom; she must be firmly convinced that you are in her arms. It is your part to pave the way for this deception; mine to maintain it. You will not have much difficulty in making her understand that you will have to leave her before dawn. Nor need you be at a loss for a pretext as to the necessity for perfectly mute caresses when you return at night, as you will promise to return. To avert all danger of discovery at the last moment, I shall, when the time comes for me to leave, act as if I heard a suspicious noise outside the window. Seizing my cloak—or rather yours, which you must of course lend me for the occasion—I shall disappear through the window, never to return. For, of course, I shall take my leave this evening. But halfway back to Mantua, telling the coachman that I have forgotten some important papers, I shall return here, and, entering the garden by the side door (you must give me the master key, Lorenzi), I shall creep to Marcolina's window, which will be opened at midnight. I shall have taken off my clothes in the carriage, even to my shoes and stockings, and shall wear only your cloak, so that when I take flight nothing will be left to betray either you or me. The cloak and the two thousand ducats will be at your disposal at five o'clock tomorrow morning in the inn at Mantua, so that you may fling the money at the marchese's feet even before the appointed hour. I pledge my solemn oath to fulfill my side of the bargain. I have finished."

Suddenly he stood still. The sun was near to setting. A gentle breeze made the yellow ears rustle; the tower of Olivo's house glowed red in the evening light. Lorenzi, too, halted. His pale face was motionless, as he gazed into vacancy over Casanova's shoulder. His arms hung limp by his sides, whereas Casanova's hand, ready for any emergency, rested as if by chance upon the hilt of his sword. A few seconds elapsed, and Lorenzi was still silent and motionless. He seemed immersed in tranquil thought, but Casanova remained on the alert, holding the kerchief with the ducats in his left hand, but keeping the right upon his sword hilt. He spoke once more.

"You have honorably fulfilled my conditions. I know that it has not been easy. For even though we may be free from prejudices, the atmosphere in which we live is so full of them that we cannot wholly escape their influence. And just as you, Lorenzi, during the last quarter of an hour, have more than once been on the point of seizing me by the throat; so I, I must confess, played for a time with the idea of giving you the two thousand ducats as to my friend. Rarely, Lorenzi, have I been so strangely drawn to anyone as I was to you from the first. But had I yielded to this generous impulse, the next moment I should have regretted it bitterly. In like manner you, Lorenzi, in the moment before you blow your brains out, would desperately regret having been such a fool as to throw away a thousand nights of love with new and ever new women for one single night of love which neither night nor day was to follow."

Lorenzi remained mute. His silence continued for many seconds, for many minutes, until Casanova began to ask himself how long his patience was to be tried. He was on the point of departing with a curt salutation, and of thus indicating that he understood his proposition to have been rejected, when Lorenzi, without a word and hardly hastily moved his right hand backward into the tail pocket of his coat. Casanova, ever on his guard, instantly stepped back a pace and was ready to duck. Lorenzi handed him the key of the garden door. Casanova's movement, which had certainly expressed fear, brought to Lorenzi's lips the flicker of a contemptuous smile. Casanova was able to repress all sign of his rising anger, for he knew that had he given way to it he might have ruined his design. Taking the key with a nod, he merely said, "No doubt that means yes. In an hour from now—an hour will suffice for your understanding with Marcolina—I shall expect you in the turret chamber. There, in exchange for your cloak, I shall have the pleasure of handing you the two thousand gold pieces without further delay. First of all, as a token of confidence; and secondly because I really do not know where I should put the money during the night."

They parted without further formality. Lorenzi returned to the house by the path along which they had both come. Casanova made his way to the village by a different route. At the inn there, by putting down a considerable deposit, he was able to arrange for a carriage to await him at ten o'clock that evening for the drive from Olivo's house into Mantua.

Returning to the house, Casanova disposed of his gold in a safe corner of the turret chamber and descended to the garden, where a spectacle awaited him, not in itself remarkable, but one which touched him strangely in his present mood. Upon a bench at the edge of the meadow Olivo was sitting beside Amalia, his arm round her shoulders. Reclining at their feet were the three girls, tired out by the afternoon's play. Maria, the youngest, had her head in her mother's lap and seemed to be asleep; Nanetta lay at full length on the grass with her head pillowed on her arm; Teresina was leaning against her father's knee, while his fingers rested tenderly in her curls. As Casanova drew near, Teresina greeted him, not with the look of lascivious understanding which he had involuntarily expected, but with a frank smile of childlike confidence, as if what had passed between them only a few hours before had been nothing more than some trivial pastime. Olivo's face lighted up in friendly fashion, and Amalia nodded a cordial and grateful greeting. It was plain to Casanova that they were receiving him as one who had just performed a noble deed, but who would prefer, from a sense of refinement, that no allusion should be made to the matter.

"Are you really determined to leave us tomorrow, Chevalier?" inquired Olivo.

"Not tomorrow," answered Casanova, "but, as I told you, this very evening."

Olivo would have renewed his protests, but Casanova shrugged, saying in a tone of regret, "Unfortunately, my letter from Venice leaves me no option. The summons sent to me is so honorable in every respect that to delay my return home would be an unpardonable affront to my distinguished patrons." He asked his host and hostess to excuse him so that he could prepare for departure and then be able to enjoy the last hours of his stay undisturbed in his dear friends' company.

Disregarding further protests, he went to the turret chamber and first of all changed from his more splendid to his simpler suit, which would have to suffice for the journey. He then packed his travel bag, and listened for Lorenzi's footsteps with an attentiveness which grew keener from moment to moment. Before the time was up, Lorenzi, knocking once at the door, entered, wearing a dark blue riding cloak. Without a word, he slipped the cloak from his shoulders and let it fall to the floor, where it lay between the two men, a shapeless mass of cloth. Casanova withdrew his kerchief filled with the gold pieces from beneath the bolster, and emptied the money on the table. He counted the coins under Lorenzi's eyes—a process which was soon over, for many of the gold pieces were worth several ducats each. Putting the stipulated sum into two purses, he handed these to Lorenzi. This left about a hundred ducats for himself. Lorenzi stuffed the purses into his tail pockets, and was about to leave without a word.

"Wait a moment, Lorenzi," said Casanova. "Our paths in life may cross once again. If so let us meet as friends. We have made a bargain like many another bargain; let us call it even."

Casanova held out his hand. Lorenzi did not take it, but now spoke for the first time. "I cannot recall that anything like this was included in our agreement." Turning on his heel, he left the room.

"Do we stand so strictly upon the letter, my friend?" thought

Casanova. Then I must be all the more sure that I am not the one who is duped in the end." In truth, he had given no serious thought to this possibility. He knew from personal experience that such men as Lorenzi have their own peculiar code of honor, a code which cannot be written in formal propositions, but which in each individual case leaves little cause to doubt. He packed Lorenzi's cloak in the top of the travel bag. Having stowed away upon his person the remaining gold pieces, he took a final glance round the room which he was never likely to enter again. Then with sword and hat, ready for the journey, he made his way to the hall, where he found Olivo, Amalia, and the children already seated at table. At the same instant, Marcolina entered by the garden door. The coincidence was interpreted by Casanova as a propitious sign. She answered his greeting with a frank inclination of the head. Supper was now served. The conversation dragged a little at first, as if all were oppressed by the thought of the imminent leave-taking. Amalia seemed conspicuously busy with her girls, concerned to see that they were not given too much or too little on their plates. Olivo, somewhat irrelevantly, began to speak of a trifling lawsuit he had just won against a neighboring landowner. Next he referred to a business journey to Mantua and Cremona, which he would shortly have to undertake. Casanova expressed the hope that before long he would be able to entertain his friend in Venice, a city which, by a strange chance, Olivo had never visited. Amalia had seen the marvelous city many long years before as a child. She could not say how she had gotten there but could only remember having seen an old man wrapped in a scarlet cloak, who, disembarking from a long black boat, had stumbled and had fallen prone.

"Have you never been to Venice either?" asked Casanova of Marcolina, who was seated facing him, and was looking over his shoulder into the deep gloom of the garden. She shook her head. Casanova thought, "If I could only show you the city in which I spent my youth! Had you only been young with me!" Another thought, almost as senseless as both of these, crossed his mind: "What if I took you there with me now?"

But even while these thoughts crossed his mind, with the ease of manner peculiar to him in moments of great excitement, he had begun to speak of his native city. At first his language was cool; he used an artist's touch, as if painting a picture. Unconsciously warming his tone, he entered into details of personal history, so that of a sudden his own figure appeared in the center of the canvas, filling it with life. He spoke of his mother, the celebrated actress, for whom her admirer Goldoni had written his admirable comedy, *La Pupilla*. Next he recounted the unhappy days spent in Dr. Gozzi's boarding school. Then he spoke of his childish passion for the gardener's little daughter, who had subsequently run away with a lackey; of his first sermon as a young abbot, after which he found in the offertory bag, in addition to the usual collection, a number of love letters; of his mischievous doings as a fiddler in the orchestra of the San Samueli Theater, when he and his companions had played in the alleys, taverns, dancing halls, and gaming houses of Venice—sometimes masked and sometimes unmasked. In telling the story of these riotous escapades, he was careful to avoid the use of any offensive epithet, indeed, he transformed his narrative into a kind of poetry, as if paying due regard to the presence of the young girls, who, like their elders, including Marcolina, listened with rapt attention. The hour grew late, and Amalia sent her daughters to bed. Casanova kissed them all tenderly, treating Teresina exactly like her sisters. He made them promise that they would soon come with their father and mother to visit him in Venice. When they had gone, he spoke with less restraint, but continued to avoid any unsuitable innuendo or display of vanity. His audience might have imagined themselves listening to the story of a soulful fool of love rather than to a dangerous seducer and half-savage adventurer. He told them of the fair Unknown who had traveled with him for weeks disguised as a man in officer's uniform and one morning had suddenly disappeared from his side; of the daughter of the gentleman cobbler in Madrid who, in the intervals between their embraces, had studiously endeavored to make a good Catholic of him; of Lia, the lovely Jewess of Turin, who had a better bearing on horseback than any princess; of Manon Balletti, sweet and innocent, the only woman he had almost married; of the singer whom he had hissed in Warsaw because of her bad performance, whereupon he had had to fight a duel with her lover, General Branitzky, and to flee the city; of the wicked woman Charpillon, who had made such an abject fool of him in London; of the night when he crossed the lagoons to Murano on the way to his adored nun, the night when he nearly lost his life in a storm; of Croce the gamester, who, after losing a fortune at Spa, had taken a tearful farewell of Casanova upon the highroad and had set off on his way to St. Petersburg, just as he was, wearing silk stockings and a coat of apple-green satin and carrying nothing but a walking cane. He told of actresses, singers, dressmakers, countesses, dancers, chambermaids; of gamblers, officers, princes, envoys, financiers, musicians, and adventurers. So carried away was he by the rediscovered magic of his own past, so completely did these splendid though irrecoverable experiences triumph over the wretched shadows of the present, that he was on the point of telling the story of a pale but pretty girl who in a twilit church at Mantua had confided her love troubles to him—absolutely forgetting that this same girl, sixteen years older, now sat at the table before him as the wife of his friend Olivo—when the maid came in with heavy steps to say that the carriage was waiting. Instantly, with his incomparable talent for pulling himself together without hesitation, whether dreaming or awake, Casanova rose to bid adieu. He again pressed Olivo, who was too much affected to speak, to bring wife and children to visit him in Venice. Having embraced his friend, he approached Amalia with intent to embrace her also, but warding him off slightly she held out her hand, and he kissed it respectfully. When he turned to Marcolina, she said, "You ought to write down everything you told us this evening, Chevalier, and a great deal more, just as you have written the story of your flight from The Leads."

"Do you really mean that, Marcolina?" he inquired, with the shyness of a young author.

She smiled with gentle mockery, saying, "I imagine such a book might prove far more entertaining than your polemic against Voltaire."

"Very likely," he thought. "Perhaps I may follow your advice some day. If so, you, Marcolina, shall be the theme of the last chapter."

This notion, and still more the thought that the last chapter was to be lived through that very night, made his face light up so strangely that Marcolina, who had given him her hand in farewell, drew it away again before he could lean forward to kiss it. Without betraying either disappointment or anger, Casanova turned to depart, after signifying, with one of those simple gestures of which he was a master, his desire that no one, not even Olivo, should follow him.

He strode rapidly through the chestnut avenue, handed a gold piece to the maid who had brought his travel bag to the carriage, took his seat, and drove away.

The sky was overcast. In the village lamps were still burning in some of the cottages; but by the time the carriage regained the open road, the only light piercing the darkness was supplied by the yellow rays of the lantern dangling from the shaft. Casanova opened his bag, took out Lorenzi's cloak, flung it over his shoulders, and under this cover undressed with all requisite caution. He packed the discarded clothing, together with shoes and stockings, in the travel bag, and wrapped himself more closely in the cloak. Then he called to the coachman,

"Stop, we must drive back!"

The coachman turned heavily in his seat.

"I have left some of my papers in the house. Don't you understand? We must drive back."

When the coachman, a surly, thin graybeard, still hesitated, Casanova said, "Of course I will pay you extra for your trouble. Here you are!" He pressed a gold piece into the man's hand.

The coachman nodded, muttered something, gave his horse a wholly superfluous lash with the whip, and turned the carriage round. When they drove back through the village, all the houses were dark. A little farther on, the coachman was about to turn into the byroad leading up the gentle ascent to Olivo's house.

"Halt!" cried Casanova. "We won't drive any nearer, otherwise we will wake them all up. Wait for me here at the corner. I shall be back in a minute or two. If I should happen to keep you longer, you shall have a ducat for every hour!"

The man by his nod seemed to show he understood what was afoot.

Casanova descended and hurried out of the sight of the coachman past the closed door and along the wall to the corner. Here began the path leading through the vineyards, turning right at an angle. Having walked it twice by daylight, Casanova had no difficulty in the dark. Halfway up the hill came a second angle in the wall. Here he had again to turn to the right, across soft meadowland, and in the pitchy night had only to take care not to miss the garden door. At length his fingers recognized the change from smooth stone to rough wood, and he could easily make out the framework of the narrow door. Rapidly finding the key, he unlocked it, entered the garden, and closed up again behind him. Across the meadow he could now discern house and tower. They seemed incredibly far off and yet incredibly large. He stood where he was for a while, looking around. What to other eyes would have been impenetrable darkness, was to him no more than deep twilight. The gravel path being painful to his bare feet, he walked upon the meadow, where, moreover, his footfall made no sound. So light was his tread that he felt as if soaring.

"Has my mood changed," he thought, "since those days when, as a man of thirty, I sought such adventures? Do I not now, as then, feel all the ardors of desire and all the sap of youth course through my veins? Am I not, as of old, Casanova? Being Casanova, why should I be subject, as others are, to the pitiful law which is called age!"

Growing bolder, he asked himself, "Why am I creeping in disguise to Marcolina? Is not Casanova a better man than Lorenzi, even though he be thirty years older? Is not she the one woman who would have understood the incomprehensible? Was it necessary to commit this small roguery and to mislead another man into committing a somewhat greater one? Would I not, with a little patience, have reached the same goal? Lorenzi would in any case have gone tomorrow, while I should have remained. Five days, three days, and she would have given herself to me, knowingly given herself." He stood close to the wall of the house beneath Marcolina's window, which was still closed. His thoughts ran on: "Is it too late? I could come back tomorrow or the next day. Could begin the work of seduction—in honorable fashion, so to speak. Tonight would be but a foretaste of the future. Marcolina must not learn that I have been here today—or not until much later."

Marcolina's window was still closed. There was no sign from within. It was probably still a few minutes before midnight. Should he make his presence known in any way? By tapping gently at the window? Since nothing of this sort had been arranged, it might arouse Marcolina's suspicions. Better wait. It could not be much longer. The thought that she might instantly recognize him, might detect the fraud before he had achieved his purpose, crossed his mind—not for the first time, yet as a passing fancy, as a remote possibility which it was logical to take into account, but not anything to be seriously feared. A ludicrous adventure now occurred to him. Twenty years ago he had spent a delicious night with a middle-aged ugly vixen in Soleure, when he had imagined himself to be possessing a beautiful young woman whom he adored. He recalled how next day, in a shameless letter, she had derided him for the mistake that she had so greatly desired him to make and that she had orchestrated with such infamous cunning. He shuddered at the thought. It was the last thing he would have wished to think of just now, and he drove the detestable image from his mind. It must be midnight! How long was he to stand shivering there, pressed against the wall in the chilly night? Waiting in vain, perhaps? Cheated, after all? Two thousand ducats for nothing? Lorenzi behind the curtain, mocking at the fool outside? Involuntarily he gripped the hilt of the sword he carried beneath the cloak, pressed to his naked body. With a fellow like Lorenzi one must in the end be prepared for even the most painful surprises. At that instant he heard a gentle rattling and knew it was made by the grating of Marcolina's window as it opened. Then both wings of the window were drawn back, though the curtain still veiled the interior. Casanova remained motionless for a few seconds more, until the curtain was pulled aside by an unseen hand. Taking this as a sign, he swung himself over the sill into the room, and promptly closed window and grating behind him. The curtain had fallen across his shoulders, so that he had to push his way beneath it. Now he would have been in absolute darkness had there not been shining from the depths of the chamber, incredibly far away, as if awakened by his own gaze, the faintest possible illumination to show him the way. No more than three paces forward, and eager arms enfolded him. Letting the sword slip from his hand, the cloak from his shoulders, he gave himself up to his bliss.

From Marcolina's sigh of surrender, from the tears of happiness which he kissed from her cheeks, from the ever-renewed warmth with which she received his caresses, he felt sure that she shared his rapture; and to him this rapture seemed more intense than he had ever experienced, seemed to possess a new and strange quality. Pleasure became worship; passion was transfused with an intense consciousness. Here at last was the reality which he had often falsely imagined himself to be on the point of attaining, and which had always eluded his grasp. Fulfillment was here at Marcolina's breast. He held in his arms a woman upon whom he could squander himself, and still feel inexhaustible; the woman upon whose breast the moment of ultimate self-abandonment and of renewed desire seemed to coalesce into a single instant of hitherto unimagined spiritual ecstasy. Were not life and death, time and eternity, one upon these lips? Was he not a god? Were not youth and age merely a fable; mere fanciful creations? Were not home and exile, splendor and misery, renown and oblivion, meaningless distinctions, fit only for the use of the restless, the lonely, the idle; had not the words become senseless to one who was Casanova, and who had found Marcolina? More contemptible, more absurd, as the minutes passed, seemed to him the prospect of keeping the resolution which he had made when still pusillanimous, of acting on the determination to flee out of this night of miracle, mute, unrecognized, like a thief. With the infallible conviction that he must be the bringer of delight even as he was the receiver, he felt prepared for the venture of disclosing his name, even though he knew all the time that he would thus play for a great stake, the loss of which he would have to pay for with his very existence. He was still shrouded in impenetrable darkness, and until the first glimmer of dawn made its way through the thick curtain, he could postpone a confession upon whose favorable acceptance by Marcolina his fate, even his life, depended. Besides, was not this mute, passionately sweet association the very thing to bind Marcolina to him more firmly with each kiss that they enjoyed? Would not the ineffable bliss of this night transmute into truth what had been conceived in falsehood? His duped beloved, the one and only, had she not already an inkling that it was not Lorenzi, the stripling, but Casanova, the man, with whom she was mingling in these divine ardors? He began to think that it was possible that he might be spared the so greatly desired and yet so intensely dreaded moment of revelation. He imagined that Marcolina, thrilling, entranced, transfigured, would spontaneously whisper his name. Then, when she had forgiven him in this way—no, had accepted his forgiveness—he would take her with him that very hour. Together they would leave the house in the gray dawn; together they would seek the carriage that was waiting at the turn of the road; together they would drive away. She would be his forevermore. This would be the crown of his life; that at an age when others were doomed to a sad senility, he, by the overwhelming power of his unconquerable personality, would have won for himself and forever the youngest, the most beautiful, the most gifted of women. For this woman was his as no woman had ever been before. He glided with her through mysterious, narrow canals, between palaces in whose shadows he was once more at home, under high-arched bridges which blurred figures were swiftly crossing. Many of the wayfarers waved down for a moment over the parapet, and vanished before their faces could be discerned. Now the gondola drew alongside. A marble stairway led up to the stately mansion of Senator Bragadino. It was the only festively lit palace. Masked guests were ascending and descending. Many of them paused with inquisitive glances; but who could recognize Casanova and Marcolina in their dominoes? He entered the hall with her. Here was a great company playing for high stakes. All the senators, Bragadino among them, were seated round the table in their purple robes. As Casanova came through the door, they whispered his name as if terror-stricken, for the flashing of his eyes behind the mask had disclosed his identity. He did not sit down; he did not take any cards, and yet he joined in the game. He won. He won all the gold on the table, and this was not enough. The senators had to give him promissory notes. They lost their possessions, their palaces, their purple robes; they were beggars; they crawled around him clad in rags, kissing his hands. Nearby, in a hall with crimson hangings, there were music and dancing. Casanova wished to dance with Marcolina, but she had vanished. Once again the senators in their purple robes were seated at the table; but now Casanova knew that the hazards at stake were not those of a game of cards; he knew that the destinies of accused persons, some criminal and some innocent, hung in the balance. What had become of Marcolina? Had he not been holding her by the hand the whole time? He rushed down the staircase. The gondola was waiting. On, on, through the maze of canals. Of course the gondolier knew where Marcolina was; but why was he, too, masked? That had not been the custom of old in Venice. Casanova wished to question him, but was afraid. Does a man become so cowardly when he grows old? Onward, ever onward. How huge Venice had grown during these five-and-twenty years! At last the houses came to an end; the canal opened out; they were passing between islands; there stood the walls of the Murano nunnery, to which Marcolina had fled. There was no gondola now; he had to swim; how delightful! It was true that in Venice the children were playing with his gold pieces. But what was money to him? The water was now warm, now cold; it dripped from his clothing as he climbed over the wall.

"Where is Marcolina?" he inquired in the parlor, in loud, challenging tones such as only a prince would dare to use.

"I will summon her," said the Lady Abbess, and disappeared.

Casanova wandered about; he had wings; he fluttered to and fro along the gratings, fluttered like a bat. "If I had only known sooner that I can fly," he thought. "I will teach Marcolina."

Behind the gratings, the figures of women were moving hither and thither. They were nuns—and yet they were all wearing secular dress. He knew it, though he could not really see them. He knew who they were. Henriette the Unknown; Corticelli and Cristina, the dancers; the bride; Dubois the Beautiful; the accursed vixen of Soleure; Manon Balletti; a hundred others—but Marcolina was not among them!

"You have betrayed me," he cried to the gondolier, who was waiting for him beneath. Never had he hated anyone as he hated this gondolier, and he swore to take an exquisite revenge. But how foolish he had been to seek Marcolina in the Murano nunnery when she had gone to visit Voltaire. It was fortunate that he could fly, since he had no money left with which to pay for a carriage. He swam away. But he was no longer enjoying himself. The water grew colder and colder; he was drifting out into the open sea, far from Murano, far from Venice, and there was no ship within sight; his heavy gold-embroidered garments were dragging him down; he tried to strip them off, but it was impossible, for he was holding his manuscript, the manuscript he had to give to Monsieur Voltaire. The water was pouring into his mouth and nose; deadly fear seized him; he clutched at impalpable things; there was a rattling in his throat; he screamed; and with a great effort he opened his eyes. Between the curtain and the window frame the dawn was making its way through in a narrow strip of light. Marcolina, in her white nightdress and with hands crossed upon her bosom, was

standing at the foot of the bed contemplating Casanova with un-
utterable horror. Her glance instantly recalled him to his senses.
Involuntarily he stretched out his arms toward her with a gesture
of appeal. Marcolina, as though in answer, waved him away with
her left hand, while with the right she continued to grasp her gown
convulsively. Casanova sat up, supporting himself with both hands
on the bed, and stared at her. Neither was able to look away from
the other. His expression was one of rage and shame; hers was
one of shame and disgust. Casanova knew how she saw him, for
he saw himself figured in imagination, just as he had seen himself
yesterday in the bedroom mirror. A yellow, evil face, deeply lined,
with thin lips and staring eyes—a face three times worse than that
of yesterday, because of the excesses of the night, the ghastly dream
of the morning, and the terrible awakening. And what he read in
Marcolina's countenance was not what he would a thousand times
rather have read there; it was not thief, libertine, villain. He read
only something which crushed him to earth more ignominiously
than could any terms of abuse; he read the word which to him
was the most dreadful of all words, since it passed a final judgment upon him—old man. Had it been within his power to annihilate himself by a spell, he would have done so, that he might be
spared from having to creep out of the bed and display himself to
Marcolina in his nakedness, which must appear to her more loathsome than the sight of some loathsome beast. But Marcolina, as if
gradually collecting herself, and clearly in order to give him the
opportunity which was, after all, unavoidable, turned her face to
the wall. He seized the moment to get out of bed, to raise the
cloak from the floor, and to wrap himself in it. He was quick, too,
to make sure of his sword. Now, when he conceived himself to
have at least escaped the worst humiliation of all, that of ludi-
crousness, he began to wonder whether it would not be possible,
through skillful words, of which he usually had such command,
to throw another light upon this affair in which he cut so pitiful
a figure. Could he not somehow or other give matters a favorable
turn? From the nature of the circumstances, it was evidently impossible for Marcolina to doubt that Lorenzi had sold her to Casanova. Yet however intensely she might hate her wretched lover
at that moment, Casanova felt that he himself, the cowardly thief,
must seem a thousand times more hateful. Perhaps another course

offered better promise of satisfaction. He might degrade Marcolina by mockery and lascivious phrases, full of innuendo. But this spiteful idea could not be sustained in face of the aspect she had now assumed. Her expression of horror had gradually been transformed into one of infinite sadness, as if it had been not Marcolina's womanhood alone which had been desecrated by Casanova, but as if during the night that had just closed a nameless and inexpiable offense had been committed by cunning against trust, by lust against love, by age against youth. Beneath this gaze which, to Casanova's greatest torment, reawakened for a brief space all that was still good in him, he turned away. Without looking around at Marcolina, he went to the window, drew the curtain aside, opened casement and grating, cast a glance round the garden which still seemed to slumber in the twilight, and swung himself across the sill into the open. Aware of the possibility that someone in the house might already be awake and might spy him from a window, he avoided the meadow and sought cover in the shaded alley. Passing through the door in the wall, he had hardly closed it behind him, when someone blocked his path. "The gondolier!" was his first idea. For now he suddenly realized that the gondolier in his dream had been Lorenzi. The young officer stood before him. His silver-braided scarlet tunic glowed in the morning light.

"What a splendid uniform," was the thought that crossed Casanova's confused, weary brain. "It looks quite new. I am sure it has not been paid for." These cool reflections helped him to the full recovery of his wits; and as soon as he was aware of the situation, his mind was filled with gladness. Drawing himself up proudly, and grasping the hilt of his sword firmly beneath the cloak, he said in a tone of the utmost amiability, "Does it not seem to you, Lieutenant Lorenzi, that this notion of yours has come somewhat too late?"

"By no means," answered Lorenzi, looking handsomer than any man Casanova had ever seen before. "Only one of us two shall leave the place alive."

"What a hurry you are in, Lorenzi," said Casanova in an almost tender tone. "Cannot the affair rest until we reach Mantua? I shall be delighted to give you a lift in my carriage, which is waiting at the turn of the road. There is a great deal to be said for observing the forms in these matters, especially in such a case as ours."

"No forms are needed. You or I, Casanova, at this very hour." He drew his sword.

Casanova shrugged. "Just as you please, Lorenzi. But you might at least remember that I shall be reluctantly compelled to appear in a very inappropriate costume." He threw open the cloak and stood there nude, the sword, as though playfully, in his hand. Hate welled up in Lorenzi's eyes. "You shall not be at any disadvantage," he said, and began to strip with all possible speed.

Casanova turned away, and for the moment wrapped himself in his cloak once more, for though the sun was already piercing the morning mists, the air was uncomfortably chill. Long shadows lay across the fields, cast by the sparse trees on the hilltop. For an instant Casanova wondered whether someone might not come down the path. Doubtless it was used only by Olivo and the members of his household. It occurred to Casanova that these were perhaps the last minutes of his life, and he was amazed at his own calmness.

"Monsieur Voltaire is a lucky fellow," came as a passing thought. But in truth he had no interest in Voltaire, and he would have been glad at this moment to have been able to call up more noble images than that of the old author's repulsive birdlike face. How strange it was that no birds were piping in the trees over the wall. A change of weather must be imminent. But what did the weather matter to him? He would rather think of Marcolina, of the ecstasy he had enjoyed in her arms, and for which he was now to pay dear. Dear? Cheap enough! A few years of an old man's life in penury and obscurity. What was there left for him to do in the world? To poison Bragadino? Was it worth the trouble? Nothing was worth the trouble. How few trees there were on the hill! He began to count them. "Five . . . seven . . . ten.—Have I nothing better to do?"

"I am ready, Casanova."

Casanova turned smartly. Lorenzi stood before him, splendid in his nakedness like a young god. No trace of meanness lingered in his face. He seemed equally ready to kill or to die.

"What if I were to throw away my sword?" thought Casanova. "What if I were to embrace him?" He slipped the cloak from his shoulders and stood like Lorenzi, lean and naked.

Lorenzi lowered his point in salute, in accordance with the rules of fence. Casanova returned the salute. Next moment they crossed blades, and the steel glittered like silver in the sun.

"How long is it," thought Casanova, "since last I stood thus measuring sword with sword?" But none of his serious duels now recurred to his mind. He could think only of fencing practice such as ten years earlier he used to have every morning with his valet Costa, the rascal who afterward bolted with a hundred and fifty thousand lire. "All the same, he was a fine fencer; nor has my hand forgotten its cunning! My arm is as true, my vision as keen, as ever. . . . Youth and age are fables. Am I not a god? Are we not both gods? If anyone could see us now. There are women who would pay a high price for the spectacle!"

The blades bent, the points sparkled; at each contact the rapiers sang softly in the morning air. "A fight? No, a fencing match! Why this look of horror, Marcolina? Are we not both worthy of your love? He is but a youngster; I am Casanova!"

Lorenzi sank to the ground, thrust through the heart. The sword fell from his grip. He opened his eyes wide, as if in utter astonishment. Once he raised his head for a moment, while his lips were distorted with pain. Then the head sank again, his nostrils dilated, there was a slight rattling in his throat, and he was dead.

Casanova bent over him, kneeled beside the body, saw a few drops of blood ooze from the wound, held his hand in front of Lorenzi's mouth—but the breath was stilled. A cold shiver passed through Casanova's frame. He rose and put on his cloak. Then, returning to the body, he glanced at the fallen youth, lying stark on the turf in incomparable beauty. The silence was broken by a soft rustling, as the morning breeze stirred the treetops beyond the garden wall.

"What shall I do?" Casanova asked himself. "Shall I call someone? Olivo? Amalia? Marcolina? To what purpose? No one can bring him back to life."

He pondered with the calmness invariable to him in the most dangerous moments of his career. "It may be hours before anyone finds him; perhaps no one will come by before evening; perchance later still. That will give me time, and time is of the first importance."

He was still holding his sword. Noticing that it was bloody, he wiped it on the grass. He thought for a moment of dressing the corpse, but to do this would have involved the loss of precious and irrecoverable minutes. Paying the last duties, he bent once more and closed Lorenzi's eyes. "Lucky fellow," he murmured; and then, dreamily, he kissed the dead man's forehead. He strode along beside the wall, turned the angle, and regained the road. The carriage was where he had left it, the coachman fast asleep on the box. Casanova was careful to avoid waking the man at first. Not until he had cautiously taken his seat did he call out, "Hullo, drive on, can't you?" and prodded him in the back. The startled coachman looked round, greatly astonished to find that it was broad daylight. Then he whipped up his horse and drove off. Casanova sat far back in the carriage, wrapped in the cloak which had once belonged to Lorenzi. In the village only a few children were to be seen in the streets, but it was plain that the men and women were already at work in the fields. When the houses had been left behind Casanova drew a long breath. Opening the travel bag, he withdrew his clothes, and dressed beneath the cover of the cloak, somewhat concerned lest the coachman should turn and discover his fare's strange behavior. But nothing of the sort happened. Undisturbed, Casanova was able to finish dressing, to pack away Lorenzi's cloak, and wear his own. Glancing skyward, Casanova saw that the heavens were overcast. He had no sense of fatigue, but rather felt tense and wakeful. He thought over his situation, considering it from every possible point of view, and coming to the conclusion that, though grave, it was less alarming than it might have seemed to timid spirits. He would probably be suspected of having killed Lorenzi, but who could doubt that it had been in an honorable fight? Besides, Lorenzi had been lying in wait, had forced the encounter upon him, and no one could consider him a criminal for having fought in self-defense. But why had he left the body lying on the grass like that of a dead dog? Well, nobody could reproach him on that account. To flee away swiftly had been well within his right, had been almost a duty. In his place, Lorenzi would have done the same. But perhaps Venice would hand him over? Immediately upon his arrival, he would claim the protection of his patron Bragadino. Yet this might involve his accusing himself of a deed which would after all remain undiscovered, or at any rate would perhaps never be laid to his charge. What proof was there against him? Had he not been summoned to Venice? Who could say that he went thither as a fugitive from justice? The coachman maybe, who had waited for him half the night? One or two additional gold pieces would stop the fellow's mouth. Thus his thoughts ran in a circle. Suddenly he thought he heard the sound of horses' hooves from the road behind him. "Already?" was his first thought. He leaned over the side of the carriage to look backward. The street was empty. The carriage had driven past a farm, and the sound he had heard had been the echo of his own horse's hooves. The discovery of this momentary self-deception quieted his apprehensions for a time, so that it seemed to him the danger was over. He could now see the towers of Mantua. "Drive on, man, drive on," he said under his breath, for he did not really wish the coachman to hear. The coachman, nearing the goal, had given the horse his head. Soon they reached the gate through which Casanova had left the town with Olivo less than forty-eight hours earlier. He told the coachman the name of the inn, and in a few minutes the carriage drew up at the sign of the Golden Lion.

Casanova leaped from the carriage. The hostess stood in the doorway. She was bright and smiling, in the mood apparently to give Casanova the warm welcome of a lover whose absence has been regretted and whose return has been eagerly desired. But Casanova looked warningly toward the coachman, implying that the man might be an inconvenient witness, and then told him to eat and drink to his heart's content.

"A letter from Venice arrived for you yesterday, Chevalier," announced the hostess.

"Another?" inquired Casanova, going upstairs to his room.

The hostess followed. A sealed dispatch was lying on the table. Casanova opened it in great excitement. "A revocation?" he thought anxiously. But when he had finished reading, his face cleared. The missive contained no more than a few lines from Bragadino, enclosing a draft for two hundred and fifty lire, in order that Casanova, should he have made up his mind to accept, might instantly set out for Venice. Turning to the hostess, Casanova explained with an air of simulated irritation that he was unfortunately compelled to continue his journey instantly. Were he to delay, he would risk losing the post which his friend Bragadino had procured for him in Venice, a post for which there were fully a hundred applicants. Threatening clouds gathered on the hostess's face, so Casanova was prompt to add that all he proposed was to make sure of the appointment and to receive his patent as secretary to the Supreme Council. As soon as he was installed in office, he would ask permission to return to Mantua, that he might arrange his affairs. Of course this request could not be refused. He was going to leave most of his effects here. When he returned, it would only depend upon his beloved and charming friend whether she would give up inn-keeping and accompany him to Venice as his wife. She threw her arms round his neck, and with brimming eyes asked him whether before starting he would not at least have a hearty breakfast in his room. He knew she had in mind to provide a farewell feast, and though he felt no appetite for it, he agreed to the suggestion simply to be rid of her. As soon as she was gone, he packed his bag with such underclothing and books as he urgently needed. Then, making his way to the parlor, where the coachman was enjoying a generous meal, he asked the man whether, for a sum which was more than double the usual fare, he would with the same horse drive along the Venice road as far as the next posting station. The coachman agreed immediately, thus relieving Casanova of his principal worry for the time. Now the hostess entered, flushed with annoyance, to ask whether he had forgotten that his breakfast was awaiting him in his room. Casanova nonchalantly replied that he had not forgotten for a moment, and begged her, since he was short of time, to take his draft to the bank, and to bring back the two hundred and fifty lire. While she was hastening to fetch the money, Casanova returned to his room and began to eat with truly wolfish voracity. He continued his meal when the hostess came back; stopping merely for an instant to pocket the money she brought him. When he had finished eating, he turned to the woman. Thinking that her hour had at length come, she had drawn near, and was pressing up against him in a manner which could not be misunderstood. He clasped her vigorously, kissed her on both cheeks, and, although she was obviously ready to grant him the last favors then and there, exclaimed, "I must be off. Till our next meeting!" He tore himself away with such violence that she fell back on to the corner of the couch. Her expression, with its mingling of disappointment, rage, and impotence, was so irresistibly funny that Casanova, as he closed the door behind him, burst out laughing.

The coachman could not fail to realize that his fare was in a hurry, but it was not his business to ask questions. He sat ready on the box when Casanova came out of the inn, and whipped up the horse the very moment the passenger was seated. On his own initiative he decided not to drive through the town, but to skirt it, and to rejoin the posting road upon the other side. The sun was not yet high, since it was still three hours till noon. Casanova reflected, "It is likely enough that Lorenzi's body has not been found yet." It hardly entered his consciousness that he himself had killed Lorenzi. All he knew was that he was glad to be leaving Mantua farther and farther behind, and glad to have rest at last. He fell into a deep sleep, the deepest he had ever known. It lasted practically two days and two nights. The brief interruptions to his slumber necessitated by the change of horses from time to time, and the interruptions that occurred when he was sitting in inns, or walking up and down in front of posting stations, or exchanging a few casual words with postmasters, innkeepers, customhouse officers, and travelers, did not linger in his memory as individual details. Later the memory of these two days and nights merged as it were into the dream he had dreamed in Marcolina's bed. Even the duel between the two naked men upon the green turf in the early sunshine seemed somehow to belong to this dream, wherein often enough, in enigmatic fashion, he was not Casanova but Lorenzi; not the victor but the vanquished; not the fugitive, but the slain around whose pale young body the lonely wind of morning played. Neither he nor Lorenzi was any more real than were the senators in the purple robes who had knelt before him like beggars; nor any less real than such as that old fellow leaning against the parapet of a bridge, to whom at nightfall he had thrown alms from the carriage. Had not Casanova bent his powers of reason to the task of distinguishing between real experiences and dream experiences, he might well have imagined that in Marcolina's arms he had fallen into a mad dream from which he did not awaken until he caught sight of the Campanile of Venice.

It was on the third morning of his journey that Casanova, having reached Mestre, sighted once more the bell tower after over twenty years of longing—a pillar of gray stone looming distantly in the twilight. It was but two hours now to the beloved city in which he had been young. He paid the driver without remembering whether this was the fifth or the sixth with whom he had had to settle since leaving Mantua, and, followed by a lad carrying his baggage, walked through the wretched streets to the harbor from which today, no different from twenty-five years ago, the boat was to leave for Venice at six in the morning. It seemed to have been waiting for him; hardly had he seated himself upon a narrow bench, among petty traders, manual workers, and women bringing their wares to market, when it cast off. It was a cloudy morning; mist was rolling across the lagoons; there was a smell of bilge water, damp wood, fish, and fresh fruit. The Campanile grew ever higher; additional towers appeared; cupolas became visible. The light of the morning sun was reflected from one roof, from two, from many. Individual houses were distinguishable, growing larger by degrees. Boats, large and small, appeared from out of the mist; greetings were shouted from one to the other. The chatter around him grew louder. A little girl offered him some grapes for sale. Consuming the purple berries, he spat the skins over the side after the manner of his countrymen. He entered into friendly talk with someone who expressed satisfaction that the weather seemed to be clearing at last.

"What, has it been raining here for three days? That is news to me. I come from the south, from Naples and Rome."

The boat had entered the canals of the suburbs. Sordid houses stared at him with dirty windows, as if with vacant, hostile eyes. Twice or thrice the vessel stopped at a quay, and passengers came aboard; young fellows, one of whom had a large portfolio under his arm; women with baskets. Here, at last, was familiar ground. Was not that the church where Martina used to go to confession? Was not that the house in which, after his own fashion, he had restored the pallid and dying Agatha to ruddy health? Was not that the place in which he had dealt with the charming Sylvia's rascal of a brother, by beating him black and blue? Up that canal to the right, in the small yellow house upon whose splashed steps the fat, barefooted woman was standing . . . Before he had fully recaptured the distant memory attaching to the house in question, the boat had entered the Grand Canal, and was passing slowly up the broad waterway with palaces on either side. To Casanova, in his dreamy reflections, it seemed as if it had been only yesterday that he had traversed the same route. He disembarked at the Rialto Bridge, for, before visiting Signor Bragadino, he wished to make sure of a room and leave his baggage in a modest hostelry nearby—he knew where it was, though he could not recall the name. The place seemed more decayed, or at least more neglected, than he remembered it to have been. A sulky waiter, badly in need of a shave, showed him to an uninviting room looking upon the blind wall of a house opposite. But Casanova did not want to lose any time. Moreover, since he had spent nearly all his cash on the journey, the cheapness of these quarters was a great attraction. He decided, therefore, to stay there for the present. Having removed the stains of travel, he deliberated for a while whether to put on his finer suit; then decided it was better to wear the more sober one, and walked out of the inn. It was only a hundred paces, along a narrow alley and across a bridge, to Bragadino's small and elegant palace. A young servant with a rather impudent manner took in Casanova's name in a way which implied that its celebrity had no meaning for him. Returning from his master's apartments with a more civil demeanor, he bade the guest enter. Bragadino was seated at breakfast beside the open window and made as if to rise, but Casanova begged him not to disturb himself.

"My dear Casanova," exclaimed Bragadino, "How delighted I am to see you once more! Who would have thought we should ever meet again?" He extended both hands to the newcomer.

Casanova seized them as if to kiss them, but did not do so. He answered the cordial greeting with warm words of thanks in the grandiloquent manner usual to him on such occasions. Bragadino invited him to be seated, and asked him whether he had breakfasted. When Casanova answered in the negative, Bragadino rang for his servant and gave the necessary orders. As soon as the man had gone, Bragadino expressed his gratification that Casanova had unreservedly accepted the Supreme Council's offer. He would certainly not suffer for having decided to devote himself to the service of his country. Casanova responded by saying that he would consider himself happy if he could win the Council's approval. Such were Casanova's words, while his thoughts ran on. He could no longer detect in himself any feeling of hatred toward Bragadino.

Instead, he realized that he was rather sorry for this man advanced in years and grown a trifle foolish, who sat facing him with a sparse white beard and red-rimmed eyes, and whose skinny hand trembled as he held his cup. The last time Casanova had seen him, Bragadino had probably been about as old as Casanova was to-day; but even then, to Casanova, Bragadino had seemed an old man.

The servant brought in Casanova's breakfast. The guest needed little pressing to induce him to make a hearty meal, for on the road he had had no more than a few hasty snacks.

"I have traveled here from Mantua without pausing for a night's rest, so eager was I to show my readiness to serve the Council and to prove my undying gratitude to my benefactor."—This was his excuse for the almost unmannerly greed with which he gulped down the steaming chocolate. Through the window, from the Grand Canal and the lesser canals, rose the manifold sounds of Venetian life, dominated above all by the monotonous shouts of the gondoliers. Somewhere close at hand, perhaps in the opposite palace (was it not the Fogazzari palace?), a woman with a fine soprano voice was practicing coloraturas; the singer was ob-viously young—someone who could not have been born at the time when Casanova escaped from The Leads. He ate rolls and butter, eggs, cold meat, continually excusing himself for his out-rageous hunger, while Bragadino looked on well pleased.

"I do like young people to have a healthy appetite," said the senator. "As far as I can remember, my dear Casanova, that is something you have never lacked!" He recalled to mind a meal which he and Casanova had enjoyed together in the early days of their acquaintance. "Or rather, as now, I sat looking on while you ate. I had not taken a long walk, as you had. It was shortly after you had kicked that physician out of the house, the man who had almost done me in with his perpetual bleedings."

They went on talking of old times—when life had been better in Venice than it was today.

"Not everywhere," said Casanova, with a smiling allusion to The Leads.

Bragadino waved away the suggestion, as if this were not a suit-able time for a reference to such petty disagreeables. "Besides, you must know that I did everything I could to save you from punishment, though unfortunately my efforts proved unavailing. Of course, if in those days I had already been a member of the Council of Ten!"

This broached the topic of political affairs. Warming to his theme, the old man recovered much of the wit and liveliness of earlier days. He told Casanova many remarkable details concerning the unfortunate tendencies which had recently begun to affect some of Venice's youth, and concerning the dangerous intrigues of which infallible signs were now becoming manifest. Casanova was thus well posted for his work. He spent the day in the gloomy chamber at the inn; and, simply as a means of restoring calm to his in so many ways recently disturbed soul, he passed the hours in arranging his papers, and in burning those of which he wished to be rid. When evening fell, he made his way to the Café Quadri in the Square of St. Mark, since this was supposed to be the chief haunt of the freethinkers and revolutionists. Here he was promptly recognized by an elderly musician who had at one time been conductor of the orchestra in the San Samueli Theater, where Casanova had been a violinist thirty years before. By this old acquaintance, and without any advances on his own part, he was introduced to the company. Most of them were young men, and many of their names were those which Bragadino had mentioned in the morning as belonging to persons of suspicious character. But the name of Casanova did not produce on his new acquaintances the effect which he felt himself entitled to anticipate. It was plain that most of them knew nothing more of Casanova than that, a great many years ago, he had for one reason or another, and perhaps for no reason at all, been imprisoned in The Leads; and that, surmounting all possible dangers, he had made his escape. The booklet in which, some years earlier, he had given so lively a description of his flight, had not actually passed unnoticed; but no one seemed to have read it with the attention it deserved. Casanova found it amusing to reflect that it lay within his power to help everyone of these young gentlemen to a speedy personal experience of the conditions of prison life in The Leads, and to a realization of the difficulties of escape. He was far, however, from betraying the slightest hint that he harbored so ill-natured an idea. On the contrary, he was able to play here as elsewhere the innocent and to adopt an amiable role. After his usual fashion, he entertained the company by recounting all sorts of lively adventures, describing them as experiences he had had during his last journey from Rome to Venice. In substance these incidents were true enough, but they all dated from fifteen or twenty years earlier. While he still had an eager and interested audience, someone came to announce the news that an officer of Mantua on a visit to a friend, a neighboring landowner, had been murdered, and that the robbers had stripped him to the skin. The story attracted no particular attention, for in those days such occurrences were far from rare. Casanova resumed his narrative where it had been interrupted, resumed it as if this Mantua affair concerned him just as little as it did the rest of the company. In fact, being now freed from a disquiet whose existence he had hardly been willing to admit even to himself, his manner became brighter and bolder than ever.

It was past midnight when, after a brief farewell, he walked alone across the wide, empty square. The heavens were heavily veiled in luminous mist. He moved with the confident step of a sleepwalker. Without being really conscious that he was on a path which he had not traversed for twenty-five years, he found the way through tortuous alleys, between dark houses, and over narrow bridges. At length he reached the dilapidated inn and had to knock repeatedly before the door was opened to him with a slow unfriendliness. When, a few minutes later, having but half undressed, he threw himself upon his uneasy pallet, he was overwhelmed with a weariness amounting to pain, while on his lips was a bitter aftertaste which seemed to rise up from his innermost being. This then, at the close of his long exile, was to be his first sleep in the city to which he had so eagerly desired to return, and, when morning was about to break, it finally came, heavy and dreamless, taking pity on the aging adventurer.

The End

Postscript

It is a historical fact that Casanova visited Voltaire at Ferney. However, none of the ensuing occurrences presented in the fore-

going novella, particularly Casanova's composition of a polemic
against Voltaire, are based on any historical truth whatsoever. It
is furthermore a historical fact that Casanova, when between fifty
and sixty years of age, found it necessary to enter Venetian service
as a spy. Of this, and of many other doings of the celebrated adventurer to which casual allusion is made in the course of the
novel, fuller and more accurate accounts will be found in Casanova's *Memoirs*. For the rest, *Casanova's Homecoming* is purely
a work of fiction.

A.S.

Translated by Eden and Cedar Paul
and revised by Caroline Wellbery

LIEUTENANT
GUSTL

How much longer is this thing going to last? Let's see what time it is . . . perhaps I shouldn't look at my watch at a serious concert like this. But no one will see me. If anyone does, I'll know he's paying just as little attention as I am. In that case I certainly won't be embarrassed. . . . Only quarter to ten? . . . I feel as though I'd been here for hours. I'm just not used to going to concerts. . . . What's that they're playing? I'll have a look at the program. . . . Yes that's what it is: an oratorio. Thought it was a mass. That sort of thing belongs in church. Besides, the advantage that church has is that you can leave whenever you want to.—I wish I were sitting on the aisle! Steady, steady! Even oratorios end some time. Perhaps this one's very beautiful, and I'm just in the wrong mood. Well, why not? When I think that I came here for diversion . . . I should have given my ticket to Benedek. He likes this sort of thing. Plays violin. But in that case Kopetzky would have felt insulted. It was very nice of him; meant well, at least. He's a good fellow, Kopetzky! The only one I can really trust. . . . His sister is singing up there on the platform. There are at least a hundred women up there—all of them dressed in black. How am I to know which one is Kopetzky's sister? They gave him a ticket because she was singing in the chorus. . . . Why then, didn't Kopetzky go?—They're singing rather nicely now. It's inspiring! Bravo! Bravo! . . . Yes, I'll applaud along with the rest of them. The fellow next to me is clapping as if he were crazy. Wonder if he really likes it as much as all that?—Pretty girl over there in the box! Is she looking at me or at the man with the blond beard? . . . Ah, here we have a solo! Who is it? ALTO: FRÄULEIN

251

WALKER, SOPRANO: FRÄULEIN MICHALEK . . . that one is probably the soprano . . . I haven't been at the opera for an awfully long time. Opera always amuses me, even when it's dull. I could actually go again the day after tomorrow. They're playing *Traviata*. To think, day after tomorrow I might already be dead as a corpse! Oh, nonsense; I can't even believe that myself! Just wait, mister, you'll stop making remarks like that! I'll scrape the skin off the tip of your nose!

I wish I could see the girl in the box more clearly. I'd like to borrow an opera glass. But this fellow next to me would probably kill me if I broke in on his reveries. . . . Wonder in which section Kopetzky's sister is standing? Wonder if I'd recognize her? I've met her only two or three times, the last time at the Officer's Club. Wonder if they're all good girls, all hundred of them? Oh, Lord! . . . ASSISTED BY THE SINGER'S CLUB—Singer's Club . . . that's funny! I'd always imagined that members of a Singer's Club would be something like Vienna chorus girls; that is, I actually knew all along that it wasn't the same thing! Sweet memories! That time at the *Green Gate* . . . What was her name? And then she once sent me a postcard from Belgrade . . . that's also a nice place! Well, Kopetzky's in luck, he's been sitting in some bar, smoking a good cigar!

Why's that fellow staring at me all the time? I suppose he notices how bored I am and that I don't belong here. . . . I'll have you know that if you keep on looking fresh like that I'll meet you in the lobby later and settle with you! He's looking the other way already! They're all so afraid of my eyes. . . . "You have the most beautiful eyes I've ever seen!" Steffi said that the other day. . . . Oh Steffi, Steffi, Steffi!—It's Steffi's fault that I'm sitting here listening to them wail at me for hours. Oh, these letters from Steffi postponing engagements—they're getting on my nerves! What fun this evening might have been! I'd love to read Steffi's letter again. I've got it right here. But if I take it out of my pocket, I'll annoy the fellow next to me—Well, I know what it says . . . she can't come because she has to have dinner with "him." . . . That was funny a week ago when she was at the Gartenbau Café with him, and I was sitting opposite Kopetzky; she kept winking at me in the way we had arranged. He didn't notice a thing—why, it's amazing! He's probably a Jew. Sure, works in a bank. And his black mustache. . . . Supposed to be a lieutenant in the reserve as well! Well, he'd better not come to practice in our regiment! If they keep on commissioning so many Jews—then what's the point of all this anti-Semitism? The other day at the club, when the affair came up between the lawyer and the Mannheimers . . . they say the Mannheimers themselves are Jews, baptized, of course . . . they don't look it—especially Mrs. Mannheimer . . . blond, beautiful figure. . . . It was a good party, all in all. Great food, excellent cigars. . . . Well, the Jews are the ones with the money.

Bravo, bravo! Shouldn't it be over soon? Yes, the whole chorus is rising . . . looks fine—imposing!—Organ too! I like the organ. . . . Ah! that sounds good! Fine! It's really true, I ought to go to concerts more often. . . . I'll tell Kopetzky how beautiful it was. . . . Wonder whether I'll meet him at the café today?—Oh Lord, I don't feel like going there; I was furious yesterday! Lost a hundred and sixty gulden in one round—how stupid! And who won all the money? Ballert. Ballert, who needed it least of all. . . . It's Ballert's fault that I had to go to this rotten concert. . . . Otherwise I might have played again today, and perhaps won back something. But I'm glad I gave myself my solemn word to stay away from cards for a whole month. . . . Mother'll make a face again when she gets my letter!—Ah, she ought to go and see Uncle. He's loaded; a couple of hundred gulden never made any difference to him. If I could only get him to send me a regular allowance . . . But, no, I've got to beg for every penny. Then he always says that crops were poor last year! . . . Wonder whether I ought to spend a two weeks' vacation there again this summer? I'll be bored to death there. . . . If the . . . What was her name? . . . Funny, I can't ever remember a name! Oh, yes: Etelka! . . . Couldn't understand a word of German . . . nor was it necessary. . . . I didn't need to say a thing! . . . Yes, it ought to be all right, fourteen days of country air and fourteen nights with Etelka or someone else. . . . But I ought to spend at least a week with Papa and Mama. She looked awful at Christmas. . . . Well, she'll have gotten over feeling insulted by now. If I were in her place I'd be happy that Papa's retired.—And Clara'll find a husband. Uncle will contribute something. . . . Twenty-eight isn't so old. . . . I'm sure Steffi's no younger. . . . It's really remarkable: the fast girls stay young much longer. Maretti, who played in *Sans Gêne* recently—she's thirty-seven, for sure, and looks . . . Well, I wouldn't have said no! Too bad she didn't ask me. . . .

Getting hot! Not over yet? Ah, I'm looking forward to the fresh air outside. I'll take a little walk around the Ring. . . . Today: early to bed, so as to be fresh for tomorrow afternoon! Funny, how little I think of it; it means nothing to me! The first time it worried me a bit. Not that I was afraid, but I was nervous the night before. . . . Lieutenant Bisanz was a tough opponent.—And still, nothing happened to me! . . . It's already a year and a half since then! Time sure flies! Well, if Bisanz didn't hurt me, the lawyer certainly won't! Still, these inexperienced fencers are often the most dangerous ones. Doschintzky's told me that on one occasion a fellow who had never had a sword in his hand before almost killed him; and today Doschintzky is the fencing instructor of the militia.—Though I wonder whether he was as good then as he is now? . . . Most important of all: keep cool. I don't feel the least angry now—and yet what an insult—unbelievable! He'd probably not have done it if he hadn't been drinking champagne. . . . Such insolence! He's probably a Socialist. All these shysters are Socialists these days. They're a gang. . . . They'd like to do away with the whole army; but they never think of who would help them out if the Chinese ever invaded the country. Fools! Every now and then you have to make an example of one of them. I was quite right. I'm really glad that I didn't let him get away with that remark. I'm furious whenever I think of it! But I behaved superbly. The colonel said I did exactly the right thing. I'll get something out of this affair. I know some who would have let him get away with it. Muller certainly would have taken an "objective" view of it, or something. This being "objective" makes anyone look foolish. "Lieutenant"—just the way in which he said "Lieutenant" was annoying. "You will have to admit—" . . . —How did the thing start? How did I ever get into conversation with a Socialist? . . . As I recall it, the brunette I was taking to the buffet was with us, and then this young fellow who paints hunting scenes—whatever is his name? . . . Good Lord, he's to blame for it all! He was talking about the maneuvers; and it was only then that the lawyer joined us and said something or other I didn't like—about playing at war—something like that—but I couldn't say anything just then. . . . Yes, that's it. . . . And then they were talking about the military school. . . . Yes, that's the way it was. . . . And I was telling them about a patriotic rally. . . . And then that lawyer said—not immediately, but it grew out of my talk about the rally— "Lieutenant, you'll admit, won't you, that not all your friends have gone into military service for the sole purpose of defending our Fatherland!" What nerve! How dare anyone say a thing like that to an officer! I wish I could remember exactly how I answered him—Oh, yes, something about "fools rushing in where angels fear to tread" . . . Yes, that was it. . . . And there was a fellow there who wanted to smooth over matters—an elderly man with a cold in the head—but I was too furious! The lawyer had said it in a way that meant me personally. The only thing he could have added was that they had expelled me from college, and for that reason I had to go into military service. . . . Those people don't understand our point of view. They're too dull-witted. . . . Not everyone can experience the thrill I did the first time I wore a uniform. . . . Last year at the maneuvers—I would have given a great deal if it had suddenly been in earnest. . . . Mirovic told me he felt exactly the same way. And then when His Highness rode up at the front and the colonel addressed us—only a cad wouldn't have felt proud. . . . And now a boor comes along who has been a penpusher all his life and has the gall to make a fresh remark. . . . Oh, just wait my dear. Unfit for battle—yes, that's what I'll make him!

Well, what's this? It ought to be over by now. . . . "Ye, his Angels, praise the Lord"—Surely, that's the final chorus. . . . Beautiful, there's no denying it, really beautiful! And here I've completely forgotten the girl in the box who was flirting with me before. . . . Where is she now? . . . Already gone. . . . That one over there seems rather nice. . . . Stupid of me—I left my opera glasses at home. Brunnthaler's smart, he always keeps his with the cashier at the café—you can't go wrong if you do that. I wish the cute little one over there would turn around. She sits there so properly. The one next to her is probably her mother. . . . I won- der whether I ought to consider marriage seriously? Willy was no older than I when he took the leap. There's something to be said for always having a pretty little wife home at your disposal. . . . Too bad that just today Steffi didn't have any time! If I only knew where she were. I'd sit down facing her again. That'd be a good one! If he'd ever catch me, he'd palm her off on me. When I think what Fliess's affair with that Winterfeld woman must cost him!— and even at that, she cheats on him right and left. One of these days the whole thing will end with a bang. . . . Bravo, bravo! Ah, it's over. . . . Oh, it feels good to get up and stretch. Well! How long is he going to take to put that opera glass into his pocket?

"Pardon me, won't you let me pass?"

What a crowd! Better let the people go by. . . . Gorgeous person. . . . Wonder whether they're genuine diamonds? . . . That one over there's rather attractive. . . . The way she's giving me the eye! . . . Why, yes, my lady, I'd be glad to! . . . Oh, what a nose!—Jewess. . . . Another one. It's amazing, half of them are Jews. One can't even hear an oratorio unmolested these days. . . . Now let's get into line. Why is that idiot back of me pushing so? I'll teach him better manners. . . . Oh, it's an elderly man! . . . Who's that bowing to me over there? . . . How do you do. Charmed! I haven't the slightest idea who he is. . . . I think I'll go right over to Leidinger's for a bite, or should I go to the Gartenbau? Maybe Steffi'll be there after all. Why didn't she write and let me know where she's going with him? She probably didn't know herself. Actually terrible, this dependency. . . . Poor thing— So, here's the exit. . . . Oh! that one's pretty as a picture! All alone? She's smiling at me. There's an idea—I'll follow her! . . . Now, down the steps. . . . Oh, a major—from the 95th—very nice, the way he returned my salute. I'm not the only officer here after all. . . . Where did the pretty girl go? . . . There she is, standing by the banister. . . . Now to the wardrobe. . . . Better not lose her. . . . She's nabbed him already. What a brat! Having someone call for her, and then laughing over at me! They're all worthless. . . . Good Lord, what a mob there at the wardrobe. Better wait a little while. Why doesn't the idiot take my coat check?

"Here, Number two hundred and twenty-four! It's hanging there! What's the matter—are you blind? Hanging there! There! At last. . . . Thank you." That fatso there is taking up most of the wardrobe. . . . "If you please!" . . .

"Patience, patience."

What's the fellow saying?

"Just have a little patience."

I'll have to answer him in kind. "Why don't you allow some room?"

"You'll get there in time." What's he saying? Did he say that to me? That's rather strong! I won't swallow that. "Keep quiet!"

"What did you say?"

What a way to talk! That's the limit!

"Don't push!"

"Shut your mouth!" I shouldn't have said that. That was a bit rough. . . . Well, I've done it now.

"Exactly what did you mean by that?"

Now he's turning around. Why I know him!—Heavens, it's the baker, the one who always comes to the café. . . . What's he doing here? He probably has a daughter or something in the chorus. Well, what's this?—What's he trying to do? It looks as though . . . Yes, great Scott, he has the hilt of my sword in his hand! What's the matter? Is the man crazy? . . . "You Sir! . . . "

"You, Lieutenant, hush your mouth."

What's he saying? For Heaven's sake, I hope no one's heard it. No, he's talking very softly. . . . Well, why doesn't he let go of my sword? Great God! Now I've got to get tough. I can't budge his hand from the hilt. Let's not have a rumpus here! Isn't the major behind me? Can anyone notice that he's holding the hilt of my sword? Why, he's talking to me! What's he saying!

"Lieutenant, if you dare to make the slightest fuss, I'll pull your sword out of the sheath, break it in two, and send the pieces to your regimental commander. Do you understand me, you young fathead?"

What did he say? Am I dreaming? Is he really talking to me? How shall I answer him? But he's in earnest. He's really pulling the sword out. Great God! he's doing it! . . . I can feel it! He's already pulling it! What is he saying? For God's sake, no scandal!—What's he forever saying?

"But I have no desire to ruin your career. . . . So just be a good boy. . . . Don't be scared. Nobody's heard it. . . . Everything's all right. . . . And so that no one will think we've been fighting I'll act most friendly toward you. . . . I am honored, Sir Lieutenant. It has been a pleasure—a real pleasure."

Good God, did I dream that? . . . Did he really say that? . . . Where is he? . . . There he goes. . . . I must draw my sword and run him through—Heavens, I hope nobody heard it. . . . No, he talked very softly—right in my ear. Why don't I go after him and crack open his skull? . . . No, it can't be done. It can't be done.

. . . I should have done it at once. . . . Why didn't I do it immediately? . . . I couldn't. . . . He wouldn't let go the hilt, and
he's ten times as strong as I am. . . . If I had said another word,
he would actually have broken the sword in two. I ought to be
glad that he spoke no louder. If anyone had heard it, I'd have had
to shoot myself on the spot. . . . Perhaps it was only a dream.
Why is that man by the pillar looking at me like that?—Maybe he
heard? . . . I'll ask him . . . ask him?!—Am I crazy?—How do I
look? Does anyone notice?—I must be pale as a sheet—Where's
the swine? I've got to kill him! . . . He's gone. . . . The whole
place is empty. . . . Where's my coat? . . . Why, I'm already
wearing it. . . . I didn't even notice it. . . . Who helped me on
with it? . . . Oh, that one there. I'll have to tip him. . . . So. But
what's it all about? Did it really happen? Did anyone really talk
to me like that? Did anyone really call me a fathead? And I didn't
cut him to pieces on the spot? . . . But I couldn't. . . . He had a
fist like iron. I just stood there as though I were nailed to the floor.
I think I must have lost my senses. Otherwise, I would have used
my other hand. . . . But then he would have drawn out my sword,
and broken it, and everything would have been over. . . . Over
and done with! And afterward, when he walked away, it was too
late. . . . I couldn't have run my sword through him from the
back.

What, am I already on the street? How did I ever get here?—
It's so cool. . . . Oh, the wind feels fine! . . . Who's that over
there? Why are they looking over at me? I wonder whether they
didn't hear something. . . . No, no one could have heard it. . . .
I'm sure of it—I looked around immediately! No one paid any
attention to me. No one heard a thing. . . . But he said it anyhow. Even if nobody heard it, he certainly said it. I just stood
there and took it as if someone had knocked me silly. . . . But I
couldn't say a word—couldn't do a thing. All I did was stand
there—hush, hush your mouth! . . . It's awful; it's unbearable; I
must kill him on the spot, wherever I happen to meet him! . . . I
let a swine like that get away with it! And he knows me. . . .
Great Heavens, he knows me—knows who I am! . . . He can tell
everybody just exactly what he said to me! . . . No, he wouldn't
do that. Otherwise, he wouldn't have talked so quietly. . . . He
just wanted me to hear it alone! . . . But how do I know that he

won't repeat it today or tomorrow, to his wife, to his daughter, to his friends in the café—for God's sake, I'll see him again tomorrow. As soon as I step into the café tomorrow, I'll see him sitting there as he does every day, playing Tarok with Schlesinger and the paper-flower merchant. No, that can't happen. I won't allow it to. The moment I see him I'll run him through. . . . No, I can't do that. . . . I should have done it right then and there! . . . If only I could have! I'll go to the colonel and tell him about the whole affair. . . . Yes, right to the colonel. . . . The colonel is always friendly—and I'll say to him—Colonel, I wish to report, Sir. He grasped the hilt of my sword and wouldn't let go of it; it was just as though I were completely unarmed. . . . What will the colonel say?—What will he say? There's just one answer: dishonorable discharge! . . . Are those one-year volunteers over there? Disgusting. At night they look like officers. . . . Yes, they're saluting!—If they knew—if they only knew! . . . There's the Hochleitner Café. Probably a couple of officers in my company are there now. . . . Perhaps one or more whom I know. . . . Wonder if it wouldn't be best to tell the first one I meet all about it—but just as if it had happened to someone else? . . . I'm already going a bit crazy. . . . Where the devil am I walking? What am I doing out here in the street?—But where should I go? Wasn't I going to the Leidinger Café? Haha! If I were to sit down in public, I'm sure everyone would see what had happened to me. . . . Well, something must happen. . . . But what? . . . Nothing, nothing at all— no one heard it. No one knows a thing. At least for the time being. . . . Perhaps I ought to visit him at his home and beg him to swear to me that he'll never tell a soul.—Ah, better to put a bullet through my head at once. That would be the smartest thing to do. The smartest? The smartest?—there's just nothing else left for me— nothing. If I were to ask the colonel or Kopetzky, or Blany, or Friedmair:—they'd all tell me the same thing. How would it be if I were to talk it over with Kopetzky? Yes, that seems the most sensible thing to do. Not to mention because of tomorrow—tomorrow—yes, that's right, tomorrow—at four o'clock, in the armory, I'm to fight a duel. But I can't do it, I'm no longer qualified for dueling. Nonsense, nonsense, not a soul knows it, not a soul!— There are hundreds of people walking around to whom worse things have happened. . . . What about all those stories I've heard about Deckener—how he and Rederow fought with pistols. . . . And the dueling committee decided that the duel could take place at that. . . . But what would the committee decide about me?— Fathead, fathead, and I just stood there and took it—! Great heavens, it makes no difference whether anyone knows it or not! The main thing is: *I* know he said it! *I* feel as though I'm not the same man I was an hour ago—*I* know that I'm not qualified for dueling, and that I must shoot myself. I wouldn't have another calm moment in my life. I'd always be afraid that someone might find out about it in some way or another, and that some time someone might tell me to my face what happened this evening!—What a happy man I was an hour ago! . . . Just because Kopetzky gave me a ticket, and just because Steffi canceled her date—destiny hangs on things like that. . . . This afternoon, all was sailing smoothly, and now I am a lost man about to shoot himself. . . . Why am I running this way? No one is chasing me. What's the time? One, two, three, four, five, six, seven, eight, nine, ten, eleven. . . . Eleven, Eleven. . . . I ought to go and get something to eat. . . . After all, I've got to go somewhere. I might go and sit down in some little restaurant where no one would know me.—At any rate, a man must eat even though he kill himself immediately afterward. Haha! Death is no child's play. . . . Who said that recently?—It makes no difference.

I wonder who'll be most upset, . . . Mama or Steffi? . . . Steffi, Great God, Steffi! . . . She won't allow anyone to notice how she feels. Otherwise "he" will throw her out. . . . Poor little thing!— At my regiment. . . . No one would have the slightest idea why I did it. They'd all wrack their brains. . . . Why did Gustl commit suicide? But no one will guess that I had to shoot myself because a miserable baker, a low person who just happened to have a strong fist . . . It's too silly—too silly for words!—For that reason, a fellow like myself, young and fit. . . . Well, afterward they're all sure to say he didn't have to commit suicide for a silly reason like that, what a pity! But if I were to ask anyone right now, they'd all give me the same answer. . . . And if I were to ask myself. . . . Oh, the devil, we're absolutely helpless against civilians. People think that we're better off just because we carry swords, and if one of us ever makes use of a weapon, the story goes around that we're all born murderers. The paper will carry a story: "Young Officer's Suicide" . . . How do they always put it? . . . "Motive Concealed" . . . Haha! . . . "Mourning at his Coffin." . . . —But it's true. I feel as if I were forever telling myself a story. . . . It's true. . . . I must commit suicide. There's nothing else left to do—I can't allow Kopetzky and Blany to come tomorrow morning and say to me: Sorry, we can't be your seconds. I'd be a cad if I expected them to . . . what kind of guy am I, standing quietly by and letting myself be called a fathead. . . . Tomorrow everyone will know it. Fancy myself believing for a moment that a person like that won't repeat it everywhere. . . . Why, his wife knows it already! Tomorrow everyone in the café will know it. All the waiters will know it. Schlesinger will know it—so will the cashier girl— And even if he planned not to tell anybody, he'll certainly tell them the day after tomorrow. . . . And if not then, in a week from now. . . . And even if he had a stroke tonight, I'd know it. . . . I'd know it. And I could no longer wear a cape and carry a sword if such a disgrace were on me! . . . So, I've got to do it—I've got to do it—There's nothing to it.—Tomorrow afternoon the lawyer might just as well run his sword through me. . . . Things like this have happened before. . . . And Bauer, poor fellow, got an inflammation of the brain and died three days later. . . . And Brenitsch fell off his horse and broke his neck. . . . And finally, there's nothing else to do, not for me anyhow, certainly not for me!—There are men who would take it more lightly. . . . But God, what sort of men are they! . . . a butcher slapped Ringeimer's face when he caught him with his wife, whereupon Ringeimer took his leave and is now somewhere out in the country, married. . . . There are women, I suppose, who'll marry people like that! . . . On my word, I'd never shake hands with him if he came to Vienna! . . . Well, you've heard it, Gustl:—life is over for you—finished, once and for all. Period! I know it now, it's a simple story. . . . Well! I'm actually totally calm. . . . I've always known it: if the occasion were ever to arise, I'd be calm, completely calm. . . . But I would never have believed that it would happen like this. . . . —That I'd have to kill myself just because a . . . Perhaps I didn't understand him correctly after all. . . . He was talking in an altogether different tone at the end. . . . I was simply a little out of my mind on account of the singing and the heat. . . . Perhaps I was momentarily demented, and it's all not

true. . . . Not true, haha! Not true!—I can still hear it. . . . It's
still ringing in my ears, and I can still feel in my fingers how I
tried to move his hand from the hilt of my sword. He's a husky
brute. . . . I'm no weakling myself. Franziski is the only man in
the regiment who's stronger than I.

Already at the Aspern bridge? . . . How far am I still going to
run? If I keep on this way I'll be at Kagran by midnight. . . .
Haha! . . . Good lord, how happy we were last September when
we marched into Kagran. Only two more hours to Vienna! . . . I
was dead tired when we got there. . . . I slept like a log all afternoon, and by evening we were already at Ronacher's. . . . Kopetzky and Ladinser. . . . Who else was along with us at the
time?—Yes, that's right . . . that volunteer, the one who told us
the Jewish stories while we were marching. Sometimes they're
pleasant fellows, these one-year men. . . . But they all ought to
be only substitutes. For what sense is there to it: all of us slave for
ages, and a fellow like him serves a year and receives the same
rank as we. . . . It's unfair!—But what's it to me? Why should I
bother about such things? A private in the quartermaster corps
counts for more than I do right now. . . . I no longer belong on
the face of the earth. . . . It's all over with me. Honor lost—
everything lost! . . . There's nothing else for me to do but load
my revolver and . . . Gustl, Gustl, you still don't quite believe it?
Come to your senses! . . . There's no way out. . . . No matter
how you torture your brain, there's no way out!—The point is to
behave properly at the end, like an officer and a gentleman so that
the colonel will say: He was a good fellow, we'll always honor his
memory! . . . How many companies attend the funeral of a lieutenant? . . . I really must know that. . . . Haha! Even if the whole
battalion turns out, even if the whole garrison turns out, and they
fire twenty salutes, it still won't wake me up! Last summer, after
the army Steeplechase, I was sitting in front of this café here with
Engel. . . . Funny, I've never seen the fellow since. . . . Why did
he have his left eye bandaged? I always wanted to ask him, but it
didn't seem proper. . . . There go two artillerymen. . . . They
probably think I'm following that woman. . . . Actually I ought
to have a look at her . . . Oh, Lord! I wonder how that one can
possibly earn a living. . . . I'd sooner . . . However, in time of
need a person will do almost anything. . . . In Przemsyl—I was

so horrified afterwards that I swore I'd never look at a woman again. . . . That was a ghastly time up there in Galicia. . . . Altogether a stroke of fortune that we came to Vienna. Bokorny is still in Sambor, and may stay another ten years, getting old and gray. . . . What happened to me today would never have happened if I'd remained there myself, and I'd far sooner grow old in Galicia than . . . Than what? Than what?—What is it? What is it? Am I crazy—the way I always forget?—Good God, I forget it every moment. . . . Has anyone ever heard of a man who within two hours of putting a bullet through his head digresses on all conceivable matters that no longer concern him? I feel as if I were drunk. Haha, drunk indeed! Dead drunk! Drunk with suicide! Ha, trying to be funny! Yes, I'm in a good mood—must have been born with one. Certainly, if I ever told anybody they'd say I were lying.—I feel that if I had the revolver with me now . . . I'd pull the trigger—in a second all is over. . . . Not everyone is so lucky—others have to suffer for months. My poor cousin, on her back two years, couldn't move, had the most excruciating pains, what misery! Isn't it better when you take it in hand yourself? . . . Care is the only thing necessary; to aim well, so that nothing unfortunate happens, as it did to that cadet last year. . . . Poor devil, didn't die, but ended up blind. . . . Whatever happened to him? Wonder where he's living now. Terrible to run around the way he—that is, he can't run around, he's led. A chap like him—can't be more than twenty years old right now. He took better aim on his beloved. . . . She was dead at once. . . . Unbelievable, the reasons people have for killing. How can anyone be jealous? . . . I've never been jealous in my whole life. At this very moment Steffi is sitting comfortably at the Gartenbau; then she will go home with "him." . . . Doesn't mean a thing to me. . . . Not a thing. She has a nicely furnished place—a little bathroom with a red lamp— When she recently came in, in her green kimono. . . . I'll never see the green kimono again—Steffi, herself, I'll never see again—And I'll never go up the fine broad steps in Gusshaus Strasse. Steffi will keep on amusing herself as if nothing had happened; she won't be allowed to tell a soul that her beloved Gustl committed suicide. But she'll weep—oh, yes, she'll weep. A great many people will weep. . . .Good God, Mama!—No, no, I can't think about it. Oh, no, I can't bear to. . . . You're not to think about home at all, Gustl, you understand? Not even with the faintest thought.

Not bad, I'm already at the Prater in the middle of the night . . . That's another thing I didn't think of this morning, that tonight I'd be taking a walk in the Prater. . . . Wonder what the cop there thinks. . . . Well, I'll walk on. It's rather nice here. No point in eating; no fun in the café. The air is pleasant and it's quiet. . . . Indeed, I'll have a great deal of quiet—as much as I could possibly want. Haha!—But I'm altogether out of breath. I must have been running like crazy. . . . Slower, slower, Gustl, you won't miss anything, there's nothing more to do, nothing, absolutely nothing! What's this, am I getting a chill?—Probably on account of all the excitement, and then I haven't eaten a thing. What's that strange smell? . . . Are the blossoms out yet?—What's today?—The fourth of April. It's been raining a great deal the last few days, but the trees are still almost entirely bare . . . how dark it is! Hooh! Dark enough to give you the shivers. . . . That was really the only time in my whole life I was scared—when I was a little kid that time in the woods. . . . But I wasn't so little at that. . . . Fourteen or fifteen. . . . How long ago was it?—Nine years. . . . Sure—at eighteen I was a substitute; a twenty a lieutenant and next year I'll be . . . What'll I be next year? What do I mean; next year? What do I mean; next week? What do I mean; tomorrow? . . . What's this? Teeth chattering? Oh!—Well! let them chatter a while. Lieutenant, you are altogether alone right now and have no reason for showing off. . . . It's bitter, oh, it's bitter. . . .

I'll sit on that bench. . . . Ah. . . . How far have I come?— How dark it is! That behind me there, that must be the second café. . . . I was in there, too, last summer at the time our band gave a concert. . . . With Kopetzky and with Rüttner—there were a couple of others along. . . . —Lord, I'm tired. . . . As tired as if I'd been marching for the last ten hours. . . . Yes, it would be fine to go to sleep now.—Ha, a lieutenant without shelter! . . . Yes, I really ought to go home. . . . What'll I do at home?—But what am I doing in the Prater?—Ah, it would be best never to get up at all—to sleep here and never wake up. . . . Yes, that would be comfortable! But, Lieutenant, things aren't going to be as comfortable as that for you. . . . What next?—Well I might really consider the whole affair in orderly sequence. . . . All things must be considered. . . . Life is like that. . . . Well, then, let's consider. . . . Consider what? . . . My God, doesn't the air feel good. . . . I ought to go to the Prater more often at night. . . . That should have occurred to me sooner. It's all a thing of the past—the Prater, the air and taking walks. . . . Well, then, what next?—Off with my cap. It's pressing on my forehead. . . . I can't think properly. . . . Ah. . . . That's better! . . . Now, Gustl, collect your thoughts, make your final arrangements! Tomorrow morning will be the end. . . . Tomorrow morning at seven . . . seven o'clock is a beautiful hour. Haha!—At eight o'clock when school begins, all will be over. . . . Kopetzky won't be able to teach—he'll be too broken up. . . . But maybe he'll know nothing about it yet. . . . No need to hear about it. . . . They didn't find Max Lippay until the afternoon, and it was in the morning that he had shot himself, and not a soul heard it. . . . But why bother about whether Kopetzky will teach school tomorrow. . . . Ha!—Well, then, at seven o'clock—Yes. . . . Well, what next? . . . Nothing more to consider. I'll shoot myself in my room and then—basta! The funeral will be Monday. . . . I know one man who'll enjoy it: the lawyer. The duel can't take place on account of the suicide of one of the combatants. . . . Wonder what they'll say at Mannheimers?—Well, he won't make much of it. . . . But his wife, his pretty, blond . . . She did not seem disinclined. . . .

Oh, yes, I would have had a chance with her if I'd only pulled myself together a little. . . . Yes, with her it might have been something altogether different from that broad Steffi. . . . But the thing is, you can't be lazy: it's a question of courting in the proper way, sending flowers, making reasonable conversation . . . not: meet me tomorrow afternoon at the barracks! . . . Yes, a decent woman like her—that might have been something. The captain's wife at Przemysl wasn't respectable. . . . I could swear that Lubitzsky and Wermutek . . . and the shabby substitute—they all had her, too. . . . But Mannheimer's wife . . . Yes, that would have put me in a different social circle. That might almost have made me a different man—she might have given me more polish— or have given me more respect for myself— But always those easy types . . . and I began so young—I was only a boy that time on my first vacation when I was home with my parents in Graz. . . .

Riedl was also along. . . . she was Bohemian. . . . Must have been twice as old as I—came home only the following morning. . . . The way Father looked at me . . . And Clara. I was most ashamed of all before Clara. . . . She was engaged at the time. . . . Wonder why the engagement never materialized. I didn't think much about it at the time. Poor thing, never had much luck—and now she's going to lose her only brother. . . . Yes, you'll never see me again, Clara—it's all over. You didn't foresee, little sister, did you, when you saw me at the station on New Year's Day, that you'd never see me again?—And Mother . . . Good God! Mother! . . . No, I can't allow myself to think of it. Ah, if I could only go home first. . . . When I think of that, I'm capable of doing something dishonorable. Say I have a day's leave. . . . See Papa, Mama, Clara again before it's all over. . . . Yes, I could take the first train at seven o'clock to Graz. I'd be there at one. . . . God bless you, Mama. . . . Hello, Clara! . . . How goes everything? . . . Well this *is* a surprise. . . . But they'll notice something. . . . If no one else, at least Clara will. . . . Clara for sure . . . Clara's such a smart girl. . . . She wrote me such a sweet letter the other day, and I still owe her an answer—and the good advice she always gives me. Such a wholeheartedly good creature. . . . Wonder whether everything wouldn't have turned out differently if I'd stayed at home. I might have studied agriculture and joined my uncle on his estate. . . . They all wanted me to do that when I was a kid. . . . By this time I'd be happily married to a nice, sweet girl. . . . Perhaps Anna—she used to like me a lot. . . . I just noticed it again the last time I was home—in spite of her husband and two children. . . . I could see it, just the way she looked at me. . . . And she still calls me "Gustl," just like she used to. . . . It will hit her hard when she finds out the way I ended up—but her husband will say: I might have known as much—a no-good like him!— They'll all think it was because I owed money. . . . It's not true. I've paid all my debts. . . . except the last hundred and sixty gulden—and they'll be here tomorrow. Well I must see to it that Ballert gets his hundred and sixty gulden—I must make a note of that before I shoot myself. . . . It's terrible, it's terrible! . . . If I only could run away from it all and go to America where nobody knows me. In America no one will know what happened here this evening. . . . No one cares about such things there. Just recently I read in the paper about some Count Runge, who had to leave because of some nasty story, and now he owns a hotel over there and doesn't give a hoot for the whole damn business. . . . And in a couple of years I could come back. . . . Not to Vienna, of course. . . . Nor to Graz . . . but I could go out to the estate. . . . And Mama and Papa and Clara would a dozen times rather have it that way—just so long as I stay alive. . . . And why worry about the other people at all? Who ever cares about me?—Kopetzky's the only one who'd ever miss me. . . . Kopetzky—just the one who gave me the ticket today . . . and the ticket's to blame for it all. If he hadn't given it to me, I wouldn't have gone to the concert, and all this would never have happened. . . . What did happen anyway? It's just as if a whole century had passed—and it's only two hours ago. Two hours ago someone called me a fathead and wanted to break my sword. Great God, I'm starting to shout here at midnight! Why did it all happen? Couldn't I have waited longer until the whole wardrobe had emptied out? And why did I ever tell him to shut up? How did it ever slip out of me? I'm generally polite. I'm usually not so rude, even to my orderly. . . . But of course I was nervous: all the things that happened just at the same time. . . . The tough luck in gambling and Steffi's eternal stalling—and the duel tomorrow afternoon—and I've been getting too little sleep lately, and all the drudgery in the barracks. . . . No one can stand that forever! . . . Before long I would have become ill—would have had to get a furlough. . . . Now it's no longer necessary. . . . I'll get a long furlough now—without pay—Haha! . . .

How long am I going to keep on sitting here? It must be after midnight. . . . Didn't I hear the clock strike midnight a while ago?—What's that there? A carriage driving by? At this hour? Rubber tires—I can already imagine . . . They're better off than I. Perhaps it's Ballert with his Bertha. . . . Why should it be Ballert, of all people?—Go ahead, right on! That was a good looking carriage His Highness had in Przemsyl. . . . He used to ride in it all the time on his way to the city to see the Rosenberg woman. He was a good mixer, His Highness—chummy with everyone, a good drinking companion. Those were good times. . . . Although . . . It was in a desolate part of the country, and the weather was hot enough in the summer to kill you. . . . One afternoon three

men were overcome by the heat. . . . Even the corporal in my
own company—a handy fellow he was. . . . During the afternoon
we used to lie down naked on the bed. Once Wiesner came into
the room suddenly; I must just have been dreaming. I stood up
and drew my sword—it was lying next to me. . . . Must have
looked funny! . . . Wiesner laughed himself sick. He's already been
promoted to lieutenant colonel in the cavalry—sorry I didn't go
into the cavalry myself. The old man didn't want me to—it would
have been too expensive—but it makes no difference now. . . .
Why?—Yes, I know: I must die, that's why it makes no difference—I must die. . . . How then?—Look here, Gustl, you came
down here to the Prater in the middle of the night especially so
that not a soul would bother you—now you can think everything
over quietly. . . . That's all a lot of nonsense about America and
quitting the service, and you haven't the brains to start on another
career. And when you reach the age of a hundred and think back
to the time that a fellow wanted to break your sword, and called
you a fathead and you stood there and couldn't do a thing—no,
there's nothing more to think about—what's happened has happened.—That's all nonsense about Mama and Clara—they'll get
over it—people get over everything. . . . Oh, Lord, how Mama
wept when her brother died—and after four weeks she hardly
thought about it anymore. She used to ride out to the cemetery
. . . first, every week, then every month, and now only on the day
of his death. Tomorrow is the day of my death—April fifth.—
Wonder whether they'll take my body to Graz—Haha! The worms
in Graz will enjoy it!—But that's not my problem—I'll let others
worry about that. . . . Well then, what actually *does* concern me?
. . . Oh yes, the hundred and sixty gulden for Ballert—that's all—
other than that I have no arrangements to make.—Are there letters to write? What for? To whom? . . . Taking my leave? The
devil I will—it's clear enough that a man's gone after he's shot
himself! Everyone will soon notice that he's taken his leave. . . .
If people only knew how little the whole thing bothers me, they
wouldn't feel sorry—No use pitying me. . . . What have I had
out of life?—One thing I'd like to have experienced: being in war—
but I would have had to wait a long time for that. . . . Outside
of that I've experienced everything. Whether a broad's called Steffi
or Kunigunde makes no difference. . . . And I've heard all the

best operettas—and I've been to see *Lohengrin* twelve times—and this evening I even heard an oratorio—and a baker called me a fathead.—Good God, I've had enough! I'm not in the least curious anymore. . . . Well then, I'll go home slowly, very slowly, there's really no hurry.—I'll rest for a few minutes on the bench here in the Prater, not a roof over my head. I'll never lie down in bed again. I'll have enough time to sleep.—This wonderful air! There'll be no more air. . . .

Well, what's this?—Hey, there, Johann, bring me a glass of fresh water. . . . What's this? . . . Where? . . . Am I dreaming? My head. Oh, Good Lord . . . I can't get my eyes open!—I'm all dressed!—Where am I sitting?—Holy God, I've been sleeping! How could I have been sleeping? It's already growing light. How long have I been sleeping?—Must look at my watch—can't see a thing. . . . Where are my matches? Won't a single one of them light? . . . Three o'clock, and I'm to have my duel at four.—No, not a duel—a suicide! It has nothing to do with a duel; I must shoot myself because a baker called me a fathead. . . . What, did it actually happen?—My head feels so funny. . . . My throat's all clogged up—I can't move at all—my right foot's asleep.—Get up! Get up! . . . Ah, that's better! It's already growing light, and the air . . . Just like that morning when I was doing picket duty when we were camping in the woods. That was a different kind of waking up—that was a different sort of day ahead of me. . . . It seems as though I'm having trouble believing it. There's the street—gray, empty—just now I'm probably the only person in the Prater. I was here once at four o'clock in the morning with Pansinger.—We were riding. I was on Colonel Mirovic's horse, and Pansinger on his own nag.—That was May, a year ago—everything was in bloom—everything was green. Now the trees are still bare, but spring will soon be here—it will be here in just a few days.—Lilies-of-the-valley, violets—pity I'll never see them again. Every yokel will enjoy them, but I must die! Oh, it's miserable! And others will sit in the café eating, as if nothing had happened—just the way all of us sat in the café on the evening of the day they buried Lippay. . . . And they all liked Lippay so much. . . . He was more popular in the regiment than me.—Why shouldn't they sit in the Weingartl when I kick off?—It's quite warm—much warmer than yesterday

and there's a fragrance in the air—the blossoms must be out. . . .
Wonder whether Steffi will bring me flowers?—It will never occur
to her! She wouldn't dream of going to the funeral. . . Oh, if it
were still Adele . . . Adele! I'm sure I haven't thought of her for
the last two years. . . . As long as I lived I never saw a woman
weep the way she did. . . . Come to think of it, that was the
tenderest thing I ever lived through . . . she was so modest, so
unassuming.—She loved me, I swear she did.—She was altogether
different from Steffi. . . . I wonder why I ever gave her up. What
a stupid thing! . . . It was too tame for me, yes, that was what it
was. . . . Going out with the same person every evening . . .
Then perhaps I was afraid that I'd never be able to get rid of her—
she always whimpered so.—Well, Gustl, you could have postponed it . . . after all, she was the only one who really loved you.
Wonder what she's doing now. Well, what would she be doing—
probably has someone else now. This, with Steffi, is much more
comfortable. When you're only together off and on—someone else
has all the inconvenience—and I just have the pleasant part. . . .
Well, in that case I certainly can't expect her to come to the cemetery. Wonder if there's anyone who'd go without feeling obliged
to. Kopetzky, perhaps—and that's all! Oh, it's sad, not to have
anyone. . . . Nonsense! There's Papa and Mama and Clara. It's
because I'm a son and a brother. . . . What more is there to hold
us together? They like me of course—but what do they know about
me?—That I'm in the service, that I play cards, and that I run
around with fast women. . . . Anything more? The fact I often
get good and sick of myself—*that* I never wrote to them about—
perhaps the reason is because I have never realized it myself. Well,
Gustl, what sort of stuff are you muttering to yourself? It's just
about time to start crying. . . . Disgusting!—Keep in step. . . .
So! Whether a man goes to a rendezvous or on duty or to battle.
. . . Who was it said that? . . . Oh yes, it was Major Lederer.
When they were telling us that time at the canteen about Wingle-
der—the one who grew so pale before his first duel—and vomited.
. . . Yes, a true officer will never betray by look or step whether
he goes to a rendezvous or certain death!—Therefore, Gustl—remember the major's words! Ha!—Always growing lighter. .¯ . .
Light enough to read, if you wanted to . . . What's that whistling
there?—Oh yes, there's the North Railroad Station. . . . the Te-

gethoff monument . . . It's never looked that tall before. . . . There are the carriages. Nobody except street cleaners around. They're the last street cleaners I'll ever see—Ha! I always have to laugh when I think of it. . . . I don't understand that at all . . . Wonder whether it's that way with everybody, once they're entirely sure. Three thirty by the clock at the North Railroad Station. . . . The only question now is whether I'm to shoot myself at seven o'clock railroad time or Vienna time. . . . Seven o'clock . . . Well, why exactly seven? . . . As if it couldn't be any other time as well. . . . I'm hungry—Lord, I'm hungry—No wonder. . . . Since when haven't I eaten? . . . Since—not since yesterday at six o'clock in the café! When Kopetzky handed me the ticket—café au lait and two croissants.—Wonder what the baker will say when he hears about it? . . . Damned swine. He'll know—he'll catch on, he'll realize what it means to be an Austrian officer—a fellow like that can get in a fight in the open street and think nothing of it. But if an officer is insulted even in secret, he's as good as dead. . . . If a rascal like that could fight duels—but no, then at least he'd be much more careful—he wouldn't take a chance like that. The fellow keeps on living quietly and peacefully while I—croak! He's responsible for my death. . . . Do you realize, Gustl, it is he who is responsible for your death! But he won't get off as easily as that!—No, no, no! I'll send Kopetzky a letter telling him the whole story. . . . Better yet: I'll write to the colonel. He'll make a report to the military command. . . . Just like an official report. . . . Just wait—you think, do you, that a matter like this can remain secret!—That's where you're wrong.—It will be reported and remembered forever. After that I'd like to see whether you'll venture into the café!—Ha!—"I'd like to see" is good! There are lots of things I'd like to see which unfortunately I won't be able to— It's all over!—

Johann must be going into my room this very minute. And now he notices that the lieutenant hasn't slept at home.—Well he'll imagine all sorts of things. But that the lieutenant has spent the night in the Prater—that, on my word, will never occur to him. . . . Ah, there goes the Forty-fourth! They're marching out to target practice. Let them pass.—I'll remain right here. . . . A window is being opened up there.—Pretty creature.—Well I would at least put on a shawl or something when I go to an open window.

Last Sunday was the last time. I'd never have dreamt that Steffi of all people would be the last. Oh God, that's the only real pleasure. Well, now the colonel will ride after them in two hours in his grand manner. These big fellows take life easy.—Yes, yes, eyes to the right! Very good. If you only knew how little I care about you all. Ah, that's not bad at all: there goes Katzer. Since when has he been transferred to the Forty-fourth?—How do you do, good morning! What sort of a face is he making? Why is he pointing at his head?—My dear fellow, your skull interests me not at all. . . . Oh, I see. No, my good chap, you're mistaken: I've just spent the night in the Prater. . . . You will read about it in the evening paper.—"Impossible!" he'll say, "Early this morning as we were marching out to target practice I met him on the Prater Strasse"— Who'll be put in command of my platoon? I wonder whether they'll give it to. Walterer. Well that'll be a good one! A fellow totally devoid of pizzaz—should have gone into shoe repair.—What, the sun coming up already!—This will be a beautiful day—a real spring day. The devil—on a day like this!—Every cab driver will still be here at eight o'clock this morning and I—well, what about me? Now really, it would be funny if I lost my nerve at the last minute just because of some cab drivers. . . . Why is my heart suddenly pounding this way?—Not because of *that* . . . No, oh no, it's because I haven't eaten in such a long time. But Gustl, be honest with yourself: you're scared—scared because you have never tried it before. . . . But that's no help to you. Being scared never helped anybody. Everyone has to experience it once. Some sooner, some later, and you just happen to have your turn sooner. As a matter of fact you never were worth an awful lot, so the least you can do is to behave decently at the very end, that I demand of you. I'll have to figure it out—figure out what? . . . I'm always trying to figure something out. . . . But it's so easy . . . It's lying in the drawer of my night stand—loaded—all I have to do is pull the trigger—certainly not very tricky!

That girl over there's already going to work . . . the poor girls! . . . Adele also used to have to go to work—I went and picked her up a few times in the evening. When they have a job they don't play around so much with men. If Steffi belonged only to me, I would have her sell hats or something. Wonder how she'll find out about it? . . . In the newspaper! She'll be angry that I didn't write to tell her. I believe I'm beginning to lose my mind. Why bother about whether she'll be angry or not? How long has the whole affair lasted? . . . Since January. . . . No, it must have begun before Christmas. I brought her some candy from Graz, and she sent me a note at New Year's. . . . Good Lord, that's right, I have her letters at home. Are there any I should burn? . . . 'Mm, the one from Fallsteiner. If that letter is found—the fellow will get into trouble. Why should that concern me!—Well it wouldn't be much of an exertion. . . . But I can't look through all that scrawl. . . . It would be best to burn the whole bunch. . . . Who'll ever need them? They're all junk.—My few books I could leave to Blany—"Through Night and Ice"—too bad I'll never be able to finish it. . . . Didn't have much chance to read these last few months. . . .

Organ playing? In the church there. . . . Early mass—haven't been to one in an age. . . . Last time it was in February when the whole platoon was ordered to go. But that doesn't count.—I was watching my men to see if they were reverent and behaving properly. . . . I'd like to go to church . . . there might be something to it after all. . . . Well, after lunch I'll know all about it. Ah, "this afternoon" is good!—what shall I do—go in? I think it would be a comfort to Mother if she knew! . . . It wouldn't mean as much to Clara. . . . Well, in I go. It can't hurt! Organ playing—singing—hm!—what's the matter! I'm growing dizzy. . . . Oh God, Oh, God, Oh, God! I want somebody whom I can talk to before it happens!— How would it be—if I went to confession! The old cleric would certainly open his eyes wide if he heard me say at the end, "Pardon, Reverend Father; I am now going to shoot myself!" . . . Most of all I want to lie down there on the stone floor and cry my eyes out. . . . Oh no, I don't dare do that. But crying sometimes helps so much. . . . I'll sit down a moment, but I won't go to sleep again as I did in the Prater! . . . —People who have religion are much better off. . . . Well, now my hands are beginning to tremble! If it keeps on this way, I'll soon become so disgusted at myself that I'll commit suicide out of pure shame! That old woman there—What's she still got to pray for? . . . It would be a good idea to say to her: You, please include me too. . . . I never learned how to do it properly. Ha! It seems that dying makes one stupid!—Stand up! Where have I heard that melody before?—

Holy God! Last night!—It's the melody from the oratorio! Out, out of here, I can't stand it any more. 'Pst! Not so much noise letting that sword drag—don't disturb the people in their prayers—so!—It's better in the open. . . . Light. . . . The time's always growing shorter. Wish it were over already!—I should have done it at once in the Prater. . . . I should never go out without a revolver. . . . If I'd had one yesterday evening. . . . Good Lord Almighty!—I might take breakfast in the café. . . . I'm hungry. It always used to seem remarkable that people who were condemned to death drank their coffee and smoked their cigar in the morning. . . . Heavens, I haven't even smoked! I haven't even felt like smoking!—This is funny: I really feel like going to the café. . . . Yes, it's already open, and there's none of our crowd there right now . . . and if there were—it would be a magnificent sign of cool-headedness! "At six o'clock he was eating breakfast in the café and at seven he killed himself." . . . —I feel altogether calm again. Walking is so pleasant—and best of all, nobody is forcing me. If I wanted to I could still chuck the whole damn business. . . . America. . . . What do I mean, "whole damn business"? What *"damn* business"? I wonder whether I'm getting a sunstroke. Oho!—am I so quiet because I still imagine that I don't have to? . . . I do have to! I must! No, I will! Can you picture yourself, Gustl, taking off your uniform and beating it, and the damned swine laughing behind your back? And not even Kopetzky wanting to shake hands with you anymore? . . . I blush just to think of it.—The cop is saluting me. . . . I must acknowledge it. . . . "Good morning, sir!" There now, I've treated him like an equal! . . . It always pleases a poor devil like him. . . . Well, no one ever had to complain about me. . . . Off duty I was always pleasant. . . . When we were at the maneuvers I gave my NCOs Havana cigars. One time at drill I heard an enlisted man behind me say something about "the damned drudgery," and I didn't even report him.—I merely said to him, "See here, be careful—some one else might hear it, and then you'll be in hot water." . . . The palace yard . . . Wonder who's on guard today?—The Bosniacs—they look good. Just recently the lieutenant colonel said, "When we were down there in '78, no one would have believed that they'd ever stoop to us the way they have." Good God, that's a place I'd like to have been! Those fellows are all getting up from the bench. I'll salute. It's too bad I couldn't have been part of something like that—that would have been so much more wonderful—on the field of battle for the Fatherland, than . . . Yes, mister lawyer, you're getting off easy! . . . Wonder if someone couldn't take my place? Great God, there's an idea—I'll leave word for Kopetzky or Wymetal to take my place in the duel! . . . He shouldn't get off so easy as that!—Oh well, what difference does it make what happens later on? I'll never hear anything about it!—The trees are beginning to bud. . . . I once picked up a girl here at the Volksgarten—she was wearing a red dress—lived in the Strozzi Gasse—later Rochlitz took her off my hands. . . . I think he still keeps her, but he never says anything about it— probably ashamed of it. . . . Steffi's still sleeping, I suppose. . . . She looks so pretty when she's asleep—just as if she couldn't count to five!—Well, they all look alike when they're asleep!—I ought to drop her a line. . . . Why not? Everyone does it . . . writes letters just before—I also want to write Clara to console Papa and Mama and the sort of stuff that one writes!—And to Kopetzky. My Lord, I'll bet it would be much easier if one said good-bye to a few people . . . and the report to the officers of the regiment.— And the hundred and sixty gulden for Ballert. . . . Still lots of things to do. Well, nobody insists that I do it at seven. . . . There's still time enough after eight o'clock for being deceased! Deceased! That's the word—That's all there is to it.

Ringstrasse—I'll soon be at my café. . . . Funny, I'm actually looking forward to breakfast. . . . Unbelievable.—After breakfast I'll light a cigar, then I'll go home and write. . . . First of all I'll make my report to the military command; then the letter to Clara—then the one to Kopetzky—then the one to Steffi. What on earth am I going to write that hussy? . . . *My dear child, you should probably never have thought* . . . Lord, what nonsense!— *My dear child, I thank you ever so much. . . .*—*My dear child, before I take my leave, I will not overlook the opportunity. . . .*— Well, letter writing was never my forte. . . . *My dear child, one last farewell from your Gustl. . . .*—What eyes she'll make! It's lucky I wasn't in love with her. . . . It must be sad if one loves a girl and then . . . Well, Gustl, let well enough alone: it's sad enough as it is. . . . Others would have come along after Steffi, and finally there would have been one who'd have been worth something—a young girl from a substantial family, with a good dowry—it might have been rather nice. . . . —I must write Clara a detailed letter explaining why I couldn't do otherwise. . . . *You must forgive me, my dear sister, and please console our dear parents. I know that I caused you all a good deal of worry and considerable pain; but believe me, I always loved all of you, and I hope that some time you will be happy, my dear Clara, and will not completely forget your unhappy brother. . . .* —Oh, I'd better not write to her at all! . . . No, it's too sad. I can already feel the tears in my eyes, when I think. . . . At least I'll write to Kopetzky. . . . A man-to-man farewell, and that he should let the others know. . . . —Already six o'clock—Oh no, half-past five—quarter to.— If that isn't a charming little face!—The little teenager, with her black eyes. I've met her so often in the Florianigasse!—Wonder what she'll say?—But she doesn't even know who I am—she'll only wonder why she doesn't see me any more. . . . Day before yesterday I made up my mind to speak to her the next time I met her.—She's been flirting plenty and in the end even a virgin. . . . She was so young— . . . . Yes, Gustl! Don't put off till tomorrow what you can do today. . . . That fellow over there probably hasn't slept all night either—Well, now he'll go home comfortably and lie down.—So will I!—Haha! This is getting serious, Gustl! Well if there weren't a little fear connected with it, there'd be nothing to it at all—and on the whole I must say in behalf of myself that I have been behaving very nobly. . . . Where'll I go now? There's my café. . . . They're still sweeping. . . . Well, I'll go in.

There's the table where they always play Tarok. . . . Remarkable, I can't imagine why that fellow who's always sitting next to the wall should be the same one who . . . —Nobody here yet. . . . Where's the waiter? . . . Ha!—There's one coming out of the kitchen. . . . Quickly putting on his apron . . . It's really no longer necessary! . . . Well, it is, for him. . . . He'll have to wait on other people today.

"Good morning, Lieutenant."

"Good morning."

"So early today, Lieutenant?"

"Oh that's all right—I haven't much time, I'll just sit here with my coat on."

"Your order, Sir?"

"A café au lait."

"Thank you—right away, Lieutenant."

Ah, there are the newspapers . . . are they out as early as this? Wonder what they say? Well, what? It's as though I wanted to see if they say I've committed suicide! . . . Haha!—Why am I still standing up? . . . Let's sit down by the window. . . . He's already brought in the coffee. There, I'll pull the curtain. I feel uncomfortable with people gaping in. Nobody's out yet. . . . Ah, this coffee tastes good—it wasn't a bad idea, this breakfast! . . . I feel like a new man.—The whole trouble was that I didn't eat anything last night. Why is the waiter back already? Oh, he's also brought some rolls. . . .

"Has the Lieutenant already heard?"

"Heard what?" For God's sake, does he know something about it already? . . . Nonsense, it's absolutely impossible!

"Herr Habetswallner—" What, what's that? That's the baker's name. . . . What's he going to say now? . . . Has he been here already? Was he here yesterday telling them the whole story? . . . Why doesn't he tell me more? . . . But he's talking right now. . . .

"—had a stroke last night at twelve o'clock."

"What?" . . . I mustn't shout this way. . . . No, I can't allow anybody to notice it. . . . But perhaps I'm dreaming. . . . I must ask him again. . . .

"Who did you say had a stroke?"—Rather good, that!—I said it quite innocently!—

"The baker, Lieutenant. You must know him. . . . Don't you remember the fat fellow who played Tarok at the table next to the officers' here every afternoon . . . with Herr Schlesinger and Herr Wasner—the one in the paper-flower business?!"

I'm completely awake—everything seems to check up—and still I just can't believe him.—I'll have to ask him again. . . . Altogether innocently. . . .

"You say that he was overcome by a stroke? . . . How did it happen? Who told you about it?"

"Who could know it sooner than we here, Lieutenant?—That roll you are eating there comes from Herr Habetswallner's own bakery. His delivery boy who comes here at half-past four in the morning told us about it."

Look out! I mustn't give myself away. . . . I feel like shouting.
. . . I'll burst out laughing in a minute. In another second I'll kiss
Rudolph. . . . But I must ask him something else! Having a stroke
doesn't mean that he's dead. . . . I must ask him—if he's dead.
. . . Altogether calmly—why should the baker concern me?—I
must look in the paper while I'm asking the waiter.

"You say he's dead?"

"Why certainly, Lieutenant, he died immediately."

Wonderful, wonderful! . . . Maybe all because I went to
church. . . .

"He went to the theater last night. On the way out he fell on
the stairs—the janitor heard him fall. . . . Well, they carried him
to his home, and he died long before the doctor ever arrived."

"That's sad—too bad. He was still in the prime of life." I said
that marvelously—not a soul can tell. . . . And I have to do
everything to keep from shouting my lungs out and jumping up
on the billiard table. . . .

"Yes, Lieutenant, it is very sad. He was such a nice gentleman;
he's been coming to this place for the last twenty years—he was a
good friend of the boss. And his poor wife. . . ."

I don't think I've felt as happy as this as long as I've lived. He's
dead—dead! Nobody knows about it, and nothing's happened!—
What a brilliant piece of luck that I came into the café. . . . Otherwise I'd have shot myself for nothing—it's like a benediction
from heaven. . . . Where did Rudolph go? Oh, he's talking to the
furnace man. . . . —Well, he's dead—dead. I just can't seem to
believe it! I'd better go and take a look at him myself.—He probably had a stroke out of anger—couldn't control himself. . . .
Well, what difference does it make why it happened! The main
thing is he's dead, and I can keep on living, and everything belongs to me again! . . . Funny, the way I keep on dunking the
roll—the roll Habetswallner baked for me! It tastes very good
too, Herr Habetswallner. Splendid!—Ah, now I'll light a cigar. . . .

"Rudolph! Hey, Rudolph! Don't argue so much with the furnace man."

"What is it, Lieutenant?"

"Bring me a cigar." . . . —I'm so happy, so happy! . . . What
am I doing? . . . What am I doing? . . . Something's got to hap-

pen, or I'll be overcome by a stroke of joy! In a few minutes I'll wander over to the barracks and let Johann give me a cold rub-down. . . . At half-past seven we have drill and at half-past nine formation.—And I'll write Steffi to leave this evening open for me no matter what! And this afternoon at four. . . . Just wait, my boy, I'm in wonderful form. . . . I'll knock you to smithereens!

Translated by Richard L. Simon
and revised by Caroline Wellbery

ACKNOWLEDGMENTS

This volume has been published with the kind assistance of The Austrian Institute, New York.

Every reasonable effort has been made to locate the holders of rights to translations included in this volume. We gratefully acknowledge permission to reprint the following translation:

La Ronde, trans. Eric Bentley, from *The Classic Theater,* ed. Eric Bentley (New York: Doubleday, 1959). Copyright © 1959 by Eric Bentley.

The original titles of the works included in this volume are as follows:

> *Liebelei*
> *Reigen*
> *Komtesse Mizzi*
> *Casanovas Heimfahrt*
> *Leutnant Gustl*